Charisma

A Scriptural Immersion in the Spiritual Gifts

Amanda Seipel

Scriptures are taken from HCSB Study Bible
Copyright © 2010 by Holman Bible Publishers
Nashville, Tennessee. Used by permission.
All rights reserved.

Hebrew and Greek words as well as definitions are from
www.biblehub.com

Please visit www.free2love.org to make comments
and read weekly devotionals

Follow a Tweet @F2LHeartsAblaze

Contents

(Amanda has all 3.)
Teaching, Prophecy & Exhortation gifts go together.

Introduction..	6 ✓ 1
Spiritual Gifts Unleashed.............................	8 ✓ 1
Prophecy, A Superior Gift............................	15 ✓ 2
✴The Essential Value of (Service)..................	25 ✓ 1
The Nourishment of Teaching.....................	33 3 ✓
Exhortations Goal? Transformation.............	51 4 ✓
A Copious Bestowal of Giving.....................	67 5 ✓
Leading with Diligence................................	83 5 ✓
The Compassion of Mercy..........................	88 4 ✓
The Fear of the Lord is This: Wisdom.........	98 6 ✓
The Equipping of Knowledge......................	114 7 ✓
Faith Triumphs..	129 6 ✓
The Compassion of Healing........................	156 8 ✓

Charisma

Miracles - God's Miraculous Power 177

The Brilliance of God's Discernment.................. 198

The Relevance of Speaking in Tongues
    and Giving Interpretation...................... 208

The Mission of the Apostle................................. 218

Prophets, God's Reformers................................. 231

The Evangelist ~ Bringing People to Christ...... 240

The Shepherding Role of Pastor....................... 244

Jesus, The Ultimate Teacher............................... 252

A Helper with Good Counsel............................. 263

The Leadership of Administration..................... 266

Spiritual Gifts Profile Tool................................... 269

Dedication

I am grateful and honored to have sisters in Christ I can call on to come to my aid with their powerful prayers. Thank you deeply for those who have offered their precious appeals on behalf of this project. The prayers of God's people sustain us when we grow weary and I am grateful to be a benefactor of this most precious gift. Thank you sweet things.

Thank you Debbie Harney. You envisioned this project and created the path to make it happen. You have been by my side from the very beginning with your prayers and words of edification. I am so appreciative for your guidance and friendship.

So grateful for my sons Ian and Cayson. Ian's cleverness assisted me in designing two book covers and they both rescued me from many jams when I could not find the words to express what I wanted to say. They profoundly bless me.

Other titles: *A Devotional on Faith, Hope, and Love* available through Amazon.

A leader guide is also available for *Charisma*.

Introduction

1 Cor. 12:11
1 Cor. 3:1-3
2 Cor. 3:3

This book was written to assist believers gain a thorough Scriptural understanding of the <u>Spiritual gifts identified in Romans 12, 1 Corinthians 12, and Ephesians 4.</u> The intent is not that we would gain additional intellectual knowledge to fill our minds or to fuel our debates but that we would able to recognize the Spiritual gifts in ourselves and others and put them to use serving God.

A chapter is included for each Spiritual gift and within each chapter is a description of the gift as well as scriptural references for you to locate in your Bible and complete the blanks. At the conclusion of the study there is a Spiritual gifts profile to be used as a tool to help you identify your gifts. Once you have identified your Spiritual gift please do not simply acknowledge it and go on with life as usual. ==“A demonstration of the Spirit is given to each person to produce what is beneficial." (1 Corinthians 12:7)== If you are a believer in Jesus Christ of Nazareth you have been given His Spirit. According to the Scripture, a manifestation of the Spirit is given to each person with the intent to benefit His Church. So, let's intend to get involved!

Spiritual gifts are given by God's grace alone and without any promise by the beneficiary that they will ever be used. The Spiritual gifts are also given apparently having nothing to do with how spiritual a person is. An example of this is seen in 1 Corinthians 1:7. Paul noted that the Corinthians were "not lacking spiritual gift" but yet they were not spiritually mature and were said to have self-centered interests.

When God calls, He also equips. Therefore if you are struggling in discerning God's vision for your life, concentrate on discerning your gifts. Every believer has the responsibility to discern, develop, and deploy their gifts so they will reach their full potential and fulfill their role in the Body of Christ. What do you think of that?

To operate full throttle in the Spirit requires a resolve. Jesus went into the wilderness and fasted 40 days before He came forth in the power of the Spirit.

This book is not attempting to provide evidence for the existence or non-existence of any of the Spiritual gifts identified in the Bible. Which gift to give and to whom it shall be given is at the discretion of the Spirit. In my opinion, who are we to say whether or not a gift is still in existence? When we make this claim it seems as if we are trying to stand on a sovereign piece of ground we have no right to stand on. We never were given the authority to determine which gifts this world would benefit from in order to best serve Christ, so why is it we get to say which of the gifts are no longer needed?

Perhaps we don't witness the gifts manifested as frequently because we operate more in the flesh than in the Spirit? Often times I think we deny the validity of certain Spiritual gifts because of the perversion and misuses that often occur. This can happen with any Spiritual gift. Let's also keep in mind that whatever God creates Satan mimics and abuses. If the Spirit gives Spiritual gifts to the Church for holy purposes, Satan will most certainly mimic these things for his unholy purposes. Just because there have been abuses in the past let's stop trying to minimize the Spiritual life.

I find it curious that the books informing us about the Spiritual gifts were written at least 2 decades after the ascension of Christ. If the gifts were only needed for the Church at that time, what person or group gets to decide the cut-off date for the time the Church no longer needs a particular gift? If the gifts were given to serve the Church and promote the message of Christ don't we still have the Church and aren't we still promoting the message of Christ?

In any case, my intent is to Scripturally study *all* the gifts in the above mentioned chapters and pray for the wisdom and guidance to use them if they have been bestowed on us by the Spirit for the sole purpose of victoriously serving the Church and bringing glory to God. The meat of Scripture is provided and we trust the Holy Spirit to develop the truths in our hearts. I pray this study blesses and assists you in your ministry efforts.

✳ *This book can be used for individual study or with your small group. Leader notes are available.*

Spiritual Gifts Unleashed!

When you accepted Jesus as Savior, you received the Holy Spirit. You may recall your soul (intellect, will, and emotions) and your body at that time, was more aware or yielded to the Spirit. Before long in your Christian walk however, the body and soul try to take over as dominate again. If you prioritize time to pray in the morning, the busyness of your soul and body becomes quieted and we have the opportunity to yield to the Spirit. We are then reminded that within us the life in the Spirit is very real. But as promptly as the clamor of existence begins again, you automatically begin trusting your flesh (soul and body) more than the Spirit. Soon, we loose track of the Spirit. We need to allow the Spirit to flow out from the deep place within us and fill our soul and body. This is done by simply asking, welcoming, and yielding. Our goal is to live not by the flesh but by the Spirit.

Charisma is a Greek word meaning, "the operation of grace; grace-endowment to edify the Church. (The 'ma' suffix, focusing on the end-result of the endowment of grace.) The grace-gift divinely empowers a believer to share God's work with others, i.e. Spirit-empowered service to the Church to carry out His plan for His people. (HELPS Word-studies biblehub.com) It is a divinely given gift.

Paul speaks about the Spiritual gifts in 1 Corinthians 13:1-3. "If I speak human or angelic languages but do not have love, I am a sounding gong or a clanging cymbal. If I have the gift of prophecy and understand all mysteries and all knowledge, and if I have all faith so that I can move mountains but do not have love, I am nothing. And if I donate all my goods to feed the poor, and if I give my body in order to boast but do not have love, I gain nothing." *Each Spiritual gift is motivated by God's love.*

Please list the Spiritual gifts Paul is referring to in 1 Corinthians 13:1-3.

1) ~~faith~~
2) ~~hope~~ languages
3) ~~love~~ prophecy

4) _giving_
5) _knowledge_
6) _____

sanctified - we are chosen or set apart by Christ for his service.

What is Paul saying is more important than all these gifts:

Love

The Spirit gives gifts in order to serve the Church and bring glory to God and we should desire these gifts. However, more than desiring any gift we should desire the self-sacrificing type of love that God lavishly pours into our hearts in order for us to lavishly pour out to others. This kind of love combined with the manifestation of Spiritual gifts is what Paul is speaking about. ==There is no greater expression of Spiritual ministry than that which is manifested through love!==

In 1 Peter 4:10-11, Peter also informs us about how to serve with Spiritual gifts. "Based on the gift each one has received, use it to serve others, as good managers of the varied grace of God. If anyone speaks, it should be as one who speaks God's words; if anyone serves, it should be from the strength God provides, so that God may be glorified through Jesus Christ in everything." God intends for us to serve Him from the strength and power found in Him.

Spiritual gifts are for the building up of the body of Christ:

"A demonstration of the Spirit is given to each person to produce what is beneficial." 1 Corinthians 12:7

"For the training of the saints in the work of ministry, to build up the body of Christ" Ephesians 4:12

"Based on the gift each one has received, use it to serve others" 1 Peter 4:10

==According to the measure in which you are yielded to the Spirit, will be the measure in which you will experience His presence, manifestation, and influence.== Recently, I described being yielded to the Spirit in the following way. Take both of your hands and place one in front of the other. The hand in front will represent you and the one behind will represent the Spirit. If you are in front, the Spirit will hardly get noticed. Now switch the hands. The Holy Spirit is now in front and you are behind. Now, who will get the notice? This is how a person would look yielded to the Spirit. Now switch the hands again. Spread the fingers of the hand in front and allow the fingers of the hand in back to come through. This is what it will look like for someone partially yielded to the Spirit. Keep in mind the measure you are yielded to the Spirit will be the measure of how you and others will notice the Spirit's influence.

When yielded to the Spirit we receive refreshing. Our minds come alive in a new way to God's reality. Our emotions respond, and we experience joy in Him. Our will responds, and we begin to want to do what He wants. Our bodies respond, not only by feelings of well-being, but by actual renewed strength, health, and youth. Then, it begins to flow out to others and they witness the power and love of Jesus in His people. He is now able to use His believers as refreshment to those in need and to point others towards God.

==You will know if you have a distinct gift because it will be something regularly manifested through you. Even though you may already have one of the supernatural gifts, it does not limit the Holy Spirit from manifesting any of the other gifts through you at any time He desires.== The Spiritual gifts are things that are manifested, meaning we see it or hear it. Our personal faith should be based on a personal experience of God's manifest power in our lives. As Paul was proclaiming God's word he said, "My speech and my proclamation were not with persuasive words of wisdom but with a powerful demonstration by the Spirit, so that your faith might not be based on men's wisdom but on God's power." (1 Corinthians 2:4-5) Amen!

During this study pray to be open to receive whatever revelation the Lord shall impart to you concerning these magnificent things. Your prayer might be for revelation, for increased understanding, or for an openness to the Spirit of God.

This book takes an active approach to learning by requesting you own the experience by looking up Scripture and then completing the blanks. Each time this is requested it will be identified with a ✎. If the information presented is not new to you, please take the time to prayerfully consider the material in a fresh way by asking the Spirit of Truth to electrify your heart with a new excitement for His Word. The goal is to not merely gain more information that sits in your mind, but to mediate on the workings of the Spirit of God Himself so that we recognize Him at work now and in the future. We want to be awakened to things pertaining to Him! Awaken and refresh me Lord and make these things known to me as You never have before! In Jesus name I pray and believe.

"Now there are different gifts, but the same Spirit. There are different ministries, but the same Lord. And there are different activities, but the same God activates each gift in each person. A demonstration of the Spirit is given to each person to produce what is beneficial. But one and the same Spirit is active in all these, distributing to each person as He wills. (His will or intention is a result of reflection and counsel) (1 Corinthians 12:4-7, 11)

Prayer

Heavenly Father, I praise Your name. I thank you for Your goodness and faithfulness. Your Word says that the one who believes in You will do the works You do and even greater works (John 14:12) because of the power of the Holy Spirit in us. Thank you for giving us Your Spirit. Father, I desire to do these works and fulfill the purposes you have for my life! Help me to walk in your provision. Open my eyes and speak to my heart regarding Your truths and the things of the Spirit. Father, demolish the barriers of unbelief I have held! I ask you for an increase of the presence of the Spirit in my life. You said to ask Father, and you would give the Spirit. With a humble heart and outstretched hands, I ask to be filled with Your Spirit! I give you glory and honor and praise because everything I have I owe to You. I declare You are the Alpha and Omega in my life this day and forevermore! Amen.

Here are some verses relating to the supernatural gifts of the Spirit. Please read the following and complete the blanks. The Holman version is used throughout this study. Don't be concerned if the version you are using does not line up exactly with the blanks given below. Be creative and make it work for you!

❧1 Corinthians 7:7b says "Each has his own _gift_ from God, one person in this way and another in that way."

The word 'gift' here is charisma and relates to a spiritual endowment denoting extraordinary powers which enables us to serve the church of Christ. Any gift we have is due to the power of divine grace operating in us by the Holy Spirit alone.

❧"Now there are different _gifts_, but the same Spirit. There are different ministries, but the same Lord. And there are different activities, but the same God activates each _gift_ in each person. A _____ of the Spirit is given to _____ _____ to produce what is beneficial." (1 Corinthians 12:4-6)

Charisma

is telling us that there are many different gifts, but it is the Holy Spirit who dispenses them all. Here again we see the word 'gifts' and is the same Greek word as above and has the same meaning ~ charisma.

Below is a list of Spiritual gifts and where they can be found in the Bible.

Romans 12:6-8

Prophecy (also found in 1 Corinthians 12:8-11)
Service
Teaching
Encouragement
Giving
Leadership
Mercy

1 Corinthians 12:8-11

Word of Wisdom
Word of Knowledge
Faith
Healing (also found in 1 Corinthians 12:28)
Miracles (also found in 1 Corinthians 12:28)
Prophecy (also found in Romans 12)
Discernment
Tongues (also found in 1 Corinthians 12:28)
Interpretation of Tongues

Ephesians 4:11 & 1 Corinthians 12:28

Apostle
Prophet
Evangelist
Pastor and Teacher
Working of Miracles (also found in 1 Corinthians 12:8-11)
Gifts of Healing (also found in 1 Corinthians 12:8-11)
Helping
Tongues (also found in 1 Corinthians 12:8-11)
Administration or Managing

The word 'demonstration' here also means manifestation. A manifestation is something we see or hear. If the supernatural gift was strictly for the benefit of the bearer, what benefit would it be to have a manifestation? The benefit of the manifestation is to bring glory to the Lord and edification to His believers. Praise God! Isn't it intriguing that the Apostle clearly states that every believer possesses, in some form, a supernatural gifting? Since it is the basis of the Apostle's exhortation, it is inconceivable that any believer should not possess and be conscious of possessing a gift. ==Therefore, since no one is without a supernatural gift, no one is without a duty.==

- 1 Corinthians 14:1 tell us to "pursue __love__ and __spiritual__ _____ gifts, and above all that you may __prophesy_____."

When we pursue love (God's love ~ agape, this is a self-sacrificing type of love) we will then desire the spiritual gifts in order to glorify God and bring edification and comfort to His people.

- Romans 12:6 "According to the __grace_____ given to ____us____ we have different __gifts_____."

The word 'gift' here is also the same as above ~ charisma.

- Hebrews 2:4 "God testified by __signs__ and __wonders_____, various __miracles_____, and distributions of __gifts_____ from the __Holy Spirit__ and according to __his will_____."

This particular verse is also intriguing. The word 'signs' means any miraculous event that shows what had been previously predicted (by prophecy) would certainly take place. Some time ago the Lord placed faith in my heart that He would indeed do a miraculous work in my bible study group (I must add they are with sisters I just ADORE!). A few weeks ago I asked Him if He would allow us to witness a manifestation of the Spirit as a testimony in our group. His Spirit testified with my spirt and I knew He would. I also knew in my spirit it would be "one speaking in a tongue and another giving the interpretation". The only thing I shared with my group was that there was to be a manifestation but I did not say what it would be. Two weeks later, as we were praying, someone stood up with a word that "someone would speak in tongues and another would give the interpretation." The sign indeed came and it came just as the Spirit revealed! "God testified by a sign" which came via a "distributed gift straight from His Spirit".

- Ephesians 4:8 For it says: "When He ascended on high, He took prisoners into captivity; He gave __gifts__ to people".
Jesus not only triumphed over His foes, but as Conqueror, He bestows Spiritual gifts to His believers.
Let's take one more thing into consideration…..

Charisma

We will one day stand before the tribunal of Christ (2 Corinthians 5:10) and be made aware of the rewards we have missed out on if we choose to ignore and not use our gifts. (Matthew 25:14-29) As seen in the verse in Matthew, these rewards come when the master returns. Are we willing to be satisfied with the heavenly economy of doing our Master's work now and waiting for future rewards? The worldly economy is to work and immediately receive monetary rewards. Which do you value more? Satan is fully aware that there are rewards we will receive in heaven for the work done on behalf of the Master here on earth. Our enemy is the master of the 'bait and switch' technique. We are 'baited' by things our flesh desires NOW and we therefore spend tremendous efforts to gain earthly pleasures only to find out they never really were exactly what our heart and soul was craving. The earthly race we run gives inferior rewards. Satan has cleverly deceived us into thinking that his have it now economy is superior to God's economy but the gold he offers is 'fools gold'. It is only a superficial luster that pales in comparison to the real thing.

So what are we to do? We do not allow our participation in the earthly economy to hinder our service in Kingdom purposes. Luke 12:43-48 tells us that the slave found working when the master returns will be rewarded. It will not go well for the slave that knew his master's will and did not prepare himself for service or participate in service. We have been given and entrusted with much and therefore much is required.

You are Divinely Inspired and Victoriously Anointed. Pray the prayer provided at the end of each chapter or pray one of your own, complete the scripture work, and allow the information revealed to move from your mind to your heart as the Spirit directs. Revelation the Spirit then imparts to you will be a witness to your spirit. Ask the Lord during this study to disclose to you which gifts He has given to you and thank Him in advance. As you begin to operate in your gifts you will experience contentment and joy.

Prophecy, A Superior Gift

1 Cor. 14:3 - Memory Verse

Paul opens 1 Corinthians 14 with these words, "Pursue love and desire spiritual gifts, and above all that you may prophesy." He said "and above all that you may _prophesy_." Why do you think he would say that? The role of prophesy is for believers to be edified, encouraged, and comforted. A word of prophecy strengthens the entire church! Fellow believers, we earnestly need Spiritual edification, encouragement, and comfort in this age!

We have had more than enough contempt, more than enough unbelief, more than enough discouragement, more than enough fear, and more than enough fence-sitting! I desire a powerful demonstration of the work of the Spirit in Christian lives as opposed to a few clever words (1 Co 2:4) how about you?

In His great grace, God has anointed each believer for powerful service in specific areas. If God has given you the Spiritual gift to prophesy (prophēteia), speak out with as much faith as God has given you (Romans 12:6). Prophecy is one of the supernatural gifts of God's power made manifest through the Spirit filled and yielded believer.

As far as the Spiritual gifts, we are instructed to eagerly pursue Prophecy. (1 Cor. 14:39). According to Acts 2:17-18, the prophet Joel announced that in the last days God would pour out His Spirit on all humanity. Our sons and daughters would prophesy; young men would see visions and our old men would dream dreams. God said He would pour out His Spirit on His male and female slaves and they would prophesy. All Christians have the ability to prophecy! (1 Corinthians 14:31) Since prophecy is given for edification, encouragement, and comfort, if a prophecy is given to a believer that falls out of line with one of these three areas then it did not originate from the Spirit of God. This is not to say, however, that prophecy is not for corrective counsel that leads to repentance. The result of the counsel is to bring about edification, encouragement, and comfort and never condemnation.

Charisma

Prophecy should always be presented in the presence of a gathering (no minimum number required) of believers so that it can be properly evaluated in terms of the witness to the heart by the Spirit and by the written Word of God (with which prophecy must always agree).

Unbelievers also benefit from prophecy because it brings a demonstration of the power of God. "But if all of you are prophesying, and unbelievers or people who don't understand these things come into your meeting, they will be convicted of sin and judged by what you say. As they listen, their secret thoughts will be exposed, and they will fall to their knees and worship God, declaring, "God is truly among you." (1 Corinthians 14:24-25) Let's talk about two things brought up in verse 24; the unbelievers and the uninformed. As intimate facts are revealed (during prophecy or through different gifts) regarding the condition of the unbeliever's heart, he is convinced of God's reality and immediately converted. The uninformed or uninstructed believer; one who does not fully understand the gifts of the Spirit, is often at this point convinced that these things are real (many these days are coming to receive because they have seen the gifts in operation, which they had been previously told were "not for today."). Since the day of Pentecost and the outpouring of the Holy Spirit, any yielded child of God may be moved by the Spirit to prophesy.

It is not what a man says in the natural realm that makes him a prophet; but that he is moved by the Spirit of God to speak the words God gives him. Very often, a prophet of God will naturally minister in the gift of prophecy as well as the gift of knowledge and it may be hard to distinguish between the two – declaring God's will and God's mind. Prophecy is typically associated with words that are predictive but it does not always have to be the case. A discourse of divine inspiration declaring the purposes of God which edifies, encourages, comforts and ultimately points towards Christ is prophecy.

Please read the words of Agabus in Acts 11:27-29 and 21:10-14 for an example of an individual giving predictive prophecy.

Characteristics of someone with the gift of prophecy:

❈ Advises a warning regarding sin and wrong attitudes ❈
❈ Can spiritually perceive when a doctrinal compromise is being made ❈
❈ Can be outspoken relating to spiritual truths ❈
❈ Uses Scriptures confidently ❈

Let's focus on a couple of areas of prophecy that we, as discerning members of the body of Christ, should be aware of. First, prophecy should be used in accordance with the standard of one's faith. I recently had a dear friend report a prophetic message to me. As soon as I heard it I was edified, encouraged, and comforted! What came forth was praise to God! She spoke what she heard according to her faith. After I had time to process the magnitude of the words I wanted to know more so I asked her questions. After prayerfully considering what I had done I realized she had already told me all the information and anything else she added would be coming from her own intellect and feelings. I immediately recalled times in the past when I felt I had received a word from the Lord but it was only a word or two. I felt compelled to add more to it because it did not seem to be enough. The part I added came from my own intellect or feelings and did not proceed from divine inspiration because the words added were my own. Adding to the prophecy is moving out of the Spirit and back into the flesh. To sum up, divine prophecy given in faith may only be a word or two and we should end there. Adding more to the prophecy is no longer divine but human. If you are given a word and you desire more information, take the request to the Lord through prayer and allow Him to reveal what is lacking.

Secondly, the discerner should determine if the words given in prophecy edify, exhort, or comfort the believer. 1 Corinthians 14:31 tells us prophecy is for all believers to learn and be encouraged. Praise God! There are times when a believer might be given information that stirs up fear, for example. In this situation we should always be ready to stop the person uttering the prophecy that we believe is not from the Lord because fear never edifies, never exhorts, and never comforts. Nothing else needs to be said on the matter and you should dismiss the prophecy immediately. This prophecy was uttered under the influence of a wrong spirit. In sensitivity to a believer who has uttered a false word we must also remember we are judging the spirit not the individual. We are all individuals operating with varying levels of sanctification. The Holy Spirit is life, He does not deaden or plant seeds of fear in the righteous.

Please open your bibles and prayerfully consider the following verses as you complete the blanks.

"Isaiah's _prophecy_ is fulfilled in them, which says: You will listen and listen, yet never understand; and you will look and look, yet never perceive. For this people's heart has grown callous; their ears are hard of hearing, and they have shut their eyes; otherwise they might see with their eyes and hear with their ears, understand with

Charisma

their hearts and turn back — and I would cure them." (Matthew 13:14-15)

Isaiah's prophecy will speak to a listener's heart and bring healing. If we hear a prophecy that lines up with Scripture and brings edification, encouragement and comfort let's welcome it and praise God for it. If someone else is not willing to receive it, this is a good verse for intercessory prayer. How would you turn this verse into prayer for the lost?

_____

_____

☙"And it will be in the last days, says God, that I will pour out My Spirit on _all_ _people_; then your sons and your daughters will _prophesy_, your young men will see visions, and your old men will dream dreams. I will even pour out _my_ _Spirit_ on My male and female slaves in those days, and they will _prophesy_." (Acts 2:17-18)

Those who are brought under the influence of the gospel should be remarkably equipped with ability to proclaim the will of God. I love how God says He will pour out His Spirit on "my" male and female slaves. We serve the Lord and should make ourselves available to fulfill His purposes. We are His! Expect to prophesy. Ask Jesus to be a vessel to edify His disciples through you. As you have fellowship with the Lord and with fellow believers, you may find thoughts and words of inspiration coming into your mind that you have not heard and did not construct. If they are according to Scripture, share them with the Body.

Someone operating in the Spiritual gift of prophecy will know Scripture very well and can therefore use it confidently to give a warning if needed regarding sin or if believers have adopted wrong attitudes. This person will operate with a skill above and beyond what other believers not having this gift are able to do.

☙"According to the grace given to us, we have different gifts: If _prophesy_, use it according to the standard of one's _faith_." (Romans 12:6)

If your gift is prophesying, then prophesy in accordance with your faith not above or below it. The gifts are manifested through God's will, not ours. If He has given you some words to speak then He will give the faith that is required to accomplish His purposes. I recently

Charisma

read this perfect comment. When God calls, He also equips. Therefore if you are struggling in discerning God's vision for your life, concentrate on discerning your gifts. Every believer has the responsibility to discern, develop, and deploy their gifts so that they will reach their full potential and fulfill their role in the Body of Christ. What do you think of that? Is there anything that might be hindering you in this area?

_____

ఈ"In this way, the __testimony__ about Christ was __confirmed__ among you, so that you do not __lack__ any spiritual gift as you __eagerly__ wait for the revelation of our Lord Jesus Christ." (1 Corinthians 1:6-7)

As a believer filled with the Spirit, you have as fully as any other person, those spiritual gifts which sustain you and enable you to wait for the revelation (second visible appearance) of Jesus as well as to serve His church.

The following four portions of verses are directed towards the church at Corinth. It is interesting to note that the city of Corinth had rampant sin. On top of the hill above Corinth was a temple dedicated to Aphrodite ~ the female goddess of love. Many sins were said to have been committed by her priestesses. If a person lived like a Corinthian their reputation was corrupted. Members of the church in Corinth were said to have immaturities but were also said to have been given ALL the gifts of the Spirit.

ఈ"If I have the gift of __prophecy__ and understand all mysteries and all knowledge, and if I have all __faith__ so that I can move mountains but do not have __love__, I am __nothing__." (1 Corinthians 13:2)

==We must primarily possess the love of God (agape) for fellow believers. Out of this love, we desire spiritual gifts *in order to serve*. Unless we have love (agape), which motivates the pure desire for spiritual gifts, all is lost.==

ఈ"__Love__ never ends. But as for __prophecies__, they will come to an end; as for languages, they will cease; as for knowledge, it will come to an end. For we know in __part__, and we __prophesy__ in part. But when the __perfection__ comes, the partial will come to an __end__." (1 Corinthians 13:8-10)

Even though we may know 'in part' (as a portion of the whole) that 'part' or portion is *powerfully* divine to allow us to Spiritually operate full-throttle in our gifting. There are no limits to what can be accomplished in the Spirit.

- "Pursue _love_ and desire spiritual gifts, and above all that you may _edify God_. For the person who speaks in another language is not speaking to men but to God, since no one understands him; however, he speaks mysteries in the Spirit. But the person who _____ speaks to people for _____, _____, and _____. The person who speaks in another language builds himself up, but he who _____ builds up the _____. I wish all of you spoke in other languages, but even more that you _prophesy_. The person who _prophesies_ is _greater_ than the person who speaks in languages, unless he interprets so that the church may be built up. But now, brothers, if I come to you speaking in other languages, how will I benefit you unless I speak to you with a revelation or knowledge or _prophesy_ or teaching?" (1 Corinthians 14:1-6)

Pursue love. We hear this yet again so it is worth putting our minds to the pursuit of it above all other things. Have you earnestly desired it, strived to possess it, and been influenced by it continually? While we strive after love we secondly desire the miraculous gifts of the Spirit and are motivated to excel in what He imparts to us. It is proper to desire and seek spiritual gifts, especially that which edifies the church. **Love has the** *priority* **and after that the gift of prophecy must particularly be sought.**

Prophecy is something uttered or declared and can only be known by divine revelation. It might be a sudden impulse of a lofty discourse or divine praise. Prophecy is not inspired preaching (proclaiming the Gospel through inspired intellect). Preaching should indeed be inspired by the Holy Spirit, but prophecy means the person is bringing the words the Lord gives directly, not through the intellect, training, skill, background, or education.

- "But _tongues_ is not for unbelievers but for _unbelievers_. Therefore, if the whole church assembles together and all are speaking in other languages and people who are uninformed or unbelievers come in, will they not say that you are out of your minds? But if all are _believers_ and some unbeliever or uninformed person comes in, he is convicted by all and is judged by all. The secrets of his heart will be revealed, and as a result he will fall facedown and worship God, proclaiming, "God is really among you." (1 Corinthians 14:22b-25)

Prophecy _____, however, is for the benefit of believers, not unbelievers. A word of prophecy is used for edification, exhortation, and comfort for believers; to be built up in our most holy faith. The Holy Spirit encourages, stirs up, cheers up, helps, counsels, and quickens because that is what love (agape) does.

• "Don't stifle the Spirit. Don't despise _prophesies_, but test all things. Hold on to what is good." (1 Thessalonians 5:19-21)

Let's look at an example when someone gives you a word 'in the Lord' which can indeed be refreshing and helpful. There must, however, be a witness of the Spirit on the part of the person receiving the words. Never do something just because someone says, "The Lord told me to tell you this". If the Lord has instructions for you, He will give you a witness in your own heart. When a word then comes from a friend through the gift of the Spirit, it will be confirmation to what God has already been showing you. Also remember the gifts of the Spirit are inspiration, not compulsion, and provide no excuse for erratic behavior.

We should never quench the Spirit or despise prophecies. Prophecy should be tested and we should retain what is good and reject what is false. Because at times prophecy is false we are told not to despise it as a result of it being imperfect, if we do we could quench the Spirit. We are expected instead to test prophecy because it comes through imperfect people but never should it be despised or un-welcomed.

• "Timothy, my son, I am giving you this instruction in keeping with the _prophesies_ previously made about you, so that by them you may strongly _____ in battle, having faith and a good conscience. Some have rejected these and have suffered the shipwreck of their faith." (1 Timothy 1:18-19)

Concerning Timothy, the prophecies made regarding his life and work as a future Christian leader are spoken of here. I love there is such boldness on behalf of speaking over a Christian leader's life or even at a Christian's baptism of that person's future courage in giving their life for the cause of Christ. What would our meetings be like if this truthful audacity in the Spirit was more frequent?

• "Do not _neglect_ the gift that is in you; it was given to you through _prophetic message_ with the laying on of hands by the council of elders. _____ these things; be _diligent_ to them, so that your progress may be _____ to all. Pay close attention to your life and your teaching; persevere in these things, for by doing this you will save both _yourself_ and your _hearers_." (1 Timothy 4:14-16)

Here again Timothy is being instructed to remain bold for the cause of Christ. We should be propelled forward with these same bold words of commendation and should bring others along with us with the same confidence.

🕮 "First of all, you should know this: No _prophecy_ of Scripture comes from one's own _interpretation_, because no _prophecy_ ever came by the will of _man_; instead, men spoke from God as they were moved _by_ the Holy Spirit." (2 Peter 1:20-21)

Are we wise enough to know that no true prophecy comes by way of any man's *will*? True prophecy that holds up to the test of Scripture is uttered under inspiration of the Spirit. It should be taken as such and revered as such.

The following are verses in Revelation relating to prophecy and how they should be regarded:

🕮 "The one who reads this is blessed, and those who hear the words of this _prophecy_ and keep what is written in it are blessed, because the time is near!" (Revelation 1:3)

Declaring the doctrine of divine authority and the evidence of its implications on current and future events is prophecy. When we read the words of the book of Revelation we are blessed as well as those who hear it. This seems to imply a public reading should be done of the book in order for it to be heard.

🕮 "These men have the power to close up the sky so that it does not rain during the days of their _prophesying_. They also have power over the waters to turn them into blood and to strike the earth with every plague whenever they want." (Revelation 11:6)

The ministry of these two witnesses in the last days might be similar to the ministry of Elijah and Moses. Any work of man or wicked spirit will not be able to halt the power of God. God's witnesses will speak their prophecy for as long as God intends them to speak and when the rebellious attempt to hinder them the witnesses are empowered to perform miraculous signs.

🕮 "Then I fell at his feet to worship him, but he said to me, "Don't do that! I am a fellow slave with you and your brothers who have the testimony about Jesus. Worship God, because the testimony about Jesus is the spirit of _prophecy_." (Revelation 19:10)

==The intent of prophecy is to point towards Jesus.==

- "Look, I am coming quickly! The one who keeps the _prophecy_ words of this book is blessed." (Revelation 22:7)

Remember the book of Revelation is called a prophetic book? Have you seen it maintain the notion that ==the goal of prophecy for the church is edification, encouragement, and comfort==? In what ways do you see the book bring:

edification: _____

encouragement: _____

comfort: _____

- "He also said to me, "Don't seal the _prophesy_ words of this book, because the time is near." (Revelation 22:10)

Until Jesus returns people will continue operating out of the flesh. People will either persist in acting unrighteous and unholy or people will persist in righteousness and holiness. This revelation does not deal with distant events as in the book of Daniel (parts of that prophetic book were told to be sealed), but events that are near and therefore to be communicated.

- "I testify to everyone who hears the _prophetic_ words of this book: If anyone adds to them, God will add to him the plagues that are written in this book. And if anyone takes away from the words of this _prophetic_ book, God will take away his share of the tree of life and the holy city, written in this book." (Revelation 22:18-19)

==The Scriptures are to be regarded as sacred and never to be altered.== ==“There is NO greater love than This.”== A prophetic word indeed. Of all the people who love you and of all the love you think you need, there is absolutely NO greater love than that expressed through God the Father, God the Son, and God the Spirit. When this revelation was revealed to my heart I froze in the place I was. The magnitude of the truth of that statement is more magnificent than there are words to label it. Our minds and emotions are unable to fathom it. Our experiences are so minute they can not even be measured by it. We have not mastered enough vocabulary to describe it. Even still, it beckons us to draw from the endless bounty He made available to us. For every need you have – there IS no greater source than God the Father, Jesus the Son, and the most Holy Spirit.

Charisma

Prayer

Thank you Lord! I praise you for Your gift of the Spirit in my life. Your Word says to pursue prophecy. I desire to do so and anticipate receiving and speaking as you see fit. Teach me everything you would have me know concerning prophecy. I cast down every imagination, mentality, and prior experience that might hinder my openness to the teachings of Your Spirit. Increase my faith! Break down the barrier walls of unbelief. Help me to further discern gifts of the Spirit you desire for me to operate in – all to Your glory! Amen.

Joel 2:28-32

Act 2:17-18

The Essential Value of Service

Memory Verse
Luke 12:35-37

There is no better way to begin a discussion of service than to reflect upon the words of Jesus Himself. He made the statement, "The Son of Man did not come to be served, but to serve, and to give His life — a ransom for many." Jesus came to serve AND to give His life as a ransom. (Matthew 20:28) Can you imagine how flawlessly He must have operated with the divine spiritual guidance to serve? We probably will not orchestrate the act of service as skillfully as He did but let's give it a divinely inspired attempt because we have the guidance of the same Spirit He did. Let's seek the Lord in prayer and offer our hands to Christ in all we do under the banner of His name.

The word service - diakonia is most often translated 'ministry'. The goal of someone operating in the spiritual gift of service is to invigorate the church so that the body is freed up to also fully operate in their calling.

All believers should be found performing acts of service but operating in the spiritual gifting of service enables a person to go beyond the common human potential and ingenuity. It enables the person to utilize maximum effectiveness with minimum fatigue.

You have probably known someone that always seems to make themselves available when they become aware of another's immediate tangible need. This is because a person operating in this gift of service is quick to recognize the needs in others that may even go unnoticed by most. The server will expect that by meeting the tangible needs of a person, spiritual encouragement and strength will then follow because their load has been lessened. The joy of the server does not come from the task itself but from the knowledge that through the service, peace of mind will come to the benefactor.

When evaluating the Spiritual gifts we must be mindful of the enormous benefit we all receive when each individual within the church body is functioning in their gifting. All the gifts are beneficial or the Spirit would not have seen the need to bestow them. Great joy will come to all when we are operating full-throttle in our spiritual gifting. As we become more aware of how the Spirit would have us serve we will yield more to the spirit and less to the flesh. Our own personal interest has a nauseating way of creeping into areas reserved exclusively for the work of the Spirit, doesn't it? Lord, empower us immensely to successfully crucify this self-serving flesh of ours.

With this in mind let's look at ways we can keep our personal interest at bay while we focus our hearts in the deep waters of Kingdom purposes. Because servers love to minister, the temptation can arise to over-commit which can lead to frustration and burn-out. One way to ensure this does not happen is to always pray before you volunteer your service to determine if that is where the Lord would place you. Even though we may see a need that we can easily meet, the Lord may have someone else in mind to fulfill that particular need while He places us at the side of another in need.

Servers are wonderfully skillful at seeing a job that needs to be done and just doing it. They can be found to be a perfectionist in their work probably because the work to be done is on behalf of another and they desire to perform their best for them. The negative side of this is they can be trapped into expecting the same perfectionist qualities in someone else that is helping because they want to ensure every possible aspect is covered, which others may have viewed as unimportant.

Servers, if operating out of personal interest, can become demanding of others if they feel they are not contributing as fully as they should or do not seem to be as committed. As a result they may not enjoy working with others. We need to communicate with servers how much we appreciate their work and we recognize their efforts. This is important because it lets them know they are going about the job in the right way and that their work is indeed making a difference in the lives of those they serve. Servers, however need to remember if recognition is not provided them that they are ultimately serving the Lord so that no bitter root has a chance to get a foothold.

Working within a Spiritual gift is not something to be prideful about; we do it because it is an honor. No glory should come to us nor should we expect it to as we operate in our most undeserving gift. God fashioned us to productively function in our gift and we are only humbly doing what we were gifted to do.

Servers pour out their lives as an offering for others and what a beautiful thing indeed to mirror the life of Christ is this way. We can easily be deceived into thinking we are misunderstood or unappreciated which can lead to thoughts of rebellion or jealousy. If we serve out of a prompting of the Spirit, out of a love for Christ, and a love for the body of believers, this will help keep our eyes off self and fixed on Kingdom purposes.

Some affirmations of those who have the gift of service:

❊ Assist others therefore helping them in their calling ❊
❊ Keen to others likes and dislikes ❊
❊ Have an intense desire to be with other people ❊
❊ Like to help - not just do a job ❊
❊ Quick to act ❊

Those with the Spiritual gift of service are a blessing. Oh the monumental, essential value of servers!

A Biblical example of a server was Tabitha. She was a valuable servant of God and used as a powerful witness. (Acts 9:36-42) She excelled in her gift of serving to sew dresses for the widows in the church and she operated in this way as a faithful servant of Jesus Christ. Simon Peter heard of the servant's death and the widows showed Peter the dresses she had made them and how she had blessed them by her service. Peter was so touched that he raised Tabitha from the dead! Her dedication of service was clearly not over and was still needed in the church.

Those with the gift of service may feel unqualified for spiritual leadership but they will quickly volunteer for a more 'hands-on' type of assignment.

The verses below all include the Greek word for service (diakonia) that we are investigating. These verses are impactful in different ways. If we are going to serve, it will benefit us to look at all the references that are provided for us in the Bible so that we are well equipped in the knowledge of service. Please look up these references and complete the blanks. I pray these verses open the door to your understanding of the Spiritual Gift of service.

❧"But we will devote ourselves to prayer and to the preaching of the Word." (Acts 6:4)

The twelve apostles had summoned the entire group of disciples so they could select from among themselves seven men "of good reputation, full of the Spirit and wisdom" to handle financial concerns. In this way, the apostles could devote themselves full time to prayer and the ministry of the gospel. The word 'ministry' here is 'diakonia' and refers to a servant who by the command of God proclaim and promote the gospel among people. The apostles saw that prayer and the ministry of the word should be joined together in order to be effective.

🕯"But I count my life of no value to myself, so that I may finish my course and the _____ I received from the Lord Jesus, to testify to the gospel of God's grace." (Acts 20:24)

Paul was in the thick of his hardships at this point yet his focus was on finishing the course set before him by God with exceeding joy! Regardless of the hardships and unknown trials he faced, he would not consider his personal life to be of more value than his life in the ministry of promoting the testimony of the Lord Jesus. To not finish the ministry because the path turned perilous or took all his strength was not even a consideration for Paul. When we begin our day are our first thoughts on Him and His appointed task for the day? ==Living life in service to the Lord, whatever that may look like, is living in our full-throttle ministry.== Isn't that where we truly find our joy?

🕯"Brothers, you know the household of Stephanas: They are the first fruits of Achaia and have devoted themselves to _serving_ the saints. I urge you also to submit to such people, and to everyone who works and labors with them." (1 Corinthians 16:15-16)

==In the work of service, we can also be seen serving those who minister to others.== Does your heart direct you to submit yourself in showing the proper regard and support to those who aid others in ministry? Do we receive the truths spoken by them in truth and love? Do we offer ourselves as refreshing to them? Do we lesson their burden and offer aid in their work so they can perform their ministry in abundance? Do we esteem others work of ministry to the best of our God-given ability? Those with the gift of service, as with the other gifts, are committed to spreading the Gospel of Christ wholeheartedly.

🕯"Therefore, since we have this _ministry_ because we were shown mercy, we do not _lose_ _heart_. Instead, we have renounced shameful secret things, not walking in deceit or distorting God's message, but _____ ourselves to every person's conscience in God's sight by an _____ display of the truth." (2 Corinthians 4:1-2)

The ministry spoken of here is that of the new Covenant, of the Spirit, of righteousness, and of glory. We have the ministry of joining God in His work only because of the great mercy shown us and not because of any of our righteous deeds. We find strength to continue on in ministry even as trials and difficulties present themselves. Just knowing that we have been called to such a ministry is our source of strength. We should not be surprised when we are faced with opposition either from outside sources or from the trials that persist inside our own deceiving minds.

We can openly display the truth by exhibiting veracity in our lives thus making it manifest as a testimony to others. This is done by leading with authenticity and confessing the truth by our words. The genuineness of the gospel should not be disguised nor sugar-coated to make it go down easier for people. Nor should the gospel be mixed with the traditions of man or have parts deleted to ensure it is easier on the ears. The purpose in speaking the gospel message is to make the full truth known in a valid straight-forward manner.

☙"Everything is from God, who reconciled us to Himself through Christ and gave us the ___ministry___ of reconciliation: That is, in Christ, God was reconciling the world to Himself, not counting their trespasses against them, and He has ___committed to us___ the message of reconciliation to us. Therefore, we are ___Christ's___ ___ambassadors___, certain that God is _____ through us. We plead on Christ's behalf, "Be reconciled to God." (2 Corinthians 5:18-20)

==Sinners are reconciled to God when self-interest is extinguished and motivation is shifted off of self and back to the Lord of Glory! (Romans 1:21). The ministry of reconciliation has been given to all. We all have been granted, through the grace of the Lord, a measure of ability to proclaim the Truth that through repentance God does not count our trespasses against us. Therefore, we speak with confidence on behalf of God (as ambassadors) for all to be reconciled to God!==

☙"We give no opportunity for stumbling to anyone, so that the ___ministry___ will not be blamed. But as God's ministers, we commend ourselves in everything: by great ___endurance___, by ___troubles___, by ___hardships___, by ___distresses___, by ___beatings___, by ___imprisonments___, by ___riots___, by ___hard work___, by ___sleepless nights___, by times of ___hunger___, by _____, by _____, by _____, by _____, by the _____, by sincere _____, by the message of _____, by the _____ of God; through weapons of righteousness on the right hand and the left, through glory and dishonor, through slander and good report; as deceivers yet true; as unknown yet recognized; as dying and look— we live; as being _____ yet not killed; as grieving yet always rejoicing; as poor yet enriching many; as having nothing yet possessing everything." (2 Corinthians 6:3-10)

Charisma

Whew!! Did you ever think the service ministry would require all of that? While ministering in the Spiritual gift of service, our lives should be such such that we do nothing in our knowledge (and fix it if we do) to cause stumbling in the faith to anyone. Our service to the Lord should be of the

highest regard. While ministering, we should be willing to stand in the face of any conflict with our mission in Christ ever before us.

❧"And tell Archippus, "Pay attention to the __Work__ you have received in the Lord, so that you can accomplish it." (Colossians 4:17)

The phrase 'pay attention to' means: to see, discern, of the bodily eye, to be possessed of sight, have the power of seeing, perceive by the use of the eyes: to turn the eyes to anything: to look at, look upon, gaze at to perceive by the senses. If we do not pay attention to something how do we expect to accomplish the task? Because servers are drawn to tasks that meet immediate needs, the task that might require either long-rage planning or some significant commitment of time to complete could be seen as frustrating.

Timothy was spoken highly of by Paul as an essential server to him. Timothy willingly operated in the Spiritual gift of service and proved himself invaluable in ministry to Paul. Paul went so far as to call him his son because of the way he came alongside him in ministry. Paul made note of Timothy's gift of serving in Philippians 2:20-21, "For I have no one else like-minded who will genuinely care about your interests; all seek their own interests, not those of Jesus Christ."

Paul also spoke to Timothy in 2 Timothy 4:21 that he should "make every effort to come before winter" knowing that Timothy should keep his eyes focused and finish the job that was before him.

❧"I give thanks to Christ Jesus our Lord who has strengthened me, because He considered me faithful, appointing me to the __service__ — one who was formerly a __blasphemer__, a __persecutor__, and an __violent__ man. But I received mercy because I acted out of ignorance in unbelief. And the __grace__ of our Lord _____, along with the faith and love that are in Christ Jesus." (1 Timothy 1:12-14)

Has the Lord given you a service to perform? Then He has strengthened you to perform it. He has audacious faith in you to boldly perform the ministry He has given, even though your past does not even begin to qualify you for the post. What mercy and grace indeed.

Charisma

&"But as for you, be serious about everything, endure hardship, do the work of an evangelist, _____ your _____." (2 Timothy 4:5)

This commentary will be similar to Colossians 4:17 above.

&"Now if the ___ministry___ of death, chiseled in letters on stones, came with glory, so that the Israelites were not able to look directly at Moses' face because of the glory from his face — a fading glory — how will the ___ministry___ of the Spirit not be more glorious? For if the _____ of condemnation had glory, the _____ of righteousness overflows with even more glory." (2 Corinthians 3:7-9)

The Law of Moses came with glory indeed but it was a fading glory. The service of the Spirit is more glorious because it does not fade! As we are serving we should keep in mind that the glory of the Spirit does not fade but endures through all seasons and all ages. It is always fresh and always prompts us to serve others in ministry for the purpose of the all-surpassing glory of the One who is worthy.

&"For the _____ of this service is not only supplying the needs of the saints, but is also overflowing in many acts of _____ to God. They will glorify God for your obedience to the confession of the gospel of Christ, and for your _____ in sharing with them and with others through the proof provided by this _____. And they will have _____ affection for you in their prayers on your behalf because of the surpassing grace of God _____ _____." (2 Corinthians 9:12-14)

This portion of scripture is referring to the generous gift of the believers at Corinth. When other believers would hear of the generous gift they would thank God for the generous act of faith of the Corinthians. Paul is suggesting that the church in Jerusalem will receive the financial benefits and in return will offer the spiritual blessing of intercession towards the Corinthians.

As we serve we supply the needs of the saints and while doing so our gifts of thanksgiving can't do anything but overflow to God. By our generous acts of service, others will dive a sacrifice of praise bringing glorify God through Christ.

&"Are they not all _____ spirits sent out to serve those who are going to _____ salvation? (Hebrews 1:14)

Charisma

What an amazing thought - angels are servant-spirits who are sent here with the purpose of caring for people who will inherit salvation. Amazing. If angels are called to serve people who will inherit salvation, those who have the Spiritual gift of service are in good company.

"I know your works — your love, faithfulness, _service_, and endurance. Your last works are greater than the first." Revelation 2:19

The church at Thyatira is being addressed by saying there was no lack of love, faithfulness, service, and endurance. When we are operating in our full-throttle Spiritual giftedness, meaningful spiritual effectiveness will be evidenced by our service.

If you have the Spiritual gift of service you have the power in your God-given hands to equip others and lesson their burdens. Begin learning how to perceive needs and pray to determine if the Lord shall indeed equip you for that particular service. Since you will be working closely with people pay attention to the invaluable ability to understand others before seeking to be understood. Prayer will ultimately guide you into areas where you can volunteer your valuable time and immeasurable skill. In the end our desire is for our master to say to us, "Well done, good and faithful servant! You were faithful over a few things; I will put you in charge of many things. Share your master's joy!" (Matthew 25:21) Amen to that.

Prayer

Father, lead me where you would have me go, soften my heart to the needs of others and help me suppress my personal ambitions as I know all things I do are meant only for Your glory. Instruct me in understanding the needs of others so that I truly am a blessing and not a hinderance in any sort of way. I will pray for others and pray for those I work alongside, giving the ultimate sacrifice of praise to the One who deserves it all. I anticipate your unending equipping in this area. In Jesus name I pray and receive. Amen.

Memory Verse
Acts 28:31

The Nourishment of Teaching

Exod. 4:12

Goal is to build up the body of Christ. (reveal Jesus)

Jesus is and was the ultimate teacher. If you have the Spiritual gift of teaching you will be wise to follow the Teacher's pattern. Jesus taught His truths and inspired His converts wherever He traveled using different techniques based upon the type of hearer around Him. He utilized parables and prepared speeches called sermons as well as informally teaching others during what would appear to be spontaneous conversation. The underlying current mixed with these styles was His supreme authority. Probably more significant than any of these teaching genres is the way He ordered His life to be living proof of the reality of the undying confidence He had in His Father. In this way, His life was a reflection of what He taught. Our lives should also be a witness of the truths we teach.

The motivation behind Jesus' teaching was to reveal His Father so that others would also know Him as He did. In doing so, *some* of the things He teaches us are about love, forgiveness, why not to judge, why not to store up riches on earth, about our true enemy, about grace, righteousness, justification, and about prayer.

We all are called to teach what we know about the scriptures to anyone having an ear to hear. The Spiritual gift of teaching however, goes beyond the everyday sort of teaching in which each believer is presumed to participate in.

The Greek word for teaching is didaskō (Strongs 1321) and means to teach (literally, "cause to *learn*"), instruct, impart knowledge, to improve morals, or expound on something (biblehub.com). The Spiritual gift of teaching comes with the ability to understand, explain, and apply the Word of God so that it can then be clearly imparted to others in an understandable way and edifies the Church.

Jesus was a momentous teacher. Because His examples of teaching are so abundant, I have summarized in the four paragraphs below numerous places in Scripture that use the same Greek word for teaching. (didaskō) He constantly leads us through His Word so let's be bold and follow His perfect teaching style.

Charisma

The following a summary of instances where the word teaching is found in Scripture. The paragraphs are separated only for ease in reading.

Jesus went all over Galilee **teaching**, (Matthew 4:23, 9:35) He did not stay put! He **taught** with such authority (Matthew 21:23, Matthew 7:29, John 7:46) that the demons recognized him. (Luke 4:41) Jesus **taught** and preached in all the towns he visited (Matthew 11:1, Mark 6:6) and the people were astonished. (Matthew 13:54, Mark 6:2) Jesus wisely suggested to His disciples that they needed to take refreshing breaks from their **teaching** (Mark 6:30). When the crowds came, Jesus could not refuse them and **taught** anyway (Mark 2:13, 6:34, 10:1) because His deep compassion and deep love. He **taught** what his father instructed him (John 8:28); such as the path to the cross (Mark 8:31, 9:31), that the Scriptures must be fulfilled (Mark 14:49), the beatitudes (Matthew 5:2), how to pray (Luke 11:1), and what the communion table represented (John 6:53-59).

Jesus frequently traveled, **teaching** along his journeys (Matthew 26:55, Luke 13:22, Luke 19:47, John 8:2) and His **teaching** was acclaimed by everyone (Luke 4:15). He even **taught** in parables when needed (Mark 4:1-2). He **taught** we must learn to recognize the Holy Spirit as our teacher (Luke 12:12, John 14:26, Hebrew 8:11) when He journeyed back to His Father.

When Jesus **taught**, He spoke of the ways of God truthfully (Matthew 22:16, Mark 12:14) and held nothing back in secret (John 18:20). He saw **teaching** as a high priority and spoke with authority in His interpretation of Scripture, unlike any Scribe they had heard before (Mark 1:21-22). One thing He clearly wanted us to understand is our worship would be in vain if we **taught** the doctrines and commands men (Matthew 15:9, Mark 7:7). People were stirred up by his life-giving **teaching** (Luke 23:5) and were often amazed at how well He knew the Scriptures and could communicate them (John 7:14). Jesus instructed others that **teaching** was good but knowing the Lord is what saves a soul (Luke 13:26).

Following Jesus' lead, the disciples went on to **teach** and proclaim the resurrection from the dead (Acts 4:2). In the power of the Spirit, the disciples did not shrink back from **teaching** and proclaiming anything that was profitable (Acts 20:20). The anointing we receive from Him remains in us and **teaches** us about all things (1 John 2:27). All revelations for **teaching** the gospel come by Jesus Christ (Galatians 1:12). In obedience, the disciples **taught** in the temple complex (Acts 5:21) and instructed others in the way of the Lord with a fervent spirt, speaking and **teaching** Jesus accurately (Acts 18:25). Paul felt strongly that our lives should reflect what we **teach** and preach

(Romans 2:21). Anyone hearing about the love of Jesus should be **taught** that the truth is found only in Him (Ephesians 4:21).

==The person with the Spiritual gift of teaching feels compelled to investigate Biblical definitions of words and driven to explore sections of the Bible for the deeper meaning. After spending time in study, the discovery will then be passionately presented to others with the desire to profoundly inspire the listener to consider the entire matter and the application it has for victorious living.==

We should always guard against any pride that accompanies knowledge if we work in the Spiritual gift of teaching. This problem area could arise if we are not yielded to the Spirit but instead are operating more from a fleshly motivation. Knowledge makes us feel important (1 Corinthians 8:1) and therefore can easily persuade us to incline towards pride. We will also want to shield ourselves against giving more information than is needed to prove a point if the goal is to show our vast knowledge. Let us also be cautious of possessing an opinionated attitude regarding information someone else presents. We do not want our thinking to say someone is only correct after 'I' investigate and 'I' acknowledge it to be correct.

==Teachers are adept at taking information scholars have researched and putting it together into a presentation in a way others can connect with and comprehend.== The goal is always to point others towards Jesus and the transforming truth He has provided.

Have you ever pondered why the Book of Luke is more lengthy than the Books of Matthew, Mark, or John? Or why there is information in the Book of Luke that is not found in the other Gospels such as detailed descriptions of events, circumstances, and conversations? ==Luke had the Spiritual gift of teaching.== Someone operating in this gift will outline with a systematic sequence what they intend to present with the purpose of getting across a clear central truth. An example of this can be found in Acts 1:1 as Luke emphasized the completeness of the narrative, which can at times mean more words! Luke also ordered his writing approach in this fashion as illustrated in the beginning of the Book of Luke.

Let's try an exercise. Investigate the passage below and write down what you glean from the text as examples of Luke's Spiritual gift of teaching.

"Many have undertaken to compile a narrative about the events that have been fulfilled among us, just as the original eyewitnesses and servants of the word handed them down to us. It also seemed good to me, since I have carefully investigated everything from the very first, to

write to you in an orderly sequence, most honorable Theophilus, so that you may know the certainty of the things about which you have been instructed." (Luke 1:1-4)

1) ____________________
2) ____________________
3) ____________________
4) ____________________

Some affirmations of those with the gift of teaching:

❊ Diligence and Endurance ❊
❊ Solves Problems by Starting with Scriptural Principles ❊
❊ Guides and Mentors ❊
❊ Detailed and Accurate ❊
❊ Disciplined ❊
❊ Articulate ❊

The Spiritual gift of teaching spoken of in Romans 12:7 is the Greek word didaskō (communicating) and we are told we should be teaching (didaskalia - should be teaching doctrine). Ephesians 4:11 and 1 Corinthians 12:18 also speak of the Spiritual gift of teachers (didaskalos) God gave the Church to build up the body of Christ. As you can see, these Greek words are similar. A chapter has been devoted to teaching (didaskō) and to teacher (didaskalos). The Spiritual Gifts Profile (pg. 269), only makes statements regarding Teacher.

Below are the elements and the style in which we should teach as taken from the examples of Scripture. Please prayerfully consider the verses as you complete the blanks.

❧"Restore the Joy______ of Your salvation to me, and give me a willing spirit. Then I will ______teach______ the rebellious Your ways, and sinners will return to You." (Psalm 51:12-13)

I recall praying for a friend once and I was overcome by a Spiritual response to the prayer and her current human condition. I knew the Spirit would soon reveal to her the message He was revealing to me; that she would "receive the joy of her salvation". Within a matter of days she did "receive"! Not long after that she had such joy in the Lord that her spirit could not help but speak of the wonders of the

Lord to others. How will we teach the rebellious the ways of the Lord so that they return to the Savior of their souls? By being filled with joy that only comes from the Lord. The true gift of teaching the Gospel is not done by a mere work of the human intellect. It is accomplished under the inspiration and filling of the Spirit of the Living God.

"They must __teach__ My people the difference between the __holy__ and the __common__, and explain to them the difference between the __clean__ and the __unclean__." (Ezekiel 44:23)
This Old Testament verse is found under the heading, The Priests' Duties and Privileges. In the Old Testament, the Levites were selected by God to serve as the priesthood. According to the New Testament, God calls all believers to comprise His priesthood. (1 Peter 2:5,9 Revelation 1:6). As the "royal priesthood", we shall also teach people the difference between the holy (all that is set apart for God) and the common (that not sanctified by the Spirit and grace of God) in an evangelical sense so that people might be kept free from pollutants. Teachers should also explain the difference between the clean and the unclean. We are bound to read the Word, teach the Word, and expound on it as necessary to answer the arising questions of hearts desiring to draw nearer to God.

Let's take a look at some Hebrew definitions from the Ezekiel verse (biblehub.com):

holy: set apart, sacred.
common: profane, profane place, unholy,
clean: holy or acceptable to God, can be used in a ritual sense to apply to a moral standard for living. Examples are 1) ceremonially clean animals, 2) physically pure, 3) morally and ethically pure.
unclean: unholy (such as an unclean spirit), defiled, polluted

Because we are part of the New Covenant priesthood, it is necessary to maintain holiness and knowledge of divine things, all the while teaching about it in truth, with faith, and with sincerity.

It is interesting to note that teaching the truths of these divine attributes was the responsibility of the priests but in the last years the teaching had been neglected (Malachi 2:7-9). Let's reinvigorate the teachings of the Messiah and not have this proclaimed over us during our watch. I heard it said recently that just because the end is near and society seems to be becoming more common and unclean are we just suppose to stop teaching truths and let the end just come? No. Jesus expects us to continue teaching the Gospel truths until our face sees His. We are not to sit passively in our generation with our head shaking and hands thrown up in the air. It is our watch, our time, our responsibility to continue while it is still called the day.

🙢"Come, let us go up to the mountain of the Lord, to the house of the God of Jacob. He will __teach__ us about His ways so we may __walk__ in His paths." (Micah 4:2)

The purpose of being taught the ways of the Lord is *so that* we may walk in His paths and teach others to do the same. Teachers, let's not neglect to approach the 'mountain of the Lord' by staying in our tents (Exodus 33:8) expecting to make a difference for the Kingdom. We are intimate with God when we approach Him, not by listening to someone else recount their intimacy with Him.

🙢"Let my __teaching__ fall like rain and my word settle like dew, like gentle rain on new grass and showers on tender plants. For I will proclaim Yahweh's name. Declare the greatness of our God!" (Deuteronomy 32:2-3)

Have you ever run carefree through the rain? Not running through the rain in a hurry to avoid the annoyance of getting yourself and your belongings wet. Running *carefree*. The carefree tender spirit receives the refreshing of the Word falling and settling down on them like the refreshment of gentle rain in a hot desert land. Don't 'run' through the Scriptures because you are in a hurry. Let the Word soak into your mind and settle in your heart while you tarry a while. When we then proclaim what we have learned by teaching it to others, we plant the seeds and await the harvest when the heavenly rain falls sweetly on their seeds. Shall we always remember to order our teaching steps in a way that falls gently on tender ears? Yes, and can be done while declaring the greatness of our God!

🙢"For a command is a lamp, __teaching__ is a light, and corrective discipline is the way to life." (Proverbs 6:23)

While operating in the Spiritual gift of teaching our motivation is to set an example for others by the testimony of our lives; paying attention not to be slothful or careless. In this way, we shall all prosper by paying close attention to things that can poison our minds and therefore our hearts. The 'command' is the Word of God, and teaching the Word is the brilliant light that pierces all darkness. Hallelujah!

🙢"Instead, this is the covenant I will make with the house of Israel after those days" — the Lord's declaration. "I will put My __law__ within them and write it on their hearts. I will be their God, and they will be My people. No longer will one __teach__ his neighbor or his brother, saying, 'Know the Lord,' for they will _____

Charisma

<u>all know</u> Me, from the least to the greatest of them" — this is the Lord's declaration. "For I will forgive their wrongdoing and never again remember their sin." (Jeremiah 31:33-34)

The Lord, through the His Holy Spirit will write His teachings on our tender hearts instead of hard tablets of stone. It is a sacred and holy heart indeed to have the Lord's instructions written there! Because of this, we all should know the desires of the Lord. As we go forth teaching others, one of the things we expound on is the power of repentance. God forgives and *never again remembers* the sin. Hallelujah! We must always be prepared to teach this overwhelmingly freeing fact.

❧"Therefore, whoever breaks one of the least of these commands and <u>teaches</u> people to do so will be called least in the kingdom of heaven. But whoever <u>practices</u> and <u>teaches</u> these commands will be called great in the kingdom of heaven." (Matthew 5:19)

We do not want to purposefully transgress, be a blind guide, depart from the Way, or teach a doctrine other than Jesus Christ. As disciples of Christ and as teachers of His gospel, we must not deceive ourselves by allowing disobedience in our lives. If we allow this, it becomes easier to either ignore specific teaching or to teach the same form of disobedience to others that we have accepted in our own lives.

Are we guilty of dividing the precepts of God's law into minor and greater aspects? In doing so do we adhere to the greater and ignore the minor? Jesus said, "Woe to you, scribes and Pharisees, hypocrites! You pay a tenth of mint, dill, and cumin, yet you have neglected the more important matters of the law — justice, mercy, and faith. These things should have been done without neglecting the others." (Mathew 23:23) There is no insignificant offense. If we feel judicial enough to make the distinction between minor offenses and greater offenses and thus saying the violation for minor offenses will be exempt we will be regarded as the "least in the kingdom of heaven." Teachers, let's avoid this at all cost.

❧"Then they understood that He did not tell them to beware of the yeast in bread, but of the <u>teaching</u> of the Pharisees and Sadducees." (Matthew 16:12)

Jesus did not tolerate hypocrisy. Period. One of the things the Pharisees were skillful at was hypocrisy. The outward appearance of worshiping God did not usually match the inward condition. Someone operating in the Spiritual gift of teaching should be aware of the dangers of pretense and have authenticity as the goal.

🙢"Then Jesus came near and said to them, "All authority has been given to Me in heaven and on earth. Go, therefore, and make disciples of all nations, baptizing them in the name of the Father and of the Son and of the Holy Spirit, __teaching__ them to __obey__ everything I have commanded you. And remember, I am with you always, to the end of the age." Matthew 28:18-20

On what basis do we 1) make disciples, 2) baptize, and 3) teach people? Jesus has been given all authority in heaven. He has the authority and therefore we teach from that place of authoritative truth. We teach others to obey Jesus' commands that come from His Word.

🙢"They worship Me in vain, __teaching__ as doctrines the commands of __men__." (Mark 7:7)

We **do not** teach the Gospel of Jesus effectively if it is done strictly based on the knowledge of man. It must be done out of an abundant love for Jesus and by the truth of the Word. What do we teach? THE Word of God. Nothing is added to it, nothing is taken away. How do we worship Jesus? In spirit and in truth. (John 4:24) If we worship God by teaching Jesus is the Messiah **we do well**. If we worship God by teaching the commands of men added to it...we are worshiping in vain (prideful, worthless, ineffective, foolish).

🙢"You were born entirely in sin," they replied, "and are you trying to __teach__ us?" Then they threw him out." (John 9:34)

The healed man was giving his testimony to the Pharisees and they would not receive it because they assumed a "sinner" has no testimony. God help us.

🙢"But the __Counselor__, the Holy __Spirit__ — the Father will send Him in My name — will __teach__ you all things and remind you of everything I have told you." (John 14:26)

How do you feel knowing the function of the Spirit is to teach you? Wow. The Lord expects you to know things, expects you to want to know things, and expects you to learn. He has given you THE ultimate teacher to accomplish this task. Hallelujah and Amen!

🙢"So they called for them and ordered them not to preach or __teach__ at all in the name of Jesus." (Acts 4:18) "Someone came and reported to them, "Look! The men you put in jail are standing in the temple complex and __teaching__ the people." (Acts 5:25) "Didn't we strictly order you not to __teach__ in this name? And look, you have filled Jerusalem with your __teaching__ and are determined to bring this man's blood on us!" (Acts 5:28) "Every day, in the temple complex, and in various homes, they continued __teaching__ and proclaiming the good news that Jesus is the Messiah." (Acts 5:42)

"Then he stayed two whole years in his own rented house. And he welcomed all who visited him, __proclaiming__ the kingdom of God and __teaching__ the things concerning the Lord Jesus Christ with full __boldness__ and without __hindrance__." (Acts 28:30-31)

==People may feel they are being prevented therefore they think they are hindered but the Word is _never hindered_. God is responsible for His Word being heard, taught, and received with power.== He watches over His Word and never returns to Him until it accomplishes what it was set out to do.

Shall we welcome all that come to us and proclaim the kingdom of God and teach all things concerning the Lord Jesus Christ with *full boldness* and without hinderance? There shall be no other way. Do we accept people into our home expecting the opportunity to teach them no matter the circumstance OR convenience?

☙"This is why I have sent Timothy to you. He is my dearly loved and faithful son in the Lord. He will remind you about __my__ __ways__ in Christ Jesus, just as I __teach__ everywhere in every church." (1 Corinthians 4:17)

Paul lived what he taught. This verse illustrates a perfect example of living what you teach. "And if you are convinced that you are a guide for the blind, a light to those in darkness, an instructor of the ignorant, a teacher of the immature, having the full expression of knowledge and truth in the law — you then, who teach another, don't you teach yourself? You who preach, "You must not steal" — do you steal? You who say, "You must not commit adultery" — do you commit adultery? You who detest idols, do you rob their temples?" (Romans 2:19-22)

Timothy was a witness of the ways Paul lived. He testified that Paul lived out the truths he taught.

☙"And He personally gave some to be apostles, some prophets, some evangelists, some pastors and __teachers__, for the _____ of the saints in the work of ministry, to __build up__ the body of Christ, until we all reach __unity__ in the faith and in the knowledge

Charisma

of God's Son, growing into a mature man with a stature measured by Christ's fullness. Then we will no longer be little children, _____ by the waves and blown around by every wind of _____, by _____ cunning with _____ in the techniques of deceit. But speaking the truth in love, let us _____ in every way into Him who is the head — Christ. From Him the whole body, fitted and knit together by every supporting ligament, _____ the growth of the body for _____ _____ itself in love by the proper working of each individual part." (Ephesians 4:11-14)

I just love this. If you are operating full-throttle in the Spiritual gift of teaching then your mission is to **build up** the body of Christ, until **all** have reached **unity** in the faith and in the knowledge of God's Son. Not only that but we should be teaching until we have all grown into a "mature man" with a stature measured by Christ's fullness. This means to me that we shall be forever teaching! We should also teach so that no one we educate behaves with the spiritual mind of a child. We should teach in the truth of love. We should teach unity of the body supporting each other and building each other up in love.

⁍"We _proclaim_ Him, warning and _teaching_ everyone with all wisdom, so that we may present everyone _perfect_ in Christ." (Colossians 1:28)

In teaching we Proclaim and Warn everyone in the fullness of spiritual wisdom SO THAT we may present all those we teach mature in Christ. Wow. That is a full plate to gobble down with an eager mouth salivating at the honor of helping a fellow believer stand mature before Christ. Honored for the opportunity.

⁍"Therefore, as you have received Christ Jesus the Lord, _continue_ in Him, _rooted_ and _built_ _up_ in Him and _strengthened_ in the faith, just as you were _taught_, _overflowing_ with gratitude." (Colossians 2:6-7)

What does it do to your soul as you read the words, 'you have received Christ Jesus the Lord'! Therefore, walk in Him! Be rooted in Him! Know that His truth builds you up! Be strongly established in the faith! Do all these things just as you were taught and be sure to teach these things as well. While you are at it, do it from a heart that is overflowing with gratitude. It will be so captivating to others they can't help but learn. Praise God teachers!

⁍"Let the message about the Messiah _dwell_ richly among you, _teaching_ and admonishing one another in all wisdom,

Charisma

and singing psalms, hymns, and spiritual songs, with gratitude in your hearts to God." (Colossians 3:16)

Where do we possibly begin with this commentary? <mark>In order to teach the Messiah the message must *already* dwell richly in us.</mark> RICHLY. Muse on the word richly. How can we imagine 'richly'? In a beautiful and expensive way, in a pleasingly strong way, in a generous way. This speaks of nothing more than Jesus Himself. When the message dwells richly what else can we do but teach, admonish, and sing of the richness found nowhere else but in Jesus himself.

The next 6 scripture verses will speak of the <mark>same common theme - sound teaching.</mark> 1 Timothy 1:9-11 is this first place in the New Testament Holman translation where this word is used. I have bolded the words for emphasis. A commentary will follow at the end of the 7 sets of verses.

> ❧ (1) "We know that the law is not meant for a righteous person, but for the lawless and rebellious, for the ungodly and sinful, for the unholy and irreverent, for those who kill their fathers and mothers, for murderers, for the sexually immoral and homosexuals, for kidnappers, liars, perjurers, and for whatever else is contrary to the **sound teaching** based on the glorious gospel of the blessed God, which was entrusted to me." (1 Timothy 1:9-11)

> ❧ (2) "Teach and encourage these things. If anyone teaches other doctrine and does not agree with the **sound teaching** of our Lord Jesus Christ and with the teaching that promotes godliness, he is conceited, understanding nothing, but has a sick interest in disputes and arguments over words. From these come envy, quarreling, slander, evil suspicions, and constant disagreement among people whose minds are depraved and deprived of the truth, who imagine that godliness is a way to material gain." (1 Timothy 6:2b-5)

> ❧ (3) "Hold on to the pattern of **sound teaching** that you have heard from me, in the faith and love that are in Christ Jesus." (2 Timothy 1:13)

> ❧ (4) "For the time will come when they will not tolerate **sound doctrine**, (doctrine is didaskalia which as you can see is a form of the word didaskō) but according to their own desires, will multiply teachers for themselves because they have an itch to hear something new." (2 Timothy 4:3)

Charisma

- (5) "For an overseer, as God's administrator, must be blameless, not arrogant, not hot-tempered, not addicted to wine, not a bully, not greedy for money, but hospitable, loving what is good, sensible righteous, holy, self-controlled, holding to the faithful message as taught, so that he will be able both to encourage with **sound teaching** and to refute those who contradict it." (Titus 1:7-9)

  - (6) "But you must say the things that are consistent with **sound teaching**." (Titus 2:1)

  - (7) "Make yourself an example of good works with integrity and dignity in your teaching. Your message is to be **sound** beyond reproach, so that the opponent will be ashamed, having nothing bad to say about us." (Titus 2:7-8)

So what is sound teaching and why is it important? Sound teaching encompasses the whole council of Scripture from Genesis to Revelation. The importance of this is that we will know and love God and love the brethren. Without sound teaching the path of life would not be clearly revealed to the Christian or for the Church. The better we know the Gospel through sound teaching the more equipped we are to share the Gospel as well as to embolden evangelism. This foundation of truth and love cultivates a life of holiness and ignites our worship.

Looking at the seven Scriptures we can extract the following things. From number (1), sound teaching based on _glorious_ _gospel_ of the _blessed_ _God_, which was entrusted to me. Sound teaching is entrusted to the one with the Spiritual gift of teaching.

From number (2), If someone teaches a doctrine other than the sound teaching of Jesus Christ that promotes godliness then what kind of search is this and teacher is this and what shall be expected of them?

___

From number (3), sound teaching that we have been taught from the Scriptures should be bound tight with _____ and _____.

From number (4), why will sound teaching no longer be tolerated?
___

From number (5), why is there a list here of qualities necessary to possess in order to encourage and to refute those who contradict

Charisma

sound teaching? Verse 10-16 gives us the reason. "For there are also many rebellious people, full of empty talk and deception, especially those from Judaism. It is necessary to silence them; they overthrow whole households by teaching what they shouldn't in order to get money dishonestly. One of their very own prophets said, Cretans are always liars, evil beasts, lazy gluttons. This testimony is true. So, rebuke them sharply, that they may be sound in the faith and may not pay attention to Jewish myths and the commands of men who reject the truth. To the pure, everything is pure, but to those who are defiled and unbelieving nothing is pure; in fact, both their mind and conscience are defiled. They profess to know God, but they deny Him by their works. They are detestable, disobedient, and disqualified for any good work."

From number (6) and (7) we must _____ things that are consistent and _____ _____ so that the opponent will be ashamed and have nothing to say. The enemy knows all about authority. Are you familiar enough with it that you can teach about it?

❧"I do not allow a woman to _teach_ or to have authority _over_ a man; instead, she is to be silent. (1 Timothy 2:12)

Let's begin by breaking this down into phrases (1) I do not allow a woman to teach or (2) to have authority over a man (3) she is to be silent.

(1) I do not allow a woman to teach or to have authority over a man. What Paul seems to be indicating in this verse regarding authority is that he does not permit women to fill the office of elder in the church. An elder is responsible for the primary leadership and oversight of a church. Since both of these things go together Paul is probably indicating that he does not permit a woman to take the position of elder in the church.

(2) I do not allow a woman to teach. In order to evaluate what Paul seems to be indicating in this verse regarding teaching, let's take a look at other verses. Titus 2:3 tells us, "In the same way, older women are to be reverent in behavior, not slanderers, not addicted to much wine. They are to **teach** what is good." 2 Timothy 3:14 tells us, "But as for you, continue in what you have **learned** and firmly believed." The ones who taught him were Eunice and Lois, his mother and grandmother. Acts 18:26 tells us, "He began to speak boldly in the synagogue. After Priscilla and Aquila heard him, they took him home and **explained** the way of God to him more accurately." Overall, what Paul seems to be saying is that women should not teach in a way that relates to

authority over men. So what about authority? Probably what Paul is meaning is that he does not permit a woman to teach and use authority over men. He taught that women should not have the responsibility or the authority as an elder in the church.

(3) Let a woman learn in silence. Combining these phrases together we can see that this kind of silence goes along with respecting and honoring the leadership of the men God has put in His church. I don't think the idea is that women are not speak but that they are submissive and do not talk in a way that indicates a lack of respect for authority.

Paul did not undervalue women in ministry. Many women served alongside Him as he indicated in Romans 16:3-15.

⁕"Therefore, brothers, stand __firm__ and hold to the traditions you were __taught__, either by our message or by our letter." (2 Thessalonians 2:15)

The word 'stand firm' is interesting in that it implies a sort of military objective. If an officer told his soldier to stand firm in the command given, the officer would expect the soldier might be tempted to sway from the original command due to an approaching danger. The soldier's mind must be set and his will must [not be] uncertain or discouraged.

The word 'tradition' implies something conveyed to another and in this case it indicates doctrines. The Pharisees' doctrine is called tradition (Matthew 15:3). The true doctrine of the gospel is what the apostles conveyed to the people (1 Corinthians 11:23, Romans 6:13) (Poole, biblehub.com)

Teachers, we stand firm in the traditions taught in the Scriptures so that we might obtain the glory of our Lord Jesus Christ. Anything else are commands of men and should not be taught.

⁕"If you point these things out to the brothers, you will be a good servant of Christ Jesus, __brought up__ by the words of the faith and the good __teaching__ that you have followed." (1 Timothy 4:6)

We should busy ourselves pointing out truths to the brethren. Not pointing out truth as one knowing better than the other but pointing out the truth in love to build each other up. We shall always remember that as we point out the truth to our brethren that we expect the same to be done regarding out lives.

⁕"Command and __teach__ these things." (1 Timothy 4:11)

Charisma

"These things refers to the preceding verses. We are to have "nothing to do with irreverent and silly myths." We should "train ourself in godliness, for the training of the body has a limited benefit, but godliness is beneficial in every way, since it holds promise for the present life and also for the life to come." (verse 7-8)

We are instructed to (1) command and (2) teach the following: the truth of the Word, godliness requires training (it will not come naturally or easily), and being physically 'in-shape' has limited benefit compared to the benefit you will receive from being 'in-shape' spiritually.

☙"Until I come, give your attention to public reading, exhortation, and _____teaching_____." (1 Timothy 4:13)

There is no other thing that should take priority than speaking the truth, exhorting each other, and teaching the truth of the Word. This should be what thrills us! This should be our undoing! This should be what our next breath longs for. If you have the Spiritual gift of teaching do you look for opportunities to read or speak the Word?

☙"Pay _____ attention to your life and your _____; _____ in these things, for by doing this you will save both _____ and your _____." (1 Timothy 4:16)

Not only do we teach others but we must adhere to the same message we ourselves teach. Our life should be an open book to teach our trials and the victories we have received in Christ. The only benefit of teaching our failures in the flesh is to bring glory to our Rescuer, the Darling of Heaven Himself. We must speak of our testimonies because this is how we defeat the enemy and encourage others to do the same. We must be *bold* for the cause of Christ.

What things exactly shall we teach and encourage? The primary motive of ministry is love.

☙"You, therefore, my son, be strong in the grace that is in Christ Jesus. And what you have heard from me in the presence of many witnesses, commit to _____ men who will be _____ to _____ others also." (2 Timothy 2:1-2)

We shall be STRONG in the grace that is in Christ Jesus! There is no other well from which to draw strength that has the power and sufficiency to equip us to face the trials of this age. We must commit our time and service to faithful men who will serve with us and will also be able to teach others the same courageous message found in the life of Christ.

Charisma

☙"The Lord's slave must not quarrel, but must be gentle to everyone, able to _____, and _____, instructing his _____ with gentleness. Perhaps God will grant them repentance leading them to the knowledge of the truth." (2 Timothy 2:24-25)

What does this look like in our lives when operating in the Spiritual gift of teaching? No quarreling, gentle to everyone, and patient. These qualities possessed in the believer is what leads the sinner to God. We must be like Jesus and our lives must be a testimony to the power of the Messiah which is available to all those who search for Him.

☙"All Scripture is inspired by God, and is profitable for _____, for rebuking, for correcting, for _____ in righteousness, so that the man of God may be _____, equipped for every good work." (2 Timothy 3:16)

Scripture is remarkable and is profitable for all things. Teaching. Rebuking. Correcting. Training. Praise God. Scripture teaches us how to be men and women of God. We can be complete and equipped for every good work purely by the power God *gives to His Word*. Remarkable.

☙"Proclaim the message; persist in it whether _____ or not; rebuke, correct, and encourage with great patience and _____." (2 Timothy 4:2)

If you are operating in the Spiritual gift of teaching what are you to do? Proclaim the message. What do you think of when you contemplate convenience? Easy? Comfortable? Opportune? Friendly? Favorable? Persist in proclaiming the message because we are told the convenience factor should not enter into our decision to be obedient. Teaching the word will also encompass rebuking, correcting, and encouraging in all seasons. Teaching the Gospel should be done with GREAT patience. What if we are not accepted? Already determine in your mind it will be a strong possibility. This should not modify the message nor is it a reason to shrink back from it.

☙"For there are also many rebellious people, full of empty talk and deception, especially those from Judaism. It is necessary to silence them; they _____ whole households by _____ what they shouldn't in order to get money dishonestly." (Titus 1:10-11)

This section is describing false teachers. The people group in Titus 1:10-13 that stand out and are used as an example are the Cretans. The Cretans were known to be dishonest and to have unjust morals.

Charisma

Paul called them "always liars, evil beasts, and lazy gluttons." These people were "greedy for money" (verse 7) and would prey on and overturn entire households.

In our generation we should stay away from all sorts of false teachers. So how would we identify someone like this? They would be (1) rebellious, (2) full of empty talk, and (3) deceptive. Once this type of teacher is identified they should not be allowed to have our ear. The verse said they should also be silenced. The word silenced paints a picture of having a muzzle put over a mouth. That is a strong move on the offense as opposed to merely defending your ground by allowing them to continue speaking.

If we desire someone to guide us in a difficult situation, "empty talkers" are not what we need. Empty talk will build up our frustrations, agree with our wrong turns, tell us what we want to hear, and help solidify our unwavering positions. We need the truth of the Word settled into our hearts in order to mend our souls. A false teacher does not have this as the motivation. The motivation of a false teacher is self gratification.

❧"In the same way, older women are to be reverent in behavior, not slanderers, not addicted to much wine. They are to _____ what is good, so they may _____ the young women to love their husbands and to love their children, to be self-controlled, pure, homemakers, kind, and submissive to their husbands, so that God's message will not be slandered." (Titus 2:3-5)

Please see the commentary associated with 1 Timothy 2:12 above.

❧"Although by this time you ought to be _____, you need someone to _____ you the basic principles of God's revelation again. You need milk, not solid food. Now everyone who lives on milk is _____ with the message about righteousness, because he is an infant. But solid food is for the _____ — for those whose senses have been trained to _____ between good and evil." (Hebrews 5:12-14)

You should be able to instruct others. Not all have the Spiritual gift of teaching and are not expected to act in this capacity but everyone ought to be able to explain Christian truths to the one that is curious.

❧"Anyone who does not remain in Christ's _____ but goes _____ it, does not have God. The one who remains in that _____, this one has _____ the Father and the Son. If anyone comes to you and does not bring this _____, do not receive him into your home, and don't say, "_____," to him;

Charisma

for the one who says, "Welcome," to him shares in his evil works." (2 John 1:9-10)

Christ's teaching was the truth He Himself taught. We must remain in His teaching as well as spread His teaching. "Going beyond it" implies an extreme departure of the faith; a sort of wandering away in which there is a loss of eternal life. Not only are we instructed to remain in the teaching of Christ but we should be about the business of teaching the message of Christ. We should live and teach that if anyone comes to us and speaks a message other than the truth of the Messiah we should not accept it and further more they should not even be welcome in our homes. We shall never align ourselves with those who intend to derail the teachings of Christ.

No matter what pain you suffer, no matter what trial you endure, no matter what you may consider to be lack, the inspired Word of God taught to your mind, and settled into your heart and soul will always surpass your greatest need. Thank you Lord for that. Please continue to inspire us so that it never slips from our memory.

Prayer

I am thankful Jesus demonstrated the most perfect teaching pattern. Equip me with Your wisdom to modify my teaching technique depending on who is listening and the way they will be most able to relate and receive. Jesus has supreme authority and I will teach from the authority that the Word represent. Empower me to order my life to be living proof of the truths I teach others. My ultimate desire is to have God revealed and magnified to Believers as well as unbelievers. Permit me to go beyond the everyday sort of teaching and to have a powerful demonstration of the Spirit through my teaching. All for Your glory and honor. Amen.

Exhortations Goal?
Spiritual Transformation.

James was an exhorter.

The exhorter tells people how to do it

If you are operating in the spiritual gift of exhortation (parakaleo) you will be motivated to encourage other believers on to maturity in Christ. "Until I come, give your attention to public reading, exhortation, and teaching." (1 Timothy 4:13) We should not stop exhorting others because the motivating goal is unity in the faith and maturity in Christ. What I find absolutely eye-opening is the realization that people operate in Spiritual gifts whether they realize it or not. If they have not realized it, they will at times operate in the flesh which will not always come across the way the Lord intended. It also may be perceived by others strangely if we do not recognize someone is operating in their gifting. We should always serve God with our Spiritual gifts in the spirit and not in the flesh.

One example of what I am describing is the difference between the gift of mercy and the gift of exhortation. Someone with the gift of mercy might offer to bring a meal, clean a house or yard, or run an errand for someone trying to get back on their feet. On the other hand, a person with a gift of exhortation will favor offering spiritual assistance instead. If we are not aware of these differences, it will be hard to understand at times why (1) some people offer assistance the way they do and (2) we will wonder why someone is not as quick to offer assistance in ways we think are needed because we see things from the perspective of the gift we operate in. All Spiritual gifts are needed in the body in order to perform successful ministry work.

An exhorter will read through the Bible with an eye for Scripture that would be helpful to pass on to someone in need. They also desire to memorize and have a good understanding of Scripture. This person can emphasize with someone but the strength of their gifting is experienced when they are able to encourage boldly with the Word of God. The exhorter can see how the person feels a certain way but will not linger there because the Spirit will instruct them to lead the person in how they can strengthen themselves by applying the power of the Word to their life.

The exhorters goal is to move forward, transformed by the power of the Word and not to linger in the hurts of the flesh. Therefore, the exhorter will want to offer a systematic way of achieving the goal of becoming spiritually strong in the situation with a plan of action.

Some weaknesses to watch out for:

❊ Could oversimplify solutions/problems. This could lead to discouragement instead of encouragement

❊ May not be the greatest listeners because they don't want the person to linger in their troubles and recant their worries but to move on to victory.

This spiritual gift called exhortation will be broken down into 6 categories and we will take a look at Scripture that falls into these categories. The categories are (1) beseeching, (2) comforting, (3) entreating, (4) exhortation, (5) desiring, and (6) praying.

Beseeching. A definition of beseech is: 'to implore urgently, to beg eagerly, solicit, to make an urgent appeal'. (dictionary.com) It indicates to 'call to one's side or aid'. We can beseech the Lord urgently during prayer as well as plead with other believers to grow in the grace and knowledge of Jesus Christ.

The following verses relate to Beseeching:

"When He entered Capernaum, a centurion came to Him, ____________ with Him." (Matthew 8:5)

"Then a man with a serious skin disease came to Him and, on his knees, ______________ Him: "If You are willing, You can make me clean." Moved with compassion, Jesus reached out His hand and touched him. "I am willing," He told him. "Be made clean." (Mark 1:40-41)

❧"They brought to Him a deaf man who also had a speech difficulty, and ______________Jesus to lay His hand on him." (Mark 7:32)

Some people brought a man who was deaf and could hardly talk. Out of concern for the man, the people begged Jesus to lay His hands on him, desperate for His healing to be made manifest. Could the man not make the request himself? Do we know people who are unable to beseech the Lord themselves due to poor health or because they do not know Him? Are you willing to 'bring' someone to Him and intercede on their behalf?

꙳"Therefore, brothers, by the mercies of God, I _____ you to present your bodies as a living _____, holy and pleasing to God; this is your spiritual _____. Do not be conformed to this age, but be _____ by the _____ of your mind, so that you may discern what is the good, pleasing, and perfect will of God." (Romans 12:1-2)

Paul begins this discussion by speaking of the fundamental requirements of a Christian life. He is not merely instructing believers but urging them based upon all that God has done for them. A person operating in the Spiritual gift of exhortation should be moved to also beseech others in this regard.

꙳"Now I _____ you, brothers, through our Lord Jesus Christ and through the love of the Spirit, to _____ with me in fervent prayers to God on my behalf." (Romans 15:30)

Paul is beseeching his fellow sojourners to join with him in a powerful prayer request. I love how he appeals through the Darling of heaven Himself, Jesus Christ and by the love of the Spirit! Lovely indeed. Having others come alongside us during our petitions is helpful for two simple reasons. 1) Jesus assured us if two agree about a matter in prayer it will be done and when we are gathered together in His name He is there among us and 2) It increases our faith when we are able to witness affirmatively answered prayer.

꙳"Now I _____ you, brothers, to watch out for those who _____ dissensions and obstacles _____ to the doctrine you have learned. _____ them, for such people do not serve our Lord Christ but their _____ appetites. They deceive the hearts of the _____ with smooth talk and flattering words." (Romans 16:17-18)

We are being beseeched here to be on the look out for agitators who would be a stumbling block to our faith and we should also urge others to watch out for the same type of troublemakers. Do you know people that talk about the Lord but do not serve Him? We will find many that can easily talk intellectually about the Lord but their true desire is to serve their own motives. We must not allow someone to

Charisma

deceive our hearts with smooth talk and flattering words. One of the problems is when we are weak in soul and spirit these type of people always seem to know just what to say to deceive our hearts. Be on the look out!

🙢"Now I _____ you, brothers, in the name of our Lord Jesus Christ, that all of you agree in what you say, that there be no divisions among you, and that you be united with the same understanding and the same conviction." (1 Corinthians 1:10)

This beseeching immediately comes out bold: in the name of Jesus Christ. As fellow believers there is unity in being in agreement regarding the testimony of Christ. Divisions should not exist among believers it only serves as a cloud of confusion which allows the enemy to slip in.

🙢"Therefore I _____ you to imitate me." (1 Corinthians 4:16)

What is it Paul is beseeching that we imitate? His ways in Christ Jesus. The Lord has entrusted us with people we have the power to influence. What are we doing to ensure our influence profits them? All the words of advice we speak to those under our influence should be filtered by the Word, not the opinion of our sadness, disappointments, or bitterness. Strengthen us Lord to not do such things!

🙢"Brothers, you know the household of Stephanas: They are the first fruits of Achaia and have devoted themselves to serving the saints. I _____ you also to _____ to such people, and to everyone who works and labors with them." (1 Corinthians 16:15-16)

Let's assist and have ears tuned to people that serve us.

🙢"If anyone has caused pain, he has caused pain not so much to me but to some degree — not to exaggerate — to all of you. The punishment inflicted by the majority is _____ for that person. As a result, you should instead forgive and _____ him. Otherwise, this one may be overwhelmed by _____ grief. Therefore I urge you to reaffirm your love to him." (2 Corinthians 2:5-8

We all make missteps. The inner suffering caused by the misstep is enough and we are under no obligation to inflict more suffering. God disciples those he loves and thus should be left to Him. Let's be considered gracious forgivers and not be the one to cause someone excessive grief due to our unforgiveness. The exhortation here is an urging of reaffirming love.

🙢"Therefore, we are ambassadors for Christ, certain that God is _____ through us. We _____ on Christ's behalf, "Be reconciled to God." (2 Corinthians 5:20)

🙢"Working together with Him, we also_____ you, "Don't receive God's grace in vain." For He says: I heard you in an acceptable time, and I helped you in the day of salvation. Look, now is the acceptable time; now is the day of salvation."
(2 Corinthians 6:1-2)

🙢"Now I, Paul, make a personal _____ to you by the _____ and _____ of Christ — I who am humble among you in person but bold toward you when absent." (2 Corinthians 10:1)

Was this also a provocation? It is easy to speak boldly regarding a situation when you are not face-to-face but would he have the courage to do so upon his visit? Provocation indeed. If we are in sin let's wise up to it and repent. Why play games when our time is so short?

🙢"Therefore I, the prisoner for the Lord, _____ you to walk _____ of the calling you have received, with all humility and gentleness, with patience, accepting, one another in love, diligently keeping the unity of the Spirit with the peace that binds us." (Ephesians 4:1-3)

This is a perfect way to edify a fellow Christ follower. What are some powerfully bold words that stand out to you?
_____

If nothing else, let's diligently keep the unity of the Spirit with the peace that binds us. This could be a prayer card taped to our mirrors.

🙢"I _____ Euodia and I _____ Syntyche to agree in the Lord." (Philippians 4:2)

🙢"Finally then, brothers, we ask and _____ you in the Lord Jesus, that as you have received from us how you must _____ and _____ God — as you are doing — do so _____ _____." (1 Thessalonians 4:1)

<u>Are you seeing a theme here? "Do so even more"? If we think we have done our best and are ready to sit back and enjoy a quiet life lets think again. Whatever good we are doing let's do so 'even more'. Praise God for the opportunity.</u>

Charisma

🙵"About brotherly love: You don't need me to write you because you yourselves are taught by God to love one another. In fact, you are doing this toward all the brothers in the entire region of Macedonia. But we _____ you, brothers, to do so even more, to seek to lead a quiet life, to mind your own business, and to work with your own hands, as we commanded you, so that you may walk properly, in the presence of outsiders and not be dependent on anyone." (1 Thessalonians 4:9-12)

We have been taught by others and taught by God about brotherly love. We should do what we have been taught and do it even more so. Even more? This verse tells us how we should be living our lives. Let's strive for these things 'even more' and not settle in for just a comfortable life.

🙵"For this reason, although I have great boldness in Christ to command you to do what is right, I appeal to you, instead, on the basis of love. I, Paul, as an elderly man and now also as a prisoner of Christ Jesus, _____ to you for my son, Onesimus., I fathered, him while I was in chains. Once he was useless to you, but now he is useful both to you and to me. I am sending him back to you as a part of myself." (Philemon 1:8-12)

A spiritual father, a spiritual son. Beautiful. A useful son that will now go and build up others in the unity of the faith.

🙵"And I especially _____ you to pray that I may be restored to you very soon." (Hebrews 13:19)

🙵"Brothers, I _____ you to receive this message of _____, for I have written to you briefly". (Hebrews 13:22)

Are you always ready to receive a message of exhortation? Do you anxiously await someone you know who possesses this gift? Oh yes! Thank you Lord!

🙵"Dear friends, I _____ you as strangers and temporary residents to abstain from fleshly desires that war against you." (1 Peter 2:11)

Comfort. God is the author of comfort (Isaiah 51:12, 2 Corinthians 1:3). As Christians we too are to function as comforters (2 Corinthians 1:4, 7:7) <u>A definition of comfort is: to soothe, console, to reassure, to bring cheer, to aid, support or encourage.</u> (dictionary.com)

Charisma

The following verses relate to Comfort:

🙢"A voice was heard in Ramah, weeping, and great mourning, Rachel weeping for her children; and she refused to be _____, because they were no more." (Matthew 2:18)

🙢"Those who mourn are blessed, for they will be _____." (Matthew 5:4)

There is no sorrow that does not have a remedy! Mourners shall be comforted by their God!

🙢"'Son,' Abraham said, 'remember that during your life you received your good things, just as Lazarus received bad things, but now he is _____ here, while you are in agony." (Luke 16:25)

Do you live more in expectation of receiving good things in the here and now or the life to come? The answer to this question will give a window into the condition of your heart. No condemnation, only a door of opportunity.

🙢"After leaving the jail, they came to Lydia's house where they saw and _____ the brothers, and departed." (Act 16:40)

🙢"There were many lamps in the room upstairs where we were assembled, and a young man named Eutychus was sitting on a window sill and sank into a deep sleep as Paul kept on speaking. When he was overcome by sleep, he fell down from the third story and was picked up dead. But Paul went down, fell on him, embraced him, and said, "Don't be alarmed, for his life is in him!" After going upstairs, breaking the bread, and eating, Paul conversed a considerable time until dawn. Then he left. They brought the boy home alive and were greatly _____." (Acts 20:8-12)

🙢"Two or three prophets should speak, and the others should evaluate. But if something has been revealed to another person sitting there, the first prophet should be silent. For you can all prophesy one by one, so that everyone may learn and everyone may be _____." (1 Corinthians 14:29-31)

🙢"Praise the God and Father of our Lord Jesus Christ, the Father of mercies and the God of all _____(paraklesis). He _____ (parakaleo) us in all our affliction, so that we may be able to _____ (parakaleo) those who are in any kind of affliction, through the _____ (paraklesis) we ourselves _____ (parakaleo) from God. For as the sufferings of Christ overflow to us, so through Christ our _____ (paraklesis) also overflows. If we are afflicted, it is for your comfort (paraklesis) and salvation. If we are comforted (parakaleo), it is for your comfort (paraklesis), which is experienced in your endurance of the same sufferings that we suffer. And our hope for you is firm, because we know that as you share in the sufferings, so you will share in the comfort (parakesis)." (2 Corinthians 1:3-7)

What a God we serve! He comforts us in *all* our affliction *so that* we can comfort others based on the comfort we received from God. He loves us! His thoughts towards us are for our good. He desires we comfort others and point them towards Christ.

☙"So even though I wrote to you, it was not because of the one who did wrong, or because of the one who was wronged, but in order that your diligence for us might be made plain to you in the sight of God. For this reason we have been _____. In addition to our comfort (paraklesis), we rejoiced even more over the joy Titus had, because his spirit was refreshed by all of you." (2 Corinthians 7:12-13)

☙"Finally, brothers, rejoice. Become mature, be _____, be of the same mind, be at peace, and the God of love and peace will be with you. Greet one another with a holy kiss. All the saints greet you. The grace of the Lord Jesus Christ, and the love of God, and the fellowship of the Holy Spirit be with all of you." (2 Corinthians 13:11-13)

☙"I am sending him to you for this very reason, to let you know how we are and to _____ your hearts. Peace to the brothers, and love with faith, from God the Father and the Lord Jesus Christ. Grace be with all who have undying love for our Lord Jesus Christ." (Ephesians 6:22-24)

Let's encourage each other's hearts. Bring words of peace, love, and faith as you build up another. We are blessed to be a blessing.

☙"I want their hearts to be _____ and joined together in love, so that they may have all the riches of assured understanding and have the knowledge of God's mystery — Christ." (Colossians 2:2)

☙"I have sent him to you for this very purpose, so that you may know how we are and so that he may _____ your hearts." (Colossians 4:8)

Charisma

ᴥ"As you know, like a father with his own children, we _____, comforted, and implored each one of you to walk worthy of God, who calls you into His own kingdom and glory." (1 Thessalonians 2:11-12)

ᴥ"And we sent Timothy, our brother and God's coworker in the gospel of Christ, to strengthen and _____ you concerning your faith, so that no one will be shaken by these persecutions. For you yourselves know that we are appointed to this." (1 Thessalonians 3:2-3)

Let no one be surprised when persecutions come. Stand firm and do not allow yourself to be shaken. We must know times like this come and to be prepared means we will not marvel at the evil intentions of man's heart. We trust and follow God at all times and in all season.

ᴥ"Therefore, brothers, in all our distress and persecution, we were _____ about you through your faith. For now we live, if you _____ _____ in the Lord. How can we thank God for you in return for all the joy we experience before our God because of you, as we pray very earnestly night and day to see you face to face and to complete what is lacking in your faith?" (1 Thessalonians 3:7-10)

ᴥ"For the Lord Himself will descend from heaven with a _____, with the archangel's _____, and with the _____ of God, and the dead in Christ will rise first. Then we who are still alive will be caught up together with them in the _____ to meet the Lord in the air and so we will always be with the Lord. Therefore _____ one another with these words." (1 Thessalonians 4:16-18)

ᴥ"For God did not appoint us to wrath, but to obtain salvation through our Lord Jesus Christ, who died for us, so that whether we are awake or asleep, we will live together with Him. Therefore _____ one another and _____ _____ _____ up as you are already doing." (1 Thessalonians 5:9-11)

ᴥ"And we _____ you, brothers: warn those who are irresponsible, comfort the discouraged, help the weak, be _____ with everyone. See to it that no one repays evil for evil to anyone, but always _____ what is good for one another and for all." (1 Thessalonians 5:14-15)

ᴥ"May our Lord Jesus Christ Himself and God our Father, who has loved us and given us eternal _____ (paraklesis) and good hope by grace, _____ (parakaleo) your hearts and

Charisma

strengthen you in every good _____ and _____." (2 Thessalonians 2:16-17)

Exhortation. A definition of exhortation is: an utterance, discourse, or address conveying urgent advice or recommendations. (dictionary.com) The Greek word translated "exhortation" (paraklesis) signifies, originally, "a calling near or for" (as an advocate or helper who should appeal on one's behalf), and carries the twofold sense of "exhortation" and "consolation". (biblestudytools.com/dictionary/exhortation/)

The following verses relate to Exhortation:

• "Then, along with many other _____, he proclaimed good news to the people." (Luke 3:18)

This is what we share with others. Do you do it at every opportunity?

• "And with many other words he testified and strongly _____ them, saying, "Be saved from this corrupt generation!" (Acts 2:40)

• "When he arrived and saw the grace of God, he was glad and _____ all of them to remain _____ to the Lord with a firm _____ of the heart, for he was a good man, full of the Holy Spirit and of faith. And large _____ of people were added to the Lord." (Acts 11:23-24)

• "After they had evangelized that town and made many disciples, they returned to Lystra, to Iconium, and to Antioch, strengthening the disciples by _____ them to _____ in the faith and by telling them, "It is necessary to pass through many troubles on our way into the kingdom of God." (Acts 14:21-22)

• "When they read it, they rejoiced because of its _____. Both Judas and Silas, who were also prophets themselves, _____ the brothers and strengthened them with a long message." (Acts 15:31-32)

• "And when he had passed through those areas and _____ them at length, he came to Greece and stayed three months." (Acts 20:2)
• "As you know, like a father with his own children, we _____, comforted, and implored each one of you to walk _____ of

Charisma

God, who _____ you into His own kingdom and glory." (1 Thessalonians 2:11-12)

❧"Finally then, brothers, we ask and _____ you in the Lord Jesus, that as you have received from us how you must walk and please God — as you are doing — do so _____ _____. For you know what commands we gave you through the Lord Jesus." (1 Thessalonians 4:1-2)

❧"And we _____ you, brothers: warn those who are irresponsible, _____ the discouraged, _____ the weak, be _____ with everyone. See to it that no one repays evil for evil to anyone, but always _____ what is good for one another and for all." (1 Thessalonians 5:14-15)

What are the powerful words in this exhortation?

_____

❧"Now we command and _____ such people by the Lord Jesus Christ that quietly working, they may eat their own food. Brothers, do not _____ weary in doing good. And if anyone does not obey our instruction in this letter, take note of that person; don't associate with him, so that he may be ashamed. Yet don't treat him as an enemy, but _____ him as a brother." (2 Thessalonians 3:12-15)

An important place to tread but tread gently. The purpose in all things is to bring glory and honor to the Lord.

"First of all, then, I _____ that petitions, prayers, intercessions, and thanksgivings be made for everyone, for kings and all those who are in authority, so that we may lead a tranquil and quiet life in all godliness and dignity. This is good, and it pleases God our Savior, who wants everyone to be saved and to come to the knowledge of the truth." (1 Timothy 2:1-4)

❧"Those who have believing masters should not be disrespectful to them because they are brothers, but should serve them better, since those who benefit from their service are believers and dearly loved. Teach and _____ these things." (1 Timothy 6:2)

❧"Proclaim the message; persist in it whether convenient or not; rebuke, correct, and _____ with great patience and teaching." (2 Timothy 4:2)
❧"For an overseer, as God's administrator, must be blameless, not arrogant, not hot-tempered, not addicted to wine, not a bully, not

Charisma

greedy for money, but hospitable, loving what is good, sensible, righteous, holy, self-controlled, holding to the faithful message as taught, so that he will be able both to _____ with sound teaching and to refute those who contradict it." (Titus 1:7-9)

☙"In the same way, _____ the young men to be self-controlled in everything. Make yourself an example of good works with integrity and dignity in your teaching. Your message is to be sound beyond _____, so that the opponent will be _____, having nothing bad to say about us." (Titus 2:6-8)

☙"Say these things, and _____ and rebuke with all authority. Let no one disregard you." (Titus 2:15)

You are worthy of repeating God's words of exhortation to anyone who needs them. Be bold and confident in the position God has placed you. Never shrink back because you feel you are not worthy.

☙"But _____ each other daily, while it is still called today, so that none of you is hardened by sin's deception. For we have become companions of the Messiah if we hold firmly until the end the reality that we had at the start." (Hebrews 3:13-14)

☙"And let us be concerned about one another in order to _____ love and good works, not staying away from our worship meetings, as some habitually do, but _____ each other, and all the more as you see the day drawing near." (Hebrews 10:24-25)

☙"Brothers, I urge you to receive this message of _____, for I have written to you briefly." (Hebrews 13:22)

☙"Therefore, as a fellow elder and witness to the sufferings of the Messiah and also a participant in the glory about to be revealed, I _____ the elders among you: Shepherd God's flock among you, not overseeing out of _____ but freely, according to God's will; not for the money but eagerly; not lording it over those _____ to you, but being _____ to the flock. And when the chief Shepherd appears, you will receive the unfading crown of glory." (1 Peter 5:1-4)

☙"I have written you this brief letter through Silvanus, (I know him to be a faithful brother) to _____ you and to testify that this is the true grace of God. Take your stand in it!" (1 Peter 5:12)

☙"Dear friends, although I was eager to write you about the salvation we share, I found it necessary to write and _____ you to

Charisma

contend for the faith that was delivered to the saints once for all. (Jude 1:3)

Desire. A definition of desire is: to wish or long for, crave, want, to express a wish to obtain, ask for, request. (dictionary.com) "How do we know if a desire is good or bad? The answer lies in the object or reason for the desire. If the desire is self-centered then it is bad, because the essence of sin is the determination to have one's own way. It is an act of idolatry in that one has put self in the place of God. Good desire is simply the opposite. It is putting the desire for God's will first. When the Lord is our greatest desire, all other desires find their proper expression." (biblestudytools.com/dictionary/desire)

The following verses relate to Desire:

⋆"Then, after he had summoned him, his master said to him, You wicked slave! I forgave you all that debt because you _____ me. Shouldn't you also have had mercy on your fellow slave, as I had mercy on you? And his master got angry and handed him over to the jailers to be tortured until he could pay everything that was owed. So My heavenly Father will also do to you if each of you does not forgive his brother from his heart." (Matthew 18:32-35)

Let's make certain we extend the same hand of mercy to others that God has extend to us. Jesus does not stand for a hypocrite.

⋆"How can I," he said, unless someone guides me? So he _____ Philip to come up and sit with him." (Acts 8:31)

⋆"So they came and apologized to them, and escorting them out, they urged them to leave town. After leaving the jail, they came to Lydia's house where they saw and _____ the brothers, and departed." (Acts 16:39-40)

⋆"There we found believers, and were _____ to stay with them for seven days. And so we came to Rome." (Acts 28:14)

Do we 'invite' people to do something? What fellow believers in need are we inviting to share our bounty with?

⋆"But God, who _____ the humble, _____ us by the arrival of Titus, and not only by his arrival, but also by the _____ he received from you. He told us about your deep

Charisma

longing, your sorrow, and your zeal for me, so that I rejoiced even more." (2 Corinthians 7:6-7)

🕮 "I testify that, on their own, according to their ability and beyond their ability, they _____ us insistently for the privilege of sharing in the ministry to the saints, and not just as we had hoped. Instead, they gave themselves especially to the Lord, then to us by God's will." (2 Corinthians 8:3-5)

Prayer. Prayer is communicating with God; really paying attention to Him. Prayer is about finding God's heart as well as confessing our burdens to Him. "Though prayer also includes adoration (Psalm 144-150, Luke 1:46-55) confession (Psalm 51, Luke 18:13), and thanksgiving (Psalm 75, 1 Thessalonians 1:2), Christian prayer has always been essentially petitionary." (biblestudytools.com/dictionary/prayer)

The following verses relate to Prayer:

🕮 "Or do you think that I cannot _____ My Father, and He will provide Me at once with more than 12 legions of angels? How, then, would the Scriptures be fulfilled that say it must happen this way?" (Matthew 26:53-54)

Jesus could have backed out of the agreement with His father. It was Jesus' choice. Otherwise, why do you think he said he would be given more than 12 legions of angels...that's a lot friend. That is coming down with a hammer against a crowd of common people. But then He says, maybe even to himself, but how then would the scriptures be fulfilled?

🕮 "The eyewitnesses described to them what had happened to the demon-possessed man and told about the pigs. Then they began to _____ Him to leave their region. As He was getting into the boat, the man who had been demon-possessed kept begging Him to be with Him. But He would not let him; instead, He told him, "Go back home to your own people, and report to them how much the Lord has done for you and how He has had mercy on you." (Mark 5:16-19)

How the once demon-possessed man 'kept begging Him to be with Him' shows how much love Jesus showed him. The man that before had only known about harassment and fear now did not want to depart from Jesus' love. Jesus does not just free people from tormenting spirits like it is just one of many task to be performed

Charisma

during the day, but sets us free out of His deep love and compassion for people and the man knew it.

☙"One of the synagogue leaders, named Jairus, came, and when he saw Jesus, he fell at His feet and kept _____ Him, "My little daughter is at death's door. Come and lay Your hands on her so she can get well and live." (Mark 22-23)

☙"During the night a vision appeared to Paul: A Macedonian man was standing and _____ with him, "Cross over to Macedonia and help us!" After he had seen the vision, we immediately made efforts to set out for Macedonia, concluding that God had called us to _____ them." (Acts 16:9-10)

☙"However, so that I will not burden you any further, I _____ you in your _____ to give us a brief hearing." (Acts 24:4)

☙"Therefore I _____ you to take some food. For this has to do with your survival, since none of you will lose a hair from your head." After he said these things and had taken some bread, he gave thanks to God in the presence of all of them, and when he broke it, he began to eat. They all became _____ and took food themselves." (Acts 27:34-36)

☙"Now I _____ you, brothers, through our Lord Jesus Christ and through the love of the Spirit, to join with me in _____ prayers to God on my behalf." (Romans 15:30)

☙"Therefore, we are ambassadors for Christ, certain that God is _____ through us. We plead on Christ's behalf, "Be reconciled to God." He made the One who did not know sin to be sin for us, so that we might become the righteousness of God in Him. Working together with Him, we also _____ you, "Don't receive God's grace in vain." (2 Corinthians 5:20-21, 6:1)

☙"First of all, then, I _____ that petitions, prayers, intercessions, and thanksgivings be made for everyone, for kings and all those who are in authority, so that we may lead a tranquil and quiet life in all godliness and dignity. This is good, and it pleases God our Savior, who wants everyone to be saved and to come to the knowledge of the truth." (1 Timothy 2:1-4)

Entreat. A definition of entreat is: to ask earnestly, beseech, implore, beg, an earnest request or petition. (dictionary.com)

The following verses relate to Entreat:

• "Your brother is here, he told him, and your father has slaughtered the fattened calf because he has him back safe and sound. Then he became angry and didn't want to go in. So his father came out and _____ with him. But he replied to his father, Look, I have been slaving many years for you, and I have never disobeyed your orders, yet you never gave me a young goat so I could celebrate with my friends. But when this son of yours came, who has devoured your assets with prostitutes, you slaughtered the fattened calf for him. Son, he said to him, you are always with me, and everything I have is yours. But we had to celebrate and rejoice, because this brother of yours was dead and is alive again; he was lost and is found." (Luke 15:27-32)

• "When we are reviled, we bless; when we are persecuted, we endure it; when we are slandered, we respond _____. Even now, we are like the world's garbage, like the dirt everyone scrapes off their sandals." (1 Corinthians 4:12-13)

Well, what do you think of that? What are you going to do with this?

• "Do not rebuke an older man, but _____ him as a father, younger men as brothers (or brethren), older women as mothers, and with all propriety, the younger women as sisters. (1 Timothy 5:1-2)

Prayer

I exhort you fellow Believers in Christ Jesus to stand firm in the Message you have received, rebuke the lies the enemy would have you believe that are contrary to this Message and exhort sojourners next to you. Always be alert, stand firm in faith, and live strong in the face of adversity! Every action you have as a Believer in Christ Jesus must be done with love. Don't allow the enemy to deceive you in any way. May you always know the hight, depth, and scope of the Messiah's love for you which surpasses all human understanding. You are dearly loved and precious to the Father. Audaciously fulfill the calling that was entrusted to you. Jesus is the only name under Heaven by which you can call on and be saved so boldly approach His throne of grace...He is waiting your arrival. Amen.

A Copious Bestowal of Giving

*G*ive, and it will be given to you; a good measure — pressed down, shaken together, and running over — will be poured into your lap. (Luke 6:38) God's ways are not the world's ways. The world methodically teaches us to believe we are prudent if we keep what we have; as this is the preeminent way to accumulate our portions. God instructs us to give and a good measure will be given to us. In case you are wondering what a good measure would look like picture a vessel being filled with precisely what you need. When it is filled, it then gets pressed down and shaken so that it fills in all the cracks and even more can be filled on top of that. So much is it filled, that the vessel can not even hold it all and it begins to run over the top. That my friend, is the good measure given you when you give. God is for us! The world appears to showcase what is best for us but it is an illusion - a so-called pot of gold at the end of the rainbow.

Giving can be viewed from different perspectives. We can give from the storehouse of our material possessions and we can impart to others from the deep well of our spiritual offerings.

The Greek word for 'giving' is metadidōmi. It combines 'meta' and 'didōmi' to get the compound word metadidōmi. 'Didōmi' has the meaning 'to give' and 'meta' adds the punch of 'beyond giving'. (biblehub.com) The Spiritual gift of giving goes beyond what is required for every Christian. This illustrates a type of giving that reaches deeper. Romans 12 informs us that the Spiritual gift of giving is accompanied by the word 'generosity'. This describes for us the copious bestowal of giving that is generated from wholehearted generosity.

There are only four verses we can examine that illustrate the Greek word metadidōmi.

❧"He replied to them, "The one who has _____ shirts must _____ _____ someone who has _____, and the one who has food must do the same." (Luke 3:11)

Charisma

The person operating in the Spiritual gift of giving is willing to offer their own personal belongings to someone having less than they do. As Christians we are without excuse to not offer our things to those in need but someone operating in this gift goes 'beyond' what others are willing to do. In order to provide for the needs of someone else we are not obligated to give away all of our things but as the verse indicates, we keep one for ourselves.

John is indicating in this verse that an expression of repentance is willingness to share with the needy. How does this stir your spirit?

🕊"For I want very much to see you, so I may _____ to you some spiritual gift to _____ you, that is, to be mutually _____ by each other's _____, both yours and mine." (Romans 1:11-12)

This probably is not indicating a *specific* charismatic gift but instead to minister to one another with the Spiritual gift each one has. We should each encourage and build each other up spiritually.

🕊"The thief must no longer _____. Instead, he must do honest _____ with his _____ hands, so that he has something to _____ with anyone in need." (Ephesians 4:28)

Instead of taking from others we should give to others. An example of self-sacrifice is being willing to work to aid others with what came honestly to us by laboring with our own hands. Do you wonder if a thief finds it easier to furnish his essentials by stealing and therefore a habit of laziness forms which inevitably leads to wickedness? Laboring with our own hands requires a certain amount of exertion which helps teach us to appreciate the cost of the gain. We are therefore less likely to squander them senselessly on folly. Are thieves more prone to common addictions because they do not appreciate the hard work required in obtaining essentials?

True christianity guides people away from laziness and draws them toward the leading of the Spirit. According to this verse that would mean working in order to have something to give to anyone in need.

🕊"We _____ so much for you that we were pleased to _____ with you _____ _____ the gospel of God but also our own lives, because you had become _____ to us." (1 Thessalonians 2:8)

Paul, Silas, and Timothy are probably the ones speaking to the Thessalonians and describing how dear an affection they had towards

Charisma

them. The desire for the Thessalonians to know and appreciate the Gospel message was such a driving force for them that they were willing to give all they had of themselves in order that the people might receive.

Do we have such a love for someone hungry for the Gospel message that we are willing to pour our heart and soul out to them and offer anything necessary to assist them and build them up in the faith?

Someone operating in the Spiritual gift of giving would have these characteristics:

❋ Does not seek compensation, an advantage, or praise ❋
❋ Willingly shares to meet a need ❋
❋ Skilled at managing finances ❋
❋ Shares with cheerfulness ❋
❋ Does not fear lack ❋
❋ Conscientious ❋
❋ Resourceful ❋
❋ Generous ❋

The following verses use the word 'give' which is the Greek word didōmi. It is found in the second part of the word metadidōmi. The word 'give' here is not associated with the Spiritual gift of giving that is described in Romans 12:8 in that it does not have the implication of 'giving beyond' what we are expected to give when living the Christian faith. Since the word is frequently found in the Bible I have included it for study. If someone was operating in the Spiritual gift of giving then 'giving' would be provided above and beyond that seen in the regular Christian life.

Giving will be separated into three different sections for emphasis: 1) what we give, 2) what the Lord gives, and 3) what we don't want to give the enemy.

❧ What we give ❧

❧"It was also said, Whoever divorces his wife must _____ her a written notice of divorce." (Matthew 5:31)

Living in the flesh we can give proof of our broken promises.

❧"_____ to the one who asks you, and don't turn away from the one who wants to borrow from you." (Matthew 5:42)

We can graciously give what we have to those who ask.

❧"Don't _____ what is holy to dogs or toss your pearls before pigs, or they will trample them with their feet, turn, and tear you to pieces." (Matthew 7:6)

We get to keep (the promises of God) and not give them away to anyone who will not value them or try to steal our faith. We discern and therefore guard the preciousness of the Gospel against those who would mock it and speak of it with contempt.

❧"As you go, announce this: 'The kingdom of heaven has come near.' Heal the sick, raise the dead, cleanse those with skin diseases, drive out demons. You have received free of charge; _____ free of charge." (Matthew 10:7-8)

We are honored to get to go forth in power and give to others what we have graciously received. You have received a largess give a largess.

❧"When he went into the house, Jesus spoke to him first, "What do you think, Simon? Who do earthly kings collect tariffs or taxes from? From their sons or from strangers? From strangers," he said. Then the sons are free," Jesus told him. But, so we won't offend them, go to the sea, cast in a fishhook, and take the first fish that you catch. When you open its mouth you'll find a coin. Take it and _____ it to them for Me and you." (Matthew 17:25-27)

We get to be citizens of the Kingdom of God as well as citizens of a nation during our earthly tenure. Our first loyalty is to the Kingdom of God and secondly to our earthly nation. We conscientiously honor rules set forth in our earthly nation and we indeed give what is required. What would we give beyond this if we were operating in the Spiritual gift of giving? Prayers for those in authority is one. What else?

❧"Why then," they asked Him, "did Moses command us to _____ divorce papers and to send her away?" He told them, "Moses permitted you to divorce your wives because of the hardness of your hearts. But it was not like that from the beginning." (Matthew 19:7-8)

We get to love those unlovable. We get to ask the Lord to soften our hearts towards those who have hurt us and we get to anticipate a longing for how it was "from the beginning". We get to give love because God pours it into us lavishly. We love with His agape love which by definition is a sacrificial love. We give sacrificially and abundantly. Never forget you are equipped to do so!

☙"Then, looking at him, Jesus loved him and said to him, "You lack one thing: Go, sell all you have and _____ to the poor, and you will have treasure in heaven. Then come, follow Me." (Mark 10:21. Also in Matthew 19:21)

We get to give what we have to someone in need knowing that God provides for our every need. Let's open up our fists and give copiously by the grace of our magnificent God.

☙"Then one of the Twelve — the man called Judas Iscariot — went to the chief priests and said, 'What are you willing to _____ me if I hand Him over to you?' So they weighed out 30 pieces of silver for him." (Matthew 26:14-15 similar to Mark 4:11)

We get to for - give others when they seem to be hindering the cause of Christ. God knows every thought and every scheme and nothing is hidden from Him. All things work together for His purposes.

☙"When Herodias's own daughter came in and danced, she pleased Herod and his guests. The king said to the girl, 'Ask me whatever you want, and I'll _____ it to you.' So he swore oaths to her: 'Whatever you ask me I will _____ you, up to half my kingdom.'" (Mark 6:22-23)

We get to be cautious in what we promise to give. We have the mind of Christ. We live by the Spirit and not by the flesh. We have no need for impulsiveness. We get to give our heart and mind time to pray before speaking or acting.

☙"Immediately she hurried to the king and said, "I want you to _____ me John the Baptist's head on a platter — right now!" (Mark 6:25)

We don't have to give in to the demands of others. Is it Biblical? Give it. If it is not Biblical, walk away. One thing we do give is our word. Therefore, prayerful consideration is a must.

☙"Send them away, so they can go into the surrounding countryside and villages to buy themselves something to eat. You _____ them something to eat, He responded". (Mark 6:36-37. Similar to Matthew 14:16)

We get to be empowered by Jesus. Jesus gives us the authority to follow in His footsteps. Let's give Him and His people our all. He is worthy, His people are worthy, and you are worthy.

☙"For what does it benefit a man to gain the whole world yet lose his life? What can a man _____ in exchange for his life? (Mark 8:36-37)

We get to give our proclamation that Jesus is our Savior and pass on this wonderful gift so that others may also receive. How do you retrieve a lost soul? Once you give your allegiance to the King don't stop until you give this life saving knowledge to anyone else with an ear to hear.

☙"And child, you will be called a prophet of the Most High, for you will go before the Lord to prepare His ways, to _____ His people knowledge of salvation through the forgiveness of their sins." (Luke 1:76-77)

We also get to give people knowledge of salvation through the forgiveness of sins. Are you giving this information to anyone who could use it?

☙"Who are you, then?' they asked. 'We need to _____ an answer to those who sent us. What can you tell us about yourself?" (John 1:22)

We get to give others a reason for our joy. Give others a bold response when they ask you to tell them about yourself. Begin by saying who you are in Jesus and ending with information about your accomplishments if need be. Give them Jesus ~ it is what everyone needs.

☙"Didn't Moses _____ you the law? Yet none of you keeps the law! Why do you want to kill Me?" (John 7:19)

Jesus is offering freedom from the law. Give someone information that will set them free.

☙"So a second time they summoned the man who had been blind and told him, _____ glory to God. We know that this man is a sinner!" (John 9:24)

Give glory to God in all seasons. We may not understand entire situations or man's interpretation of right and wrong but giving glory to God is right at all times, in all seasons.

🙣"But Peter said, 'I don't have silver or gold, but what I have, I _____ you: In the name of Jesus Christ the Nazarene, get up and walk!'" (Acts 3:6)

We get to give what we have from our physical possessions and we get to give what we have from the depths of our spirit. In this example Peter did not have the desirable silver or gold the world is eager for but he did have the all-surpassing healing power in the name of Jesus, so he gave!

🙣"He assumed his brothers would understand that God would _____ them deliverance through him, but they did not understand. (25) He is the one who was in the congregation in the wilderness together with the angel who spoke to him on Mount Sinai, and with our ancestors. He received living oracles to _____ to us." (38) (Acts 7:25, 38)

Stephen gave an example that they rejected Moses as their leader/savior. Might they also have been wrong about rejecting Jesus as well? We give people as much information as we have to give. It is up to each individual to have faith but we never stop planting seeds.

🙣"In every way I've shown you that by laboring like this, it is necessary to help the weak and to keep in mind the words of the Lord Jesus, for He said, 'It is more blessed to _____ than to receive.'" (Acts 20:35)

We are more blessed when we give than when we receive. Let's thaw some hearts with the love of Jesus and be known as generous givers. Are you up for that?

🙣"For it is written: As I live, says the Lord, every knee will bow to Me, and every tongue will give (different Greek word) praise to God. So then, each of us will _____ an account of himself to God." (Romans 14:11-12)

We must give an account of our actions to God Himself. Let's make it our aim to have such a positive impact on fellow souls that the account we give of our behavior makes Him smile. Don't hold back your giving!

🙣"We are not commending ourselves to you again, but _____ you an opportunity to be proud of us, so that you may have a reply for those who take pride in the outward appearance rather than in the heart. For if we are out of our mind, it is for God; if we have a sound mind, it is for you." (2 Corinthians 5:12-13)

Let's give of ourselves so freely that other people are proud to stand shoulder to shoulder with us. Our focus should be on tipping the scales in favor of the heart as opposed to our outward appearance. God views the heart and man views the outward appearance. Who do you primarily aim to please? Give your heart to the Lord in such a way that you might be accused of being crazy in love with Him. You can keep your wits for His people.

⁂"We _____ no opportunity for stumbling to anyone, so that the ministry will not be blamed." (2 Corinthians 6:3)

Our lives should not be such that it gives anyone a cause to stumble. Our lives should reflect the beauty and truth of our Lord and the only thing we want to give is an example of the impact Christ has and continues to have on our life.

"Now I am _____ an opinion on this because it is profitable for you, who a year ago began not only to do something but also to desire it." (2 Corinthians 8:10)

We give opinions and counsel that comes from the love of the truth. If someone is not walking in truth but is then restored we give them ample urging to finish the good thing they started.

⁂"If a brother or sister is without clothes and lacks daily food and one of you says to them, 'Go in peace, keep warm, and eat well,' but you don't _____ them what the body needs, what good is it?'" (James 2:15)

Give. If we see a brother or sister in need of essentials but offer empty words of peace what is the point? If we are aware of a need we should not expect someone else to meet the need if we can do it ourselves. Give. If you are operating in the Spiritual gift of giving, give beyond. The Lord will give you the ability.

⁂ *What the Lord gives* ⁂

"_____ us today our daily bread." (Matthew 6:11)

Thank you Lord for giving us what we need. You know everything. Let's praise Him for keeping our needs close to His heart.

🕮 "If you then, who are evil, know how to _____ good gifts to your children, how much more will your Father in heaven _____ good things to those who ask Him! Therefore, whatever you want others to do for you, do also the same for them — this is the Law and the Prophets." (Matthew 7:11-12)

The Lord gives us Spiritual gifts to accomplish what is needed for the building up of His Church, all we have to do is ask. Thank you Lord for your good gifts.

What do we want others to do for us? Do we want people to visit us in the hospital? Bring us food when we are sick? Pray for us when we have no words to pray for ourselves? Smile at us when we feel lonely? Share with us when we lack? Let's do what the Lord does and give good gifts to others as we would desire them to do for us.

🕮 "I will _____ you the keys of the kingdom of heaven, and whatever you bind on earth is already bound in heaven, and whatever you loose on earth is already loosed in heaven." (Matthew 16:19)

The Lord is giving us authority as citizens of the Kingdom. This handing over of keys symbolizes the ability to enforce the authority of the Kingdom. We speak the authority of Scripture. Thank you Lord that you have entrusted us with the authority of Your name. May we give it the honor it deserves.

🕮 "When he went out about nine in the morning, he saw others standing in the marketplace doing nothing. To those men he said, 'You also go to my vineyard, and I'll _____ you whatever is right.' So off they went. (3-4) He replied to one of them, 'Friend, I'm doing you no wrong. Didn't you agree with me on a denarius? Take what's yours and go. I want to _____ this last man the same as I gave you. Don't I have the right to do what I want with my business? Are you jealous because I'm generous?'" (13-15) (Matthew 20:3-4, 13-15)

The Lord gives His grace as He chooses. He never gives how the world gives but gives based on His absolute fairness and complete omniscience. He gives what is right.

🕮 "It must not be like that among you. On the contrary, whoever wants to become great among you must be your servant, and whoever wants to be first among you must be your slave; just as the Son of Man did not come to be served, but to serve, and to _____ His life — a ransom for many." (Matthew 20:26-28)

Charisma

The Lord gives His life for our freedom.

ख"Who then is a faithful and sensible slave, whom his master has put in charge of his household, to _____ them food at the proper time?" (Matthew 24:45)

The person the master chooses is given stewardship of the household and this good slave can be difficult to find. The slave is assigned to give meat to his master's household at the proper time. The stewards will give the flock spiritual food according to the ability, progress, and circumstances of each recipient. If you operate in the Spiritual gift of giving, do so faithfully as the Lord directs.

ख"So take the talent from him and _____ it to the one who has 10 talents. For to everyone who has, more will be _____, and he will have more than enough. But from the one who does not have, even what he has will be taken away from him." (Matthew 25:28-29)

The Lord gives us resources, talents, and the Spirit to use for the advancement of the Gospel. Let's faithfully use what we have been given and not squander the gifts we have been entrusted with.

ख"Then He instructed them to have all the people **sit down** in groups on the green grass. So they sat down in ranks of hundreds and fifties. Then He took the five loaves and the two fish, and looking up to heaven, He blessed and broke the loaves. He **kept** _____ them to His disciples to set before the people. He also divided the two fish among them all. Everyone ate and was filled." (Mark 6:39-42) "Then He commanded the crowd to **sit down** on the ground. Taking the seven loaves, He gave thanks, broke the loaves, and **kept on** _____ them to His disciples to set before the people. So they served the loaves to the crowd." (Mark 8:6 *also in Luke 9:16-17*)

The Lord keeps on giving! Did you notice He instructed the people to sit down before He distributed what they needed? Do you have a humble and quiet spirit that awaits the things the Lord intends to give you? When the Spirit is involved expect order.

ख"But to sit at My right or left is not Mine to _____; instead, it is for those it has been prepared for." (Mark 10:40. Also similar to Matthew 20:23)

God gives places of honor in His kingdom.

ख"For even the Son of Man did not come to be served, but to serve, and to _____ His life — a ransom for many." (Mark 10:45)

Charisma

❧"Therefore, what will the owner of the vineyard do? He will come and destroy the farmers and _____ the vineyard to others." (Mark 12:9)

The owner of the vineyard is the Lord. The Lord chose to give the Gospel message to the Gentiles.

❧"Jesus answered, "If you knew the gift of God, and who is saying to you, '_____ Me a drink,' you would ask Him, and He would _____ you living water." (John 4:10) "Jesus said, 'Everyone who drinks from this water will get thirsty again. But whoever drinks from the water that I will _____ him will never get thirsty again — ever! In fact, the water I will _____ him will become a well, of water springing up within him for eternal life.' 'Sir,' the woman said to Him, '_____ me this water so I won't get thirsty and come here to draw water.'" (John 4:13-15)

Jesus is the giver of living water. This provision of water has properties which allow you to never thirst again. Amen.

❧"Jesus answered, 'I assured you: You are looking for Me, not because you saw the signs, but because you ate the loaves and were filled. Don't work for the food that perishes but for the food that lasts for eternal life, which the Son of Man will _____ you, because God the Father has set His seal of approval on Him.'" (John 6:26-27)

It intrigues me that Jesus, knowing all things, knew they were not moved by the signs He performed but because of the filling they received by eating the bread He gave. They wanted more of what Jesus had given them 'to eat'. They became filled like they had never experienced! That's our Jesus. Come, be fed by Jesus and give what you have been given.

❧"Jesus said to them, "I assure you: Moses didn't give you the bread from heaven, but My Father _____ you the real bread from heaven. For the bread of God is the One who comes down from heaven and _____ life to the world." Then they said, "Sir, _____ us this bread always!" (John 6:32-34) "At that, the Jews argued among themselves, 'How can this man _____ us His flesh to eat?' 'I am the living bread that came down from heaven. If anyone eats of this bread he will live forever. The bread that I will _____ for the life of the world is My flesh." (John 6:51-52)

Moses gave the bread that was lifeless and became corrupted after a few days. The Father gives Jesus as the real and incorruptible bread.

The bread He gives contains never-ending life. All we do is come to Him and feast.

☙"My sheep hear My voice, I know them, and they follow Me. I _____ them eternal life, and they will never perish — ever! No one will snatch them out of My hand. My Father, who has _____ them to Me, is greater than all. No one is able to snatch them out of the Father's hand. The Father and I are one." (John 10:27-30)

Jesus gives eternal life to those the Father has brought to Him. No evil one is able to snatch you from the Father's hand. God gives us the choice to come to Him or to leave Him.

☙"Yet even now I know that whatever You ask from God, God will _____ You." (John 11:22)

It was obvious to those close to Jesus that whatever He asked the Father, the Father gave to Him. Be close to Jesus, receive from Him, learn from Him, and give how He gave.

☙"Jesus replied, 'He's the one I _____ the piece of bread to after I have dipped it.'" (John 13:26)

The Lord makes no obvious indication the entire time Judas was in His midst that he would betray Him. Isn't it the same in this generation? Does the Lord indicate who is His and who is not? Don't we make our own distinctions based upon the fruit? Even to the last moment when Judas left to betray Him Jesus handed him the elements of His covenant; the bread dipped in the wine. Was He giving the traitor one last extended hand of affection and ultimately leaving the choice to Judas? Let's make certain to give our love to others in a way that covers their sin from on-lookers and kindles a heart of repentance in them.

☙"I _____ you a new command: Love one another. Just as I have loved you, you must also love one another. By this all people will know that you are My disciples, if you have love for one another." (John 13:34-35)

The Lord commands us to love one another. He gives us His sacrificial love poured into us so that we can give it to others.

☙"Peace I leave with you. My peace I give to you. I do not _____ to you as the world gives. Your heart must not be troubled or fearful." (John 14:27)

Charisma

The Lord gives His peace. Expect to receive this peace daily and your heart will be free from trouble and fear.

☙"You did not choose Me, but I chose you. I appointed you that you should go out and produce fruit and that your fruit should remain, so that whatever you ask the Father in My name, He will _____ you." (John 15:16. Also similar to John 16:23)

Align your thinking with the word of God. May your desires be His desires. If this is true, ask the Father and He will give.

☙"Jesus spoke these things, looked up to heaven, and said: Father, the hour has come. Glorify Your Son so that the Son may glorify You, for You _____ Him authority over all flesh; so He may _____ eternal life to all You have _____ Him." (John 17:1-2)

Thank you Lord that you have authority over all flesh and You give eternal life!! Give the Lord authority over all your flesh and give your life as a testimony to the power of God.

☙"When Pilate heard this statement, he was more afraid than ever. He went back into the headquarters and asked Jesus, 'Where are You from?' But Jesus did not _____ him an answer." (John 19:8-9)

Pilate asked the deep question regarding where Jesus was from. Did he know Jesus was from God the Father? Why did he ask when the answer had already been given? (John 18:37) When Pilate heard the answer he could not receive it in truth. Why should the Magnificent voice speak if it can not be heard? Ask and the truth will be given to you if you have an ear to hear. Give this truth to anyone who will listen.

☙"In past generations He allowed all the nations to go their own way, although He did not leave Himself without a witness, since He did what is good by _____ you rain from heaven and fruitful seasons and satisfying your hearts with food and happiness." (Acts 14:16-17)

The Lord, in His sovereignty gives us what we need. Give to others what they need which is a witness to the goodness of God seen in creation and in our daily existence.

☙"And God, who knows the heart, testified to them by _____ the Holy Spirit, just as He also did to us." (Acts 15:8) "If you love Me, you will keep My commands. And I will ask the Father, and He will _____ you another Counselor to be with you forever."
(John 14:15-16)

The Lord gives you the Holy Spirit as a testimony that you are His! His counsels in us daily leads us towards sanctification and victorious living.

➤ "But our presentable parts have no need of clothing. Instead, God has put the body together, _____ greater honor to the less honorable, so that there would be no division in the body, but that the members would have the same concern for each other. So if one member suffers, all the members suffer with it; if one member is honored, all the members rejoice with it." (1 Corinthians 12:24-26)

The Lord gives us the Spirit and as we yield to the Spirit we experience a blessed renewal. We are members of one body in the Spirit. With the new birth we are not created to live in division with the rest of the body of Christ. Each of us has a gifting and a distinct way we are to contribute to the body. We are to operate full-throttle in our Spiritual gifting leaving no room for quarrels or rivalries. We build each other up because the unified goal is for our efforts to point others to life in Christ. We give and receive assistance from one another in unity of the Spirit. If the church suffers we all suffer and if the church is exalted we are all exalted with it. Praise God.

➤ "I pray that the God of our Lord Jesus Christ, the glorious Father, would _____ you a spirit of wisdom and revelation in the knowledge of Him." (Ephesians 1:17)

The Lord gives us wisdom and a revelation of the knowledge of who He is so that we desire to be like Him. Give this knowledge to others.

➤ "May the Lord of peace Himself _____ you peace always in every way." (2 Thessalonians 3:16)

The Lord IS peace and He gives us what He has - peace. His peace is quietness, rest, harmony, and assurance. Peace *always* and in *every* way. He gives it. Do you receive it? Let others see your peace as a testimony to His greatness so that others will also want to receive.

➤ "Consider what I say, for the Lord will _____ you understanding in everything." (2 Timothy 2:7)

The Lord gives us the ability to understand. Are we yielding to the Spirit so that we can walk in this understanding? Helps us Lord when we fall short.

➤ *What we don't want to give the enemy* ➤

❧"Again, the Devil took Him to a very high mountain and showed all the kingdoms of the world and their splendor. And he said to 'I will give You all these things if You will fall down and worship me.'" Matthew 4:8-9

We don't give the enemy our allegiance or worship.

❧"Be angry and do not sin. Don't let the sun go down on your anger, and don't give the Devil an opportunity." (Ephesians 4:26)

We don't give the Devil an opportunity by allowing our anger to simmer overnight. He is an opportunist. As the sun sets we rest our minds and settle our hearts and souls with forgiveness towards others and pray for His forgiveness towards us. This is the means by which we are freed from simmering over other's sin and becoming angry. Again, the Devil is an opportunist. Not forgiving others of their missteps gives the enemy an opportunity to invade our thoughts and provide us with bricks to begin building ill-advised barrier walls of protection.

❧"Therefore, I want younger women to marry, have children, manage their households, and give the adversary no opportunity to accuse us." (1 Timothy 5:14)

Here again we see that the Devil is an opportunist. Paul is suggesting if women marry, have children, and manage their households the enemy will not be able to tempt them because they will not be idle. Whether you agree with this statement or not, the point is that when we are idle the Devil has an opportunity to tempt. Whatever our ministry is in life, let's be aware that the enemy prowls in search of prey so let's be on our guard and aimed toward Kingdom purposes.

Scriptural Examples of People Operating in the Spiritual Gift of Giving

❊ Elijah's Experience with the Widow ~ 1 Kings 17:7-16 ❊
❊ Jesus ~ John 10:11, 14:27, Matthew 20:28 ❊
❊ The Widow's Gift ~ Mark 12:41-44 ❊
❊ Churches of Macedonia ~ 2 Corinthians 8:1-5 ❊
❊Christians in Philippi ~ Philippians 4:15-19 ❊

Prayer

Father, assist me in taking these Scriptural examples you have provided for me and teach me how to properly operate in the Spiritual gift of giving if that is where you have placed me in the body. I desire to humble myself and serve your Church. Open my eyes and heart to the ways You give so that I can follow in your footsteps. Fill me with your truth so that I can give not only from my possessions but from Your truth. Help me to not give things to the enemy because it only diminishes my faith. I anticipate Your unending strength to reside in me and equipping me in this area so that I can operate full-throttle in ministry. I joyfully relinquish all glory to You. In Jesus name I pray and receive

Leading with Diligence

Let's always have the mindset of BOLD and BIG regarding the entirety of God. While researching for 'leading with diligence' I explored synonyms for the word 'leading' which pointed me to the word 'visionary'. According to dictionary.com a visionary is one: given to audacious, highly speculative, or impractical ideas or schemes (a course of action). Do you know the God you serve is big? And whatever you might be tempted to imagine about Him, He stretches beyond that. Every bold initiative we open our heart and unfold our hands to on behalf of furthering the cause of Christ springs from the giftedness of the Spirit in us. God is a visionary! He has audacious thoughts and plans towards us. He envisions His people being bold on His behalf! Our Christian lack comes only when we do not respond to the invitations God has planned for us. A person operating in the Spiritual gift of leadership will get a vision of where God is directing their ministry group and will be able to inspire others to assist in making that vision a reality.

God has divinely radical thoughts towards you and me. If we perceived the things He anticipated regarding us we would immediately be tempted to say, "Outrageous!" "It is not practical!" and we would stop the initiative before we even had the nerve to begin it. Our human mind is tempted to contrive the big ideas of God in our lives as quixotic and therefore ultimately unattainable. Unattainable in the flesh, probably. Attainable in the Spirit, certain. What we ought to remember is that His power is made perfect in our weakness (2 Corinthians 12:9). If you operate in the spiritual gift of leadership, dare to allow the visionary dreams of God to inspires you and trust Him to see them through. Once you have this audacious mindset you are then to implement it by leading others with that same inspiration. Be courageous and prevail in leadership with God's vision.

The spiritual gift of leadership is closely related to the gift of administration and the gift of pastor/shepherd. The Greek word for this gift is proistemi and has the meaning of standing before, being a protector or guardian, and assisting and caring for others. (biblehub.com) One distinction in the gift of leadership and the gift of pastor/shepherd verses the gift of administration is that leadership tends to be more people oriented versus task oriented. Someone operating in the spiritual gift of administration most definitely cares for people but those with the Spiritual gift of leadership just tend to focus more directly on people and relationships as opposed to tasks.

A person operating in the gift of leadership will determine their successfulness based upon on how those they are leading are growing in their spiritual journey with the Lord. Spiritual leadership will spring from a deep love of the Lord as well as a desire to see others knowing and living out the truth Scripture reveals.

Characteristics of Someone Operating in the Spiritual gift of Leadership:

Leaders:
Paul
Peter
Moses
Nehemiah
Joshua
Elisha
Joseph

✻ Leads others into a deeper relationship with Jesus ✻
✻ Able to accomplish many different tasks ✻
✻ Prefers visionary thoughts as opposed to prosaic details ✻
✻ Feel protective of those which they are entrusted ✻
✻ Are not afraid to handle crisis situations ✻
✻ Able to inspire others ✻
✻ Takes calculated risks ✻

Things to Watch Out For in Leadership:

✻ Not one leader has all the answers ✻
✻ Passivity ~ don't be afraid to address issues ✻
✻ Meet with other leaders often to battle feelings of being isolated ✻
✻ The focus is not on pleasing the followers ✻
✻ Don't be afraid to learn ✻
✻ Take critiques from others to the Lord for His evaluation ✻

Please open your Bible and complete the following blanks relating to leadership which is the Greek word proistemi.

☙"Now we ask you, brothers, to give recognition to those who labor among you and _____ you in the Lord and admonish you, and to regard them very highly in love because of their work. Be at peace among yourselves." (1 Thessalonians 5:12-13)

This verse is speaking of highly esteeming the elders and overseers in the church. Our leaders in these positions work steadfastly on behalf of our welfare which they hold in high regard. Because of their dedication we should be mindful of regarding them very highly in love. As we consider this verse let's also apply the same consideration to others that lead us in the Lord. 1 Thessalonians 5 is also similar to 1 Timothy 5:17-18 as we will soon notice.

I was pondering the deep meaning of 1 Thessalonians 5:12-13 as I left for church, drove to church, walked into church, and then listened to my pastor deliver his message. As he was speaking with boldness concerning the things of God I sat thanking God for allowing me the privilege of sitting under his teaching. Our leaders have great authority *in* the Lord and great accountability *to* the Lord. The job can be overwhelming at times and a tremendous burden. Have you ever thought through the considerable load our leaders have 1) in their labors, 2) in their leadership, and 3) in their role to admonish us? What a responsibility indeed. I am so very thankful. We are blessed to have leaders willing to put themselves under such scrutiny not only by men but by God. We must pray for them as we richly receive a bounty from their hard work. Let's love them with the tenacity that calls for a continuous bold and faithful prayer given on their behalf.

Consider this thought. When our leaders determine the necessity to admonish us, God forbid we should resent this discipline nor shall we withhold love from them as they are acting as God has instructed them. Thank you Lord that you instruct us to love our leaders and to pray for them as they are a blessing to us. Thank you Lord for the opportunity to serve them with prayer. They provide for us in such enormously thankless ways.

❧"One who _____ his own household competently, having his children under control with all dignity. (If anyone does not know how to _____ his own household, how will he take care of God's church?)" (1 Timothy 3:4-5)

The 'one' this verse is referring to is an overseer or elder. The heading in the Bible for this passage is The Qualifications of Church Leaders, and it goes on to also describe deacons. Let's expect this qualification to include all those inspired by the Spirit to lead. Leadership begins within the household. I think this could be considered one of the most challenging areas in the life of the person called to lead. Your household members see you at your best and at your worst but you must be courageous enough to exhibit Godly leadership qualities even during the toughest trials. This is perfect training ground for leading a larger body of the church.

Let's keep in mind that we may not all operate in the spiritual gifting of leadership but we all have a responsibility to be a leader in some capacity. If you are a parent, you lead your children. If you are a boss, you lead your subordinates. If you are a teacher, you lead your classroom. If you are a spouse, you lead your spouse. You can think of other examples. Wherever God has placed us we must lead in that environment according to the council of Scripture.

☙"Deacons must be husbands of one wife, _____ their children and their own households competently." (1 Timothy 3:12)

Many have gazed at this verse and have applied it as proof positive that Deacons should be men due to the wording "must be husbands of one wife." Sweet things, if God willed it that is the way it is. Let's not argue with the Word, let's just take our places in the Kingdom - wherever that may be. We can also look at the verse as a plumb line. If someone desires to be a Deacon but can not competently control his household how can he possibly imagine controlling a larger church environment? The Word is always the ultimate source of wisdom for leadership or anything else in which we need direction.

☙"The elders who are good _____ should be considered worthy of an ample honorarium (or double honor), especially those who work hard at preaching and teaching. For the Scripture says: Do not muzzle an ox while it is treading out the grain, and the worker is worthy of his wages." (1 Timothy 5:17-18)

Good leaders are worthy of their wages. Let's not be stingy. Where on earth would we be without our Christian leaders? We benefit from the fruit of their intense labor. Let's honor them with the fruit of our labor. All the while thanking the Lord for the opportunity to be a blessing. After all, we are blessed to be a blessing. Amen! If you are operating in the spiritual gift of leadership you should be leading in such a way that people ultimately support you out of love and gratitude not primarily out of obligation.

☙"This saying is trustworthy. I want you to insist on these things, so that those who have believed God might be careful ___ _____ themselves to good works. These are good and profitable for everyone." (Titus 3:8)

Have you pondered lately the impact of Christ's finished work on Calvary regarding your personal life and your life of full-throttle leadership? The significance of Calvary is enough to powerfully fuel your striving, stirring you to maintain a spirit that aims to do nothing but good works to promote the cause of Christ. Believer, if you have trusted in God you should find yourself spiritually competent. Because of the grace of God given us, we are intensely diligent in leadership and all other Christian duties we are called and equipped to perform. When we have this bold endeavor before us we find it is a robust kind of good and enormously profitable for everyone.

☙"And our people must also _____ _____ _____ _____ _____ good works for cases of urgent need, so that they will not be unfruitful." (Titus 3:14)

Believers should engage in good works by helping the needy and any other Christian cause. This scripture tell us that by doing so we will produce fruit. Leaders should also encourage others in this way.

Prayer

Thank you lord for the Spiritual gift of leading. Miraculously empower me to believe the visionary thoughts You have toward me and others. I desire to extinguish thoughts I might have of the impossible and take hold of the Possible. You have uncommon thoughts and I desire to lead fellow believers not to the common but the uncommon. I choose to open my heart and mind to your leadership so that I can lead as you desire. I know I am not responsible for filling someone else's cup as that is a job reserved exclusively for You. I am willing, however, to empty my cup to others. If I do not operate in the Spiritual gift of leading assist me to lead in my surroundings in an extraordinary capacity so that others experience You through my actions. In the name of Jesus I am courageous and will prevail in the leadership in which You have appointed me. Amen.

The Compassion of Mercy

Every person craves compassion, love, forgiveness, kindness, peace, patience, gentleness, and bolstering. We *need* mercy. Above all other forms of mercy people provide, our souls need the compassionate mercy God gives - and is willing to give. Operating as God's outstretched hand, we can provide mercy to a bruised humanity. Sometimes the only thing we have to give is mercy so lets make sure we give in abundance. It is God's gifting to us that is meant to be given away and constantly refreshed again to overflowing by the Spirit.

When Jesus traveled the land of Israel people clamored, "have mercy!" His response was furnished from His storehouse of unending compassion. Most people in need of mercy are accustomed to being treated harshly by this world's inhabitants. This grim conduct can be demonstrated by unforgiveness, by not making peace when you have the ability to institute it, by not showing kindness when it is fully in your control, by not giving a gentle word when you are the one that controls your mouth, by not showing compassion because of a judgmental opinion, by not loving because the person is deemed unlovable, or by not being patient because we are too busy. It is paradoxical when we expect others to treat us with mercy but we don't esteem others in the same way. Lord, please have mercy on us and help us be different. We are not bound to continue behaving without mercy towards others because it is not given to us or because we were not raised that way. We extend a compassionate hand of mercy because God extends His audacious mercy to us.

The only way mercy will be impactful is if we extend it with cheerfulness. Mercy given because we feel we must or given with an expression that does not match the action will not be received the way the Spirit intends. I have attempted to be an example of mercy to my kids. When they have made an error I will occasionally tell them, "I will give you mercy. Even though your actions deserve justice I will give you mercy instead." They usually end up staring at me wide-eyed which gives me a perfect opportunity to say that is what Jesus does for us. He gives us mercy when we don't deserve it.

Someone operating in the gift of mercy (eleeō) has the ability to sense and respond to the needs of others with love and sympathy. They have considerable compassion for people when they face taxing trials or sufferings. The gift of mercy presented in Romans 12:8 instructs us to, "show mercy with cheerfulness." There is a huge chasm that exist between showing mercy with resentfulness or sorrow and showing mercy with cheerfulness. Mercy is not received as well or arguably not received at all if it is not extended with cheerfulness. When you give mercy, make certain you present it in the beautiful packaging of cheerfulness so that the gift you are passing along on behalf of the Giver is given in grace and received in grace. In this manner all glory is received by God! Practice being a magnificent bestower of mercy! Mercy originates from the Spirit and should be poured out from you under the influence of the Spirt with a sanguine disposition. Think about a time someone extended mercy to you and the grace it was presented. How was it received in your heart?

A person operating in the spiritual gift of mercy can be observed following and depending on their emotions and are therefore drawn to more sensitive people. They are more inclined to reach out to those who are hurting even if the person may be reluctant to admit they have a need. The merciful person is willing to stick-it-out with people to see them through their trial and suffering. This person is quick to forgive and slow to judge.

If a person operating in the spiritual gift of mercy gets out of step with the Spirit some weaknesses can present themselves. As with any gift, we must always yield our souls to the Spirit to avoid functioning from the flesh. Because of a mercy-giver's sensitivity, they must watch out for other's becoming dependent on them. The mercy-giver should continually be mindful of directing the person they are having an influence on back to God. He is the one the person ultimately must depend upon. The one operating in this gift should also be aware of the potential trap of becoming a rescuer to someone not needing a rescue. These people are manipulators and will maneuver their story to worm their way into your emotions. A merciful person typically does not like conflict and will avoid it even when a confrontation is necessary. To avoid these pitfalls we must continually be aware if we are yielding to our emotions verses yielding to the Spirit.

Charisma

Here is a summary of some places we see mercy demonstrated in Scripture:

Mercy to all God calls (Galatians 6:16) as He is rich in **mercy** (Ephesians 2:4) and He saves us according to this great **mercy** (Titus 3:5, 1 Peter 1:3, 2:10). We should expect the **mercy** of Christ for our eternal life (Jude 1:21). The atoning work of Christ is His **mercy** toward us (Hebrews 9:5) and not only that, He gave us His **mercy** to remain with us (2 John 1:3). We are God's people therefore we have received His **mercy** (1 Peter 2:10). We boldly approach His throne of grace so that we may receive **mercy** (Hebrews 4:16). All who have a holy reverence for the Mighty One will receive His **mercy** (Luke 1:50) and we rejoice with those who have received His great **mercy** (Luke 1:58). We should have **mercy** on those who doubt (Jude 1:22). Jesus showed **mercy** and instructed us to show **mercy** because our Father is **merciful** (Luke 6:36). Never should we be found neglecting **mercy** (Matthew 23:23). **Mercy** triumphs over judgment (James 2:13)! **Mercy** to those who refresh us and are not ashamed of our condition (2 Timothy 1:16). When the Lord has shown you **mercy** tell others about it (Matthew 5:19)! Now go...and show **mercy** to others (Luke 10:37).

To familiarize yourself even further with the Spiritual gift of mercy I recommend you look up and read for yourself the details found in the above Scriptures. Time spent in the Word is always rewarded.

A person operating in the gift of mercy generally is:

❈ Kind and Gentle ❈
❈ Able to empathize with others ❈
❈ Aware of the feelings involved in an experience ❈
❈ Drawn to people in need ❈
❈ Sensitive ❈
❈ Good listener ❈
❈ Supportive ❈

While operating in any spiritual gift we are wise if we are continually mindful of the shortcomings of the flesh. We must be cautious of the potential anger and bitterness that could arise if the person we have given mercy to does not receive or chooses not to change in order to improve their situation. The temptation to act impatiently or sharply with a person in whom we see our own short-comings, should be completely avoided. Mercy is not the judge, therefore if we see weaknesses in others because we dislike the trait in ourselves that is a signal to ask the Lord for His strength to dislodge our weakness. Another hinderance of not yielding to the Spirit is the temptation to avoid our enemies because we loath confrontation, even when the confrontation is necessary. Self-examination is crucial. However, we must avoid the pitfall during self-examination that causes us to dwell on our past failures which leads to feelings of unworthiness and the inability to move on and live victoriously.

The Scriptures below have instructions regarding the Greek word for mercy (eleeō) that is found in Romans 12:8. There may be some additional verses that use the word mercy but are not the exact same Greek word. I included them as well because of the richness of their application in learning more about mercy. Please open your Bibles and complete the blanks.

❧"Go and _____ what this means: I desire _____ and not _____. For I didn't come to call the righteous, but sinners." (Matthew 9:13, 12:7)

This is a quoted text from Hosea 6:6. Introspection. Are we boastful enough that we dare sit in high places and critique others without a continual self-inspection of our own sin? Mercy here is in the context of love and relating it to the verse in Hosea, it is more important than offering any ritual sacrifice. <u>Jesus is never interested in the outward appearance of religion as He is in things related to the heart.</u>

<u>One of Christ's highest duties was that of love and mercy.</u> Therefore, He desires that his people should also have as one of their highest duties love and mercy. The Pharisees were righteous in their own minds and were shocked when Jesus spent time with sinners. Because they saw themselves as righteous they justified their actions and therefore had no need for introspection or for Jesus. Let's never justify our actions but always be ready for introspection and allow Jesus to be our defender. When we show compassionate mercy for someone's poor behavior it plants a seed that Jesus can water when the time is right.

❧"The _____ are blessed, for they will be shown _____." (Matthew 5:7)

This sentence stated by Jesus was part of the Sermon on the Mount. Receiving the Lord's mercy is a great need of ours. We need His mercy in our desperate pitiful condition as well as during times when we are unable to perceive our vast need of mercy. We also need mercy shown to us by others. When our soul discerns we have received mercy from the Lord let us be quick to then pour out the same measure we have received to another in need of receiving mercy from us. In doing so we are called the merciful and we are blessed. Matthew 5:7 shows us one way to receive blessing is by showing mercy. I have included a few scriptures that support this same idea.

> Proverbs 11:25 "The generous man will be prosperous, And he who waters will himself be watered."

> Matthew 6:14 "For if you forgive men their trespasses, your Heavenly Father will also forgive you."

> Matthew 6:15 "But if you do not forgive men their trespasses, neither will your Father forgive yours."

> Matthew 18:33 "Should you not have had mercy on your fellow servant, just as I had on you?"

> James 2:13 "For judgment without mercy will be shown to anyone who has not been merciful. Mercy triumphs over judgment."

Matthew 5:7 is a terrific opening verse to begin an examination of the ways in which Jesus was merciful towards people. Let's lean in and take a look at how Jesus did it. The following (8) verses will give us a peek.

> "Just then a Canaanite woman from that region came and kept crying out, "Have mercy on me, Lord, Son of David! My daughter is cruelly tormented by a demon." (Matthew 15:22)

> "Lord," he said, "have mercy on my son, because he has seizures and suffers severely. He often falls into the fire and often into the water. (Matthew 17:15)

> "There were two blind men sitting by the road. When they heard that Jesus was passing by, they cried out, "Lord, have mercy on us, Son of David! The crowd told them to keep quiet, but they cried out all the more, "Lord, have mercy on us, Son of David!" (Matthew 20:30-31 and 9:27)

> "But He would not let him; instead, He told him, "Go back home to your own people, and report to them how

* much the Lord has done for you and how He has had mercy on you." (Mark 5:19)

* "When he heard that it was Jesus the Nazarene, he began to cry out, "Son of David, Jesus, have mercy on me!" Many people told him to keep quiet, but he was crying out all the more, "Have mercy on me, Son of David!" (Mark 10:47-48)

* "Father Abraham!' he called out, 'Have mercy on me and send Lazarus to dip the tip of his finger in water and cool my tongue, because I am in agony in this flame!' (Luke 16:24)

* "As He entered a village, 10 men with serious skin diseases met Him. They stood at a distance and raised their voices, saying, "Jesus, Master, have mercy on us!" (Luke 17:12-13)

* "So he called out, "Jesus, Son of David, have mercy on me!" Then those in front told him to keep quiet, but he kept crying out all the more, "Son of David, have mercy on me!" (Luke 18:38-39)

* "Shouldn't you also have had _____ on your _____ slave, as I had _____ on you?" (Matthew 18:33)

Since the Lord has shown us tremendous mercy we should compassionately demonstrate that same mercy toward others. Not mercy that merely comes from the words of our mouth but mercy that originates from the depths of our heart that knows what it is to receive from God. A heart eager to expose the transformation it welcomed from Jesus and is therefore zealous for the opportunity to extend mercy to another.

Since we have received mercy from the Lord we shall make certain we do not withhold mercy from someone else. In this verse Jesus is questioning if we really think it is right to withhold from someone else what He has freely given us when we ourselves did not even deserve it. Refresh our hearts Lord to the audacious ways You have been merciful towards us.

* "What should we say then? Is there _____ with God? Absolutely not! For He tells Moses: I will show _____ to whom I will show _____, and I will have _____ on whom I will have _____. So then it does not

Charisma

_____ on human will or effort, but on God who shows _____. For the Scripture tells Pharaoh: I raised you up for this reason so that I may display My power in you and that My name may be proclaimed in all the earth. So then, He shows _____ to those He wants to, and He hardens those He wants to harden." (Romans 9:14-18)

<u>There is no injustice with God. He delights to show mercy over judgment. But because He is holy, His righteousness must judge those who refuse to accept His mercy.</u>

His ways are untraceable. We will not figure out why He chooses to act or not act simply because He is God and we are not. We trust at all times in His sovereignty. We must always remember He knows all ends regarding situations that we do not begin to see or understand.

He will show mercy and compassion to those He chooses. We are instructed to show compassion. We are not told to try to determine who is worthy of our compassion because we are unable to see all ends. God is just and because of this He is free to make any decisions He deems fit. Since we do not operate in perfect knowledge and perfect wisdom, we make decisions based on what we perceive or information we have available to us. Even in this, we should always prayerfully consider the direction the Spirit would lead us. God sees and knows all things and makes His decisions out of complete information not the partial as we have. Praise God for His wholeness and distinctiveness!

❧"As you once disobeyed God, but now have received _____ through their disobedience, so they too have now disobeyed, _____ in _____ to you, so that they also now may receive _____. For God has imprisoned all in _____, so that He may have _____ on _____." (Romans 11:30-32)

We should never be surprised that through God's mercy He has a magnificent future planned for Israel. It is through their disobedience that mercy was extended to us, the Gentiles. What a pity it is that we would believe the arrogant lie that our disobedience is less significant than the disobedience of others. Would we ever be bold enough to consider that our disobedience to the Gospel is what would cause someone else to be more unyielding in their disobedience? May God have mercy on us. To the wise, disobedience amplifies God's mercy.

❧"Therefore, since we have this _ministry_ because we were shown _mercy_, we do not _give up_." (2 Corinthians 4:1)

What is this ministry? The ministry of reconciliation (2 Corinthians 5:18-19), the ministry of righteousness (2 Corinthians 3:9), the ministry of the Spirit (2 Corinthians 3:8). This ministry we are entrusted with is superior to the ministry Moses was entrusted with. This ministry involves the shed blood of the Darling of Heaven. God has, in His mercy, approved us to be His servants and expects us to not shrink back from the ministry He has entrusted to us even if threatened by danger, by increasing difficulty, by fear, or by trial.

✦ "Indeed, he was so sick that he nearly died. However, _____ had _____ on him, and not only on him but also on _____, so that I would not have one grief on top of another." (Philippians 2:27)

Paul is saying that Ephaphroditus, his brother, coworker, and fellow soldier was so sick he nearly died in service to the Lord if it had not been for the mercy of God. Paul would have had anguish upon anguish considering his recent trial of being held in chains and separated from his brothers. God had mercy on Ephaphroditus and Paul and he responded with thankfulness and joy. This should always be our rejoinder when we receive God's mercy in our lives! Never should it be received casually.

✦ "I give thanks to Christ Jesus our Lord who has _____ me, because He _____ me faithful, appointing me to the ministry — one who was formerly a blasphemer, a persecutor, and an arrogant man. But I received _____ because I acted out of ignorance in _____. And the grace of our Lord _____, along with the faith and _____ that are in Christ Jesus." (1 Timothy 1:12-14)

The beginning of this verse is similar to 2 Corinthians 4:1. Paul was formerly a blasphemer, persecutor and arrogant man. The power Saul received to turn his life over to God was fueled by the abundant undeserving mercy that flowed copiously into his life. Once he received this heavenly mercy he moved forward in the power of the Spirit to proclaim the Gospel with which he was entrusted. When Paul reflected on his past he did so with regret but not with condemnation because the reflection did not weaken his spirit or slow him down. He proceeded victoriously in the grace, power, and mercy he received in order to complete the task he was given. We shall do the same. Our past ignorances shall not hinder our triumphant future because we too have received the mercy and love that is in Christ Jesus. We shall go forth proclaiming the Gospel to anyone who has an ear inclined toward our merciful Lord.

Charisma

🕭"But I received _____ for this reason, so that in me, the _____ of them, Christ Jesus might _____ His extraordinary _____ as an _____ to those who would believe in Him for eternal life." (1 Timothy 1:16)

Have you ever considered the vast patience of Christ? He is waiting out the evil that exist in the world because in His mercy He desires everyone to have an opportunity to choose Him as Savior. Paul says that he, the worst of all sinners, received the Lord's mercy as an example demonstrated so everyone will understand God's extraordinary restraint towards sinners so that all will come to repentance and be welcomed into The Kingdom. What a merciful God we are privileged to serve! Someone operating in the Spiritual gift of mercy will use Jesus as their example.

🕭"But the _____wisdom_____ from above is first pure, then peace-loving, gentle, compliant, __full__ __of__ __mercy__ and good fruits, without favoritism and hypocrisy." (James 3:17)

> Wisdom is full of mercy. When we are blessed with the opportunity to show mercy we are to do it with cheerfulness according to Romans 12:18. In the Spirit's wisdom, we will demonstrate our good works of mercy with gentleness. When our Lord exhibits His mercy toward us it is not paired with bitterness, selfishness, with envy or with falsehood. We pattern our steps after the Lord's example. Let's always remember when we are blessed to show mercy we do it with a gentle disposition. Consider all of these facets of wisdom (James 3:17) when giving mercy.

We undoubtedly have received the words of mercy from someone that has not understood the heart-felt compassion that should accompany it. When we do *receive* mercy from someone else in a manner different than that described we shall nevertheless receive it graciously, prayerfully planting a seed of compassion! This person is not yet mature in their gifting but with the gentleness of grace given back to them they soon will be in Jesus name.

🕭"But you, dear friends, as you build _____ up in your most holy faith and pray in the Holy Spirit, keep _____ in the love of God, _____ the _____ of our Lord Jesus Christ for eternal life. Have _____ on those who _____; save others by snatching them from the fire; have mercy on others but with _____, hating even the garment defiled by the flesh." (Jude 1:20-23)

Believers, we are to build ourselves up in the truth of Scripture. We are to keep ourselves in the love of God knowing that He loves us and demonstrated that audacious love to the point of death on a cross. We constantly remind ourselves, if we are prone to doubt, that God's love is not measured by the lack of love received from anyone else. In keeping ourselves in God's love we are all the more faithful in obeying the command to demonstrate mercy to others.

We must have mercy on those who hesitate to proceed full-throttle in faith by leading, teaching, and setting an example of the truth of the Gospel. When others are entrenched in the instruction of false teachers we also have the same mercy towards them but we must be wise to fear the same trap they have fallen into. We should never rely on the flesh but on the Spirit in all Gospel work.

What are we without mercy Father? Jesus' ministry was nothing if it withheld mercy. Fill me and renew me with the knowledge of the abundant mercy I have received and continue to receive as a bearer of Your name. Strengthen me with resolve to demonstrate compassionate mercy with no bounds! I trust you Lord with all things therefore I am free from second guessing. I resolve to hold back nothing I can graciously give to nourish another's desperate soul. In the name of Jesus I am empowered and equipped to demonstrate Your compassionate mercy to others. Amen.

Prayer

Father, you have great mercy towards us and continue to have self-sacrificing love towards us even in our sin. Strengthen us to extend the same hand of mercy to others as You have extended to us. It is a merciful compassion that is beyond compare. Help me to acknowledge this amazing truth in a new way today. Allow me to understand that just as I crave compassion, love, forgiveness, kindness, peace, patience, and gentleness, so does my brother and sister in Christ. Empower me to operate as Your outstretched hand and not deny abundant mercy to anyone. It is by Your love, which fills in every space in my heart that I am able to pour out what you have mercifully poured in. I am empowered and well able by the name of Jesus Christ. Amen.

The Fear of the Lord is this: Wisdom

Godly wisdom (sophia) is a priceless gift essential to a successful Christian life. We all should consider the consequences of our actions before we act or speak as well as have understanding to recognize the right course of action needed. Help us Lord to discern the vast difference between the world's wisdom and your wisdom. Your wisdom fixed the weight of the wind, gives the ocean its boundary, and brings forth the seasons in perfection. The world's wisdom relies on humanities fallen nature which brings forth brokenness, bankrupt advice, confusion, and pain. So how do we find this kind of wisdom? (Job 28:12-27) God said to mankind, "The fear of the Lord is this: wisdom. And to turn away from evil is understanding." (Job 28:28) If we lack wisdom, we are instructed to ask God, for He gives to all generously and without criticizing (James 1:5). Expect this type of wisdom to gradually illuminate your understanding and inform your choices. The person operating in the Spiritual gift of wisdom will have an insight which exceeds the wisdom God freely gives to all His children that ask.

Just like the other gifts spoken about in 1 Corinthians 12:8-10 which originate from God and are distributed by the Spirit, so does wisdom. All of these allocations reside fully with God. A small portion of what He has is imparted to you by the Spirit as He evaluates and sees fit.

Once I was walking an amazingly difficult faith journey. On one portion of the journey there was much planting and no harvesting. I had begun to grow weary and needed wisdom to know how to proceed. I was beginning to wonder if I had even heard correctly from the Lord regarding the assignment. At that moment I received a word from someone to not grow weary because obedience was key. As I was thinking through what had been shared, it began to agree with my spirit and the power of the Lord fell on me. I dropped to the floor and for a short time I could not rise up again (nor did I care to!). When I did rise, I prayed and told the Lord over and over "I believe, I believe!" The best I could later describe was the Lord had something similar to a "dropper" above my head and a tiny portion of His power was released from that "dropper" on me. As a result, I fell to my knees under the weight of that power. What was imparted to me at that time was all I could manage. As a created being having to put aside the influence of the flesh, there is only so much of God's power our flesh can handle. Remember Paul in 2 Corinthians 12:7-8? Surprisingly, we don't even operate in what we think we can manage. Friend, God knows the quantity to impart to us because He is omniscient. Are you fully operating in the wisdom He has given you so far?

While anticipating the return of Jesus, believers have been given the Spirit as a down-payment of our Kingdom inheritance. Have you fully considered what that means? The Spirit is the power behind the Word of God. We are to be led by the Spirit and are to function in the power of the Spirit! It is a taste of what is to come. Have you tasted? Are you yielded to the Spirit so this can happen? What are you currently doing with the gift of the Spirit you have? You understand that Jesus died for all mankind. Do you have wisdom to also know the Spirit's law of life in Christ has set you free from the law of sin and death? (Romans 8:2) Jesus loves us all the same and does not favor one over the other (Romans 2:11), yet some do not have this wisdom. As yielded believers, we all have grace to operate in the 'charisma' of the Spirit. Some have this wisdom and operate in this fashion whenever possible. While others do not investigate their gifting and therefore forfeit what God would have for them, therefore they do little. (Please read Matthew 25:14-23) According to this passage, the Master gave gifts for his servants to use while He was away. When He returned He asked what His servants did with the gifts. Those who were faithful in their stewardship were then put in charge of more and were invited to share in their Master's joy. Are we living as spiritual people or letting the flesh get in the way therefore derailing the Master's purpose in our life? Do you contemplate how you function now will have an impact on your eternity (when the Master returns)?

Let's think through some different kinds of wisdom. The first is natural human knowledge without wisdom or the fallen world's wisdom, secondly is intellectual wisdom and finally, the divine word of wisdom. The verses below will assist in bringing more insight to wisdom. Which type of wisdom would you like to cultivate?

Compared to God's wisdom, natural human wisdom is foolishness (1 Co1:25) It is like applied knowledge without wisdom's guidance. It can also be a stumbling block to our personal relationship with Jesus as well as our witness to others.

✒1 Corinthians 1:19 says, "For it is written: _____ will _____ the _____ of the wise, and I will set aside the _____ of the experts."

Charisma

Natural wisdom will one day pass away and we will no longer rely on our own understanding but will be behold the Truth!

Along with human wisdom, we have the fallen world's wisdom. This type of wisdom God told Adam to stay away from. (Genesis 2:17) The wisdom received by eating the fruit of the tree (Genesis 3:6) would now inspire attempts to move away from God and rely instead on this new kind of wisdom (fallen world's wisdom). This wisdom attempts to rival God's wisdom as supreme.

Below is a summary of 1 Corinthians 2:6-16
which outlines Spiritual wisdom
(Please read the entire section in your Bible).

❊ We speak God's wisdom found in Christ to the mature ❊
❊ You can not see, hear, or imagine what God has prepared for those that love Him ❊
❊ The Spirit searches everything, even the depths of God and reveals things to us ❊
❊ The Spirit of God is the only one that knows the thoughts of God ❊
❊ We have received God's Spirit, not the spirit of the world ❊
❊ God gave us His Spirit so that we can understand what He has given us ❊
❊ We are able to speak about such things because the Spirit teaches us ❊
❊ The Spirit explains spiritual things to Spiritual people ❊
❊ Unbelievers do not welcome the Spirit and believe it to be foolish because they do not understand ~ spiritual truths can only be evaluated spiritually ❊
❊ The spiritual person can evaluate everything and things done in the Spirit cannot be evaluated by anyone in the flesh ❊
❊ We have the mind of Christ ❊

Please retrieve your Bibles and complete the following blanks.
While you are at it pray for divine wisdom and revelation...
Come Lord Jesus come.

❧"For the LORD ____________ ________________; from His mouth come knowledge and understanding." (Proverbs 2:6)

The one who seeks knowledge will find God because He is the source of wisdom and knowledge. We live our lives based on what we believe is true. What is your source?

❧"For______________ will enter your ____________, and knowledge will __________________ your heart." (Proverbs 2:10)

Has wisdom taken up residence in you?

❧"_____ is a man who _____ wisdom and who _____ understanding." (Proverbs 3:13)

Wisdom brings happiness. Do you remember the discussion from Genesis 3:6? The woman saw that the tree was desirable for obtaining wisdom. Proverbs 3:18 speaks of a different kind of tree. The tree of wisdom is a tree of life to those who seize it. God planted them both. One tree gives the fruit of worldly wisdom and the other gives the fruit of Godly wisdom. Both fruit is desirable. Which will you choose? If you are walking in the orchard, and your hunger is intense enough to 'eat anything' will you eat the fruit from the Genesis 3:6 tree or WAIT for the Proverbs 3:18 tree? You will face this decision daily, prepare yourself in advance.

Continuing on in this verse it says wisdom and understanding will profit you more than silver and gold and *nothing* you desire holds a comparison. (Also similar to Proverbs 8:11) If a table with precious stones was placed before you on the left and a Proverbs 3:18 tree on the right which would you desire most? Be honest.

_____

❧"The LORD founded the earth _____ _____ and established the heavens _____ _____." (Proverbs 3:19)

The wisdom from God that directs our paths is the same wisdom that created the universe. Someone operating in the Spiritual gift of wisdom has this as their source. Let's not neglect the wisdom found in God, it is genius.

So many times we imitate man when we should be imitating God.

❧"Get _____, get _____; don't forget or turn away from the words of my mouth. Don't abandon _____, and she will _____ you; _____ her, and she will _____ you. Wisdom is _____ – so _____ wisdom." (Proverbs 4:5-7)

And whatever else you get, get understanding. Wisdom is frequently referred to as a 'she'. The urging here is to get wisdom and understanding and don't forget! During a moment when a decision must be made or in the heat of a trial do you abandon this type of wisdom? Love and don't abandon God's wisdom and it will guard you. Thank you Lord.

Charisma

☙"I am teaching you the way of wisdom; I am guiding you on _____ paths." (Proverbs 4:11)

Wisdom is more than an instrument effective in the moment. It is a way of life. The verse goes on to say your steps will not be hindered with God's wisdom and you will not stumble when you run. God's ways are trustworthy and safe.

☙"The _____ (reverence, awe) of the LORD is the _____ of _____, and the _____ of the Holy One is _____. For _____ _____ your days will be _____, and years will be _____ to your life." (Proverbs 9:10-11)

The fear of the Lord is the foundation of all wisdom and righteousness. This foundation is expressed in reverential submission to the Lord's will and is the mark of a true worshiper.

☙"The _____ of the _____ produces _____." (Proverbs 10:31)

Righteous speech benefits all and pleases God. The wicked use perverse words without the wisdom to consider consequences.

☙"When _____ comes, _____ follows, but with _____ comes _____." (Proverbs 11:2)

This is what Expositors' (biblehub.com) has to say about this verse. "Humility describes those who know their place. The humble, will avoid disgrace and therefore find wisdom. Pride is literally a boiling up. The prideful will overstep boundaries and insubordination occurs. The proud are inflated to the level of self-bestowed divinity and will eventually have their egos deflated." Wisdom tells us to not be prideful. Here is a question to consider. If you are driven by pride and were once successfully navigating life in this way, has your ego been deflated leaving you depressed which has now brought you disgrace? Seek the Lord friend. I am in love with the verse telling us the righteous man falls seven times but God picks him up eight (Proverbs 24:16). Do you need to know that the righteous will make mistakes but God intends for you to not remain down! Hallelujah! Stand up friend, it is God's will.

☙"_____ wisdom – how much better is it than _____! And _____ understanding – it is _____ to silver." (Proverbs 16:16)

Charisma

Wisdom is supreme! Gold and silver are used several times in Scripture to describe the highest things of value you can obtain in the world. Gaining heavenly wisdom and understanding ranks higher than the gain of these worldly riches.

🕭"Wisdom is_____ to a _____; he does not open his mouth at the gate (center for community discussions, political meetings, and trying of court cases)." (Proverbs 24:7)

==Wisdom is beyond the reach of a fool. As the above verse states, disgrace is the result of lack of wisdom and will keep you from God's best.== Christian's need a voice at the 'gate'. A fall as a result of pride is a hinderance to yourself and others who need you. Remember, there is no condemnation in Christ Jesus (Romans 8:1), so get up and keep engaging.

🕭"The one who trust in _____ is a _____, but one who _____ in wisdom will be _____." (Proverbs 28:26)

Security comes from a life of wisdom. Trust God in all seasons.

🕭"This also comes from the LORD of Hosts. He _____ wonderful advice; He _____ great wisdom." (Isaiah 28:29)

Do you love the Lord? He loves you. He produces wonderful counsel, He magnifies wisdom. I read over that sentence several times and love the Lord all the more. He is for you friend. Do we need anything else?

🕭"The wise (from worldly wisdom) _____ _____ put to shame; they _____ _____ dismayed and snared. They _____ _____ the word of the LORD, so _____ wisdom do they _____ _____?" (Jeremiah 8:9)

Wow. Let's not rely on worldly wisdom and ultimately be snared and put to shame. The only true wisdom is found in the Word of the Lord. Are you in His word enough to detect the difference between wisdom and folly?

🕭"He _____ the earth by His _____, _____ the world by His _____, and _____ _____ the heavens by His _____." (Jeremiah 10:12, 51:15)

Charisma

Power and wisdom were manifested in the creation of the heavens and the earth.

☙"May the _____ of God be _____ forever and ever, for _____ and _____ _____ to Him. He _____ the times and seasons; He _____ kings and _____ kings. He gives _____ to the wise and knowledge to those who _____ understanding." (Daniel 2:20-21)

You have read many times now that wisdom originates from God and belongs to God. Someone operating in the Spiritual gift of wisdom is given impartations from the mind-blowing Source.

☙"The Son of Man came eating and drinking, and they say, 'Look, a glutton and a drunkard, a friend of tax collectors and sinners!' Yet _____ is vindicated by her deeds." (Matthew 11:19 also see Luke 7:35)

Wisdom has the ability to see beyond what is observed and understood by the flesh. What people had the unrelenting desire to judge Jesus for, He would soon be vindicated by the wisdom God imparted to His people. Now, we do not stand in the position of judge but instead choose to copy Jesus' behavior. Praise God.

☙"The queen of the south will rise up at the judgment with this generation and condemn it, because she came from the ends of the earth to hear the ___wisdom___ of Solomon; and look — something greater than Solomon is here!" (Matthew 12:42 also see Luke 11:31)

Solomon asked God for wisdom and he received it extravagantly! "Now it pleased the Lord that Solomon had requested this. So God said to him, "Because you have requested this and did not ask for long life or riches for yourself, or the death of your enemies, but you asked discernment for yourself to understand justice, I will therefore do what you have asked. I will give you a wise and understanding heart, so that there has never been anyone like you before and never will be again." (1 Kings 3:10-12) People traveled from far away places just to hear the wisdom of Solomon. No one would surpass his wisdom...until Jesus came. Now, something even greater than Solomon was present and the people did not recognize it.

The Queen of Sheba traveled to the ends of the earth to hear Solomon's wisdom. But look, something better has come! Would you yourself travel to the ends of the earth to hear His wisdom? The beauty is you are not required to because it is provided for you on the pages of His Word. It waits waits for you to open it and discover the depth and riches found within the pages. Do you go to the Word with the same longing and effort as one willing to travel long distances to hear wisdom?

What are your thoughts regarding the queen of the south rising up at the judgment and condemning this generation?

___

❧"He went to His hometown and began to teach them in their synagogue, so that they were astonished and said, "How did this _____ and these miracles come to Him?" (Matthew 13:54 also in Mark 6:2)

Jesus' teaching was filled with wisdom as well as accompanied by miraculous signs. Doubters were mystified as to why such wonders would come from someone so 'common'. Do you think they even wondered if these abilities could come to Him couldn't they just as easily come to them? Do oftentimes we confuse humility with being of little consequence?

❧"The boy grew up and became strong, filled with _____, and God's grace was on Him." (Luke 2:40)

One of the meanings of the word 'strong' is empowered. Jesus was empowered by God's grace and wisdom. Someone operating in the Spiritual gift of wisdom is empowered by God!

❧"And Jesus increased in _____ and stature, and in favor with God and with people." (Luke 2:52)

Stature here can mean maturity. Someone operating in the Spiritual gift of wisdom should also expect to grow in favor with people.

❧"Because of this, the _____ of God said, 'I will send them prophets and apostles, and some of them they will kill and persecute,' so that this generation may be held responsible for the blood of all the prophets shed since the foundation of the world, — from the blood of Abel to the blood of Zechariah, who perished between the altar and the sanctuary." (Luke 11:49-51)

The wisdom of God sees things we can never see, understands things we can never understand, and suffers things we can't comprehend.

❧"But before all these things, they will lay their hands on you and persecute you. They will hand you over to the synagogues and prisons, and you will be brought before kings and governors because of My name.

It will lead to an opportunity for you to witness. Therefore make up your minds not to prepare your defense ahead of time, for I will give you such words, and a _____ that none of your adversaries will be able to resist or contradict." (Luke 21:12-15)

During times of persecution (either at an individual level or from a group) if you are yielded to the Spirit you can expect to be directed in wisdom to speak. Have you ever been in a situation where you have thought for hours what words you would use to defend yourself as a result of a disagreement? Walk in the Spirit's wisdom and expect guidance. Replace the time you would spend thinking of your defense and devote the time to prayer and thanksgiving. This will prepare your heart for witness and allow room for your Defender's wisdom.

❧"Therefore, brothers, select from among you seven men of good reputation, _____ of the Spirit and _____, whom we can appoint to this duty." (Acts 6:3)

In ministry we need those filled with the Spirit and wisdom if we are to the best of our ability fulfill the Lord's purposes. He provided this gift of wisdom to us because He knows we require it to successfully navigate life and ministry. Thank you Lord.

❧"But they were unable to stand up against his _____ and the Spirit by whom he was speaking." (Acts 6:10)

Those operating in the Spiritual gift of wisdom have powerful understanding imparted to them that will absolutely shut the mouths of refuters.

❧"The patriarchs became jealous of Joseph and sold him into Egypt, but God was with him and rescued him out of all his troubles. He gave him favor and _____ in the sight of Pharaoh, king of Egypt, who appointed him ruler over Egypt and over his whole household." (Acts 7:9-10)

What does this tell you about times you are faced with adversity yet have God's wisdom?

_____

❧"Oh, the depth of the riches both of the _____ and the knowledge of God! How unsearchable His judgments and untraceable His ways!" (Romans 11:33)

Have you considered the goal of your work day? The goal of your discretionary time? Maybe even the goal of the New Year, as some often do? God's wisdom is deep and rich. As a Christian, the goal of our days, our refreshing, and our resources should be Jesus. Try as you might, you will never reach the depth of Him. This is an encouraging thought in that you will never out grow, out think, out maneuver, out live, out give…God. There is no end to Him. Be bold and courageous and make Him the goal of all your pursuits.

God's thoughts and ways are not worldly but are higher and come from far better things. He is sovereign and His plans are beyond what the human mind can figure out and His ways are beyond the ability of a person to trace. How does this truth bless you? Can you give an example?

_____

☙"For it is written: I will destroy the _____ of the wise, and I will set aside the understanding of the experts. Where is the philosopher? Where is the scholar? Where is the debater of this age? Hasn't God made the _____ wisdom _____? For since, in God's _____, the world did not know God through _____, God was pleased to save those who believe through the foolishness of the message preached. For the Jews ask for signs and the Greeks seek wisdom, but we preach Christ crucified, a stumbling block to the Jews and foolishness to the Gentiles. Yet to those who are called, both Jews and Greeks, Christ is God's _____ and God's _____." (1 Corinthians 1:19-24)

God's power for salvation is in the cross. Human wisdom as a means of salvation is dismissed by God. Is there any philosopher, scholar, or debater available who can do what the message of the cross is able to do? Hardly.

You want the power of God manifest in your life? It begins and ends with Christ. Know His crucifixion, resurrection and ascension to your bones then be prepared to share this wisdom with others every chance that is provided.

☙"But it is from Him that you are in Christ Jesus, who became God-given _____ for us — our righteousness, sanctification, and redemption, in order that, as it is written: The one who boasts must boast in the Lord." (1 Corinthians 1:30-31)

We do not boast because we have nothing in ourselves to boast about. Wisdom is a result of the full work of Jesus Christ and this is our only boast. We add nothing to it and can take nothing away. If we are anything at all it is because we are made able to stand in His power by grace alone. Let's live worthy of this privilege. We should be willing to teach this wisdom to anyone having an ear to hear.

☙"When I came to you, brothers, announcing the testimony of God to you, I did not come with brilliance of speech or _____. For I didn't think it was a good idea to know anything among you except Jesus Christ and Him crucified. I came to you in weakness, in fear, and in much trembling. My speech and my proclamation were not with _____ words of _____ but with a powerful _____ by the Spirit, so that your faith might not be based on _____ wisdom but on God's _____. However, we do speak a _____ among the mature, but not a _____ of this age, or of the rulers of this age, who are coming to nothing. On the contrary, we speak God's hidden _____ in a mystery, a _____ God predestined before the ages for our glory." (1 Corinthians 2:1-7)

Here again is the contrast between human wisdom and God's wisdom. The unrighteous man relies on his own wisdom and he is unable to accept enlightenment and truth from the Spirit. Because of this, God's truth is considered by him to be foolish.

Have you limited God in your life because of your crooked thinking and habits of unbelief? Let's believe God for these gifts. Come Lord with your divine wisdom and let it be made manifest in my life as you see fit. God's hidden wisdom is a mystery, a wisdom He predestined from the ages for our glory. (1 Corinthians 2:7) Not everyone knows of this wisdom which is Christ Jesus. While in the flesh, Jesus grew up and became strong in this wisdom (Luke 2:40). Because Jesus had wisdom, he grew in stature and in favor with God and men (Luke 2:52). Many have heard of the great wisdom of Solomon, yet in all his wisdom something greater (Jesus) has come that surpasses even the wisdom of Solomon! (Luke 11:31) God has placed all the treasures of wisdom and knowledge in the Darling of heaven Himself. (Colossians 2:3) Seek Him as your first priority and these things will be given to you. Amen.

☙"No one should deceive himself. If anyone among you thinks he is wise in this age, he must become foolish so that he can become wise. For the ___wisdom___ of this world is foolishness with God, since it is written: He catches the wise in their craftiness; and again, The Lord knows that the reasonings of the wise are meaningless. (1 Corinthians 3:18-20)

We should not be deceived into thinking that the wisdom of the human intellect works to obtain salvation or builds up the brethren. Do you think yourself to be wise? It is suggested we should renounce our dependence on this type of wisdom in order to receive God's wisdom. Nothing that enters the mind of man is beyond God's understanding.

🕯"For this is our confidence: The testimony of our conscience is that we have conducted ourselves in the world, and especially toward you, with God-given sincerity and purity, not by _____ wisdom but by God's _____." (2 Corinthians 1:12)

Paul is answering a charge by speaking truth from the testimony of his conscience and the Corinthians' knowledge of his conduct. If a person is being led out of fleshy wisdom then accusations will also come from that same source. A person operating full-throttle in this gift will be led and will speak by the Spirit's wisdom.

🕯"We have redemption in Him through His blood, the forgiveness of our trespasses, according to the riches of His grace that He lavished on us with all _____ and _____." (Ephesians 1:7-8)

We have the lavish gift of salvation that God, in His divine wisdom planned for us. This wisdom should be throughly known and graciously remembered by us as well as conveyed to others.

🕯"I pray that the God of our Lord Jesus Christ, the glorious Father, would give you a spirit, of _____ and revelation in the knowledge of Him." (Ephesians 1:17 also see Colossians 1:9-10)

A great prayer of proclamation to pray for yourself and others is that "I may be filled with the knowledge of His will in all wisdom and spiritual understanding so that I may walk worthy of the Lord, fully pleasing to Him, bearing fruit in every good work and growing in the knowledge of God!" Amen!

🕯"This is so God's multi-faceted _____ may now be made known through the church to the rulers and authorities in the heavens. (Ephesians 3:10)

God's multi-faceted wisdom is found in Christ Jesus. We all are able to be fortified by His unfathomable riches which He made freely available to us. However, how many do not allow themselves to do so? It is not the fault of God if we choose to not partake of these powerfully transforming truths; we can only blame ourselves.

Charisma

Can you even fathom the idea that the principalities and powers of heaven have also been enlightened to God's manifold wisdom? What do you suppose they did when the curtain was pulled back and they beheld the sublime act of the Darling of heaven stepping into time to rescue our souls from the clutches of the destroyer? I imagine after an initial slack-jawed response, joyous praise erupted and the heavens have yet been quieted!

☙"We proclaim Him, warning and teaching everyone with all _____, so that we may present everyone mature in Christ." (Colossians 1:28)

If you operate in the Spiritual gift of wisdom, from that wisdom you should warn and teach everyone until we all reach unity in the faith.

☙"All the treasures of _____ and knowledge are hidden in Him." (Colossians 2:3)

If you seek wisdom search no further than Jesus. How do you see wisdom as a treasure?

_____

☙"If you died with the Messiah to the elemental forces of this world, why do you live as if you still belonged to the world? Why do you submit to regulations: "Don't handle, don't taste, don't touch"? All these regulations refer to what is destroyed by being used up; they are commands and doctrines of men. Although these have a reputation of _____ by promoting ascetic practices, humility, and severe treatment of the body, they are not of any value in curbing self-indulgence." (Colossians 2:20-23)

Remember the earlier discussion of worldly wisdom versus God's wisdom? We can set up barriers in our lives that appear to guide us regarding self-control but real wisdom for success emanates from God and must be the result of an inward change.

☙"Let the message about the Messiah dwell richly among you, teaching and admonishing one another in all _____, and singing psalms, hymns, and spiritual songs, with gratitude in your hearts to God." (Colossians 3:16)

The *full* message of the Messiah should *dwell richly*. Search your heart and determine if this is true in your life. Possibly one of the hardest things to walk out is forgiveness. However, forgiveness is a foundational truth of the message and therefore must be done. Because corruption exist in our hearts we therefore must strive to continually be renewed. When a quarrel arises, we will then be able to quickly forgive because the truth of our own salvation is at the forefront of our heart and mind.

🙵"Act _____ toward outsiders, making the most of the time." (Colossians 4:5)

Outsiders most likely means those outside the body of believers of Christ Jesus. Even within the church there are those that are still 'outside' of the truth. Shall we draw from our memory of what brought us to a knowledge of the truth? Was the person kind and gracious towards us and it beckoned a desire to know more? Our behavior should exhibit wisdom to those inside and outside the church, making the most of the time given us to bring another soul to knowledge of the truth. What an honor.

🙵"Now if any of you lacks _____, he should ask God, who gives to all generously and without criticizing, and it will be given to him. But let him ask in faith without doubting. For the doubter is like the surging sea, driven and tossed by the wind. That person should not expect to receive anything from the Lord. An indecisive man is unstable in all his ways." (James 1:5-8)

Have you asked God for His wisdom? When you asked did you ask in faith expecting to receive? Do you ever ask someone for something anticipating their answer will be no? If so, why would you even ask them? Why ask God for equipping that is in line with His word and expect Him to say no? Let's not be doubters by not expecting God to grant what His Word clearly says He will. Ask God for wisdom and be prepared to receive ~ He gives generously.

"Listen closely to wisdom and direct your heart to understanding; furthermore, if you call out to wisdom and lift your voice to understanding, if you seek it like silver and search for it like hidden treasure, then you will understand the fear of the LORD and discover the knowledge of God." (Proverbs 2:2-5)

🙵"Who is wise and has understanding among you? He should show his works by good conduct with _____ _____. But if you have bitter envy and selfish ambition in your heart, don't brag and deny the truth. Such _____ does not come from _____ but is earthly, unspiritual, demonic. For where envy and selfish ambition exist, there is disorder and every kind of evil. But the _____ from above is first pure, then peace-loving, gentle, compliant, full of mercy and good fruits, without favoritism and hypocrisy." (James 3:13-17)

Charisma

'Such wisdom' is referring to bitter envy and selfish ambition in the heart that is spoken about in verse 14. This type of wisdom evaluates everything by worldly standards and makes personal gain of supreme importance. This wisdom does not come down from heaven. It has its origin in the world and is of the devil.

The source of true wisdom is above the wisdom humanity is capable of obtaining outside of God. Thank you Lord that You are above our thinking yet you allow Your Spirit to fill us with the wisdom You have! The absence of any sinful attitude or motive is 'pure'. The absence of a bitter spirit of competitiveness and selfish ambition is 'peace-loving'. The absence of insisting on your own rights but exercising love's leniency is 'gentle'. The absence of self-seeking and instead having a posture ready to yield is 'compliant', 'full of mercy' and with 'good fruit'.

A divine word of wisdom comes from no human ability but rather is a gift of the Spirit originating from God Himself. This word comes in a moment to give insight to a particular situation or question. A divine word of wisdom speaks to your spirit and an acknowledgement is made in agreement with the word that speaks resolution and life into the needed situation. Sometimes the wisdom will say 'wait' for the right time to reveal. Do you recall Joseph interpreting Pharaoh's dream in Genesis 41? Joseph did not study or prepare before giving the dream's interpretation, but was given a supernatural word of wisdom precisely in the moment needed.

"Also, regard the patience of our Lord as an opportunity for salvation, just as our dear brother Paul has written to you according to the _____ given to him. He speaks about these things in all his letters in which there are some matters that are hard to understand. The untaught and unstable twist them to their own destruction, as they also do with the rest of the Scriptures." (2 Peter 3:15-16)

The Lord is incredibly patient. So patient, He is waiting for all to come to a knowledge of salvation and make their choice before He judges the earth. Being around someone operating in the Spiritual gift of wisdom helps us further our pursuit of God as well as our ministry. They bless our learning and help instruct us when we have wrong thinking.

"Here is _____: The one who has understanding must calculate the number of the beast, because it is the number of a man. His number is 666. Here is the mind with _____: The seven heads are seven mountains on which the woman is seated." (Revelation 13:18 and 17:9)

Someone operating in the Spiritual gift of wisdom will guide and teach us in a greater understanding of things of the Spirit because God intends for His people to be informed. When necessary, God's Spirit will reveal knowledge to be shared with His believers.

🕊"They said with a loud voice: The Lamb who was slaughtered is worthy to receive power and riches and _____ and strength and honor and glory and blessing! I heard every creature in heaven, on earth, under the earth, on the sea, and everything in them say: Blessing and honor and glory and dominion to the One seated on the throne, and to the Lamb, forever and ever! All the angels stood around the throne, the elders, and the four living creatures, and they fell facedown before the throne and worshiped God, saying: Amen! Blessing and glory and wisdom and thanksgiving and honor and power and strength be to our God forever and ever. Amen."
(Revelation 5:12 and 7:11-12)

Amen indeed!

Facts (knowledge) + Faith = wisdom
wisdom is application - knowing what to do with the knowledge

Prayer

Father, I humbly ask to be filled with the knowledge of Your will in all wisdom and spiritual understanding so that I can walk worthy of you Lord. I rebuke the world's wisdom I have so naively trusted in so many times. I turn away from wisdom that relies on my understanding and exalts myself. I desire the source of my understanding to be You. When times are especially difficult, Lord fill me with your wisdom and increase my faith to wait and look for Your guidance. May you be the rudder of my words Father. If I am tempted to speak what does not bring comfort or edification, I ask that you would lead me in wisdom to change my thoughts. Open my eyes to behold the enormous value of Your wisdom compared to my own. Empower me with Your wisdom Lord because I lack! Give me wisdom to navigate my life, to advise those seeking salvation, to inspire other believers, and to know how and what to pray! I will learn the sacred Scriptures because Your word says all the treasures of wisdom and knowledge are hidden in Jesus! I choose to not walk in little but to walk in the riches of Your abundance. I choose Your ways Lord!

The Equipping of Knowledge

Praise God for His knowledge! We need His equipping in our lives for every occasion. The Spiritual gift of knowledge (gnōsis) assist the believer in praying more effectively, giving protection, or showing how to help others. I read something recently regarding praying with confidence in the knowledge of God. Before you make your request to God, search the Scriptures to find knowledge regarding how God feels about your need. In this way, there is no need to tack on to the end of the prayer "if it is Your will" because you have already attained the knowledge that it is. If it is not His will, then don't pray in that direction. Pray instead that your will be in line with His. Once this is settled, pray with confidence! Ask the Lord so that your joy may be complete! (John 16:24) Thank Him in faith when you finish praying and not just when your senses have beheld the reality of the answered prayer. (Mark 11:24) Search the Scripture for knowledge of particular verses to pray. The knowledge of God's will must direct our prayers.

The gift of a word of knowledge can be received in a moment when a tiny portion of God's knowledge is imparted to you by the Holy Spirit, bringing insight to a situation. A word of knowledge can speak of things only God would know, which can increase faith in believers or bring truth to an unbeliever.

Knowledge can be separated into four sorts:

(1) Natural human knowledge (an acquaintance with facts, truths, or principles attained from personal study)
(2) The fallen world's supernatural knowledge (The natural mind gaining information by supernatural means that do not involve the Spirit of God. Some examples are the occult, the psychic, and the metaphysical)
(3) True intellectual knowledge (results from knowing God through Jesus, being filled with the Spirit, and studying the Word)
(4) The gift of the word of knowledge (originates from God and is imparted by the Holy Spirit for a specific purpose). Whatever part

of your life that is yielded to wisdom and knowledge you will thrive. Where you have places of pride you will stagnate and be hindered. Humble yourself in the fear of the Lord.

When Jesus left his position in glory with his father, he took on flesh. In doing so, he laid aside many things, one being His omniscience (all-knowing). In order to fulfill His purpose He had to rely on the Spirit to receive the knowledge required for His ministry. Just as He relied on the Spirit for knowledge, we are to do the same and it is just as available to us today! Hallelujah!

1 Corinthians 8:1b is an informative verse as well as one that comes with a warning. "We know that "we all have knowledge." Knowledge inflates with pride, but love builds up." Love builds up the whole church. The love spoken of here is God's love. We receive this love from Him and it is intended to fill us so completely that our vessel then spills out onto others. Love builds us up and we apply this love to build up others. We are also told that knowledge inflates with pride. Knowledge has the ability to inflate the ego of the one possessing it. If we keep it for ourselves it brings the temptation to believe we know more than another therefore we are better. Let it not be so. Any revelation we receive from God is intended for the edification of the church. We are strictly a vessel which is not superior to any other that He uses to share His love.

Characteristics of someone operating in this gift:

✸ Shares insight, a digest, or appropriate message (which He speaks as a result of our experience with Him and with His Word) ✸
✸ Desire to investigate, research, and personally experience the assurances of God's Word ✸
✸ Insightful ✸
✸ Has Spirit-given ability to understand ✸
✸ Discovers new insights in Scripture ✸
✸ Can analyze and clarify information ✸

Please open your Bible and prayerfully consider the following verses as you complete the blanks:

❧"This extraordinary _____ is beyond me. It is lofty; I am unable to reach it." (Psalm 139:6)

The knowledge of God graciously discerns in favor of those who are loyal to the Lord. Do you find God's favor toward you too wonderful to comprehend? Do you desire to be equipped with knowledge that is 'extraordinary'? Lord, impart to me knowledge I need for life.

✒ "The _____ of the _____ is the beginning of _____; fools despise wisdom and discipline." (Proverbs 1:7)

Fear of the Lord is your foundation for success in this life and the platform from which you spring into eternity. Have you considered that nothing can be hidden from Him? God does not overlook things we might consider 'innocent' sin and He certainly does not overlook lawlessness. This reverential fear of the Lord is the prerequisite of knowledge. If you seek knowledge, first plant your heart in the fertile ground of the fear of the Lord. When YOU draw near to God, He will draw near to you (James 4:8).

✒ "Because they hated _____, didn't _____ to fear the Lord, were not _____ in my counsel, and _____ all my correction, they will _____ the _____ of their way and be _____ with their _____ _____." (Proverbs 1:29-31)

According to the verse above, the fear of the Lord is the beginning of knowledge. In this verse, the people hated knowledge so they choose not to fear God. The fruit of the Spirit is love, joy, peace, patience, kindness, goodness, faithfulness, gentleness, and self-control. This fruit is quite lovely indeed and is evident in a life yielded to the Spirit. Those who do not choose the fear of the Lord and hate knowledge will not have the fruit of the Spirit but instead will produce the fruit of corruption and rebellion. <u>The fruit you produce is a result of YOUR choosing.</u>

✒ "...then you will _____ the _____ of the Lord and discover the _____ of God." (Proverbs 2:5-6)

For the Lord gives wisdom; from His mouth come knowledge and understanding. God is the source of knowledge. From this spring of knowledge you will find THE path of life and the Word made flesh.

✒ "For wisdom will enter your mind, and _____ will _____ your heart." (Proverbs 2:10)

How glorious indeed to have a heart that is delighted! This verse asserts knowledge will do just that. Possessing God's knowledge puts you head and shoulders above the world. Being skilled to discern with

Charisma

this knowledge protects you from evil and the repercussions of naiveté.

- "The __fear__ of the Lord is the beginning of wisdom, and the __knowledge__ of the __Holy__ __One__ is understanding." (Proverbs 9:10)

Are you catching the theme here of the fear of the Lord and how it provides knowledge?"

- "Whoever _____ discipline loves _____, but one who hates correction is _____." (Proverbs 12:1)

I read something on this verse that compares one being stupid with a dumb animal. Let's 'roll around' with this for a minute. If you have ever owned a pet you will be able to quickly see the analogy. I have had the privilege of owning several dogs over the years. When choosing my pet, I am only drawn to the highly trainable. I would much prefer a not-so-cute dog that is intelligent over an adorable dog that is an imbecile. An untrainable dog is completely frustrating to me and does not fit well in my household. (I apologize in advance to anyone I might have offended by stating my preferences.) However, a clever dog is a pure delight! Now let's look back at the verse. Using the analogy provided, how do you think God appreciates your love of discipline and your 'trainability'?

_____

- "Stay _____ from a _____ man; you will gain _____ _____ from his _____." (Proverbs 14:7)

How does a foolish person add to your knowledge and understanding? There are places in Scripture where we are warned to avoid certain types of people and to seek out others...here is one of them.

- "The _____ of the _____ makes knowledge _____, but the mouth of _____ blurts out _____." (Proverbs 15:2) And "A _____ mind seeks _____, but the mouth of fools _____ on _____." (Proverbs 15:14)

Can you discern if a person is wise or foolish by what is said? A wise person discerns how to make the knowledge of God attractive. We must keep a vigilant watch over our mouths. Don't risk your testimony over an unguarded mouth.

☙"A _____ warrior is better than a strong one, and a man of _____ than one of strength; for you should wage war with sound _____." (Proverbs 24:5-6)

You are a warrior in the army of the living God! In war, brute force (pure muscle or harsh words) may win some battles but wisdom and knowledge wins the war. Do you realize you are quite often in a spiritual battle? Of course they are only battles because the Lord has ultimately won the war! The spiritual battles you are in are not against flesh and blood but against dark spiritual forces. When you realize this, you are then engaging in the war equipped with knowledge. When you fight your spiritual battle you are instructed to take up the full armor of God (Ephesians 6:13-17) and the knowledge of God will give you the sound guidance required. Battling any other way is waging war according to how the world battles. You are a child and warrior of the King and the Kingdom for which you are defending is spiritual.

☙"For to the man who is _____ in His sight, He gives wisdom, _____, and joy, but to the sinner He _____ the _____ of gathering and accumulating _____ _____ to give to the one who is _____ in God's sight." (Ecclesiastes 2:26)

Do you seek the Lord's favor? For the one who is pleasing to Him, He gives the knowledge needed to live rightly the life you have been entrusted with. The sinner toils endlessly and all the accumulating is done without the wisdom and knowledge to then properly have enjoyment. Before long it is merely passed on to someone else.

☙"Therefore My people will go into _____ because they lack _____." (Isaiah 5:13)

This is speaking of the result of Judah's sin, however, WE are God's people. If we lack knowledge, we too can go into exile (as a captive and lead away disgracefully). Desire to have knowledge of the work of the Lord and His ways. Let us have knowledge of Christ and of His mercy and grace. We have the means of knowledge so we will not be rebellious and refuse to make use of it and therefore live life as if we are excluded.

☙"You were _____ in your wickedness; you said, No one _____ me. Your wisdom and _____ led you astray. You said to yourself, ____exist, and there is no _____ _____ else." (Isaiah 47:10)

Our wisdom and knowledge will lead us astray. It tends to become prideful and exalts itself. God's knowledge is available to His children and we will prosper if we choose to live by it. Let it not be so that we feel so 'secure' in our old habits and practices. Let us not be deceived in thinking that because we have not yet received discipline from the Lord that He has not seen. God is omniscient (all-knowing) and omnipresent (present everywhere at the same time).

☙ "_____ people are _____ for lack of _____." (Hosea 4:6)

Because you have rejected knowledge, I will reject you from serving as My priest. The Old Testament priests had not been teaching the people about God and His law so the people were being destroyed for lack of knowledge. According 1 Peter 2:5,9 we are the priests of God. Hallelujah! There is knowledge needed and an accountability that goes along with that. Let us not be in lack nor reject knowledge. Fear the Lord and rise up as you are called by Him!

☙ "For I desire _____ and not sacrifice, the _____ of God rather than burnt offerings." (Hosea 6:6)

In our day, let us have our worship indeed but it must be with a proper heart. The Lord still desires our loyal hearts and a desire to have knowledge about Him. The challenge is not so much in the praise and worship alone. Praise and worship without the inward bowing of the heart is worthless. A loyal heart is just the thing the Lord desires! He instituted love and loyalty. His love is so loyal to us that instead of forgetting us because we forget Him, we are merely to turn back to Him and He will be found! Hallelujah! May the foundation of the altar of our praise be established on the fear of the Lord and may our loyalty be steadfast!

☙ "Woe to you experts in the law! You have taken away the _____ of _____! You didn't _____ _____ yourselves, and you _____ those who were going in." (Luke 11:52)

We should open the meaning of the Word with the 'key' and then enter through the 'door'! Knowledge is the only key to open heaven. Let us never substitute 'our' knowledge for 'true' knowledge ~ not ever.

☙ "I can testify about them that they have _____ for God, but not according to _____." (Romans 10:2-3)

Because they disregarded the righteousness from God and attempted to establish their own righteousness, they have not submitted themselves to God's righteousness. This begs the question. If there is zeal for God but it is not according to knowledge about Him then what is the zeal based on? Traditions? Assumptions? What is the foundation for your zeal for God? _____ We will not disregard the righteousness from God and foolishly think we are righteous according to any of the works we have been allowed to accomplish. Submit therefore to God.

❧"Oh, the _____ of the riches both of the wisdom and the _____ of God!
How _____ His judgments and _____ His ways!" (Romans 11:33)

The depth of God! You will never come to the end of discovering His knowledge. Hallelujah!!! Picture yourself standing at the edge of the abyss of knowledge. Do you desire to stand and look, or to wade in slowly only going deep enough to turn back if needed, or do you desire to dive in...head first!!! I have always loved the second part of this verse regarding his untraceable ways. We will never be able to trace out the ways of God and figure out His purposes. Whatever you think you have figured out about God, He is vastly more. Amen.

❧"Woe to you _____ in the law! You have taken away the key of _____! You didn't go in yourselves, and you _____ those who were going in." (Luke 11:52)

Those that understood the law knew enough to consider themselves an exclusive group but they did not perceive adequately to apply the Word as a key to enter through the 'door'. They refused to teach those not wealthy or those not born into the proper family and thus created a stumbling block for them. They were a hinderance because they would not teach them the knowledge they knew. (Malachi 2:8-9)

❧"If you are _____ that you are a guide for the blind, a light to those in darkness, an instructor of the ignorant, a teacher of the immature, having the full _____ of _____ and truth in the law." (Romans 2:20)

What would the full expression of knowledge look like? Is the full manifestation of the knowledge you have walked out daily in your life? If so, you not only are authentic but there will not always be a need to teach with words because your daily life will represent what you know to be true.

☙"Oh, the _depth_ of the riches both of the wisdom and the _knowledge_ of God! How _unsearchable_ His judgments and _____ His ways!" (Romans 11:33)

This is one of my favorite go-to verses when my flesh tries to figure out why or why God is not intervening in a situation I think would be a perfect time for Him to. Even if there are times I feel I should know more, truth be told I would rather know there are deep things of God that are unsearchable and things that we can never trace out. God is God and we are not. I am thankful for that. What would God be reduced to if we could reach the depth of Him? Would His wisdom and knowledge be no better than yours or mine? That indeed is a very unsettling thought. I am content in waiting to discover His depths until I see Him face to face. In the meantime fellow sojourner, let's not hesitate one minute from diving heart first into the abyss of His character and just see how far we can go.

☙"My brothers, I myself am convinced about you that you also are _____ of goodness, _____ with all _____, and _____ to instruct one another." (Romans 15:14)

This of course is not relating to knowledge of things of the world that we can learn, but of Spiritual knowledge relating to the things of God. If someone is operating in the Spiritual gift of knowledge they are able to admonish another person in full goodness and tenderness since this is what is required in order to be successful.

☙"I always thank my God for you because of God's grace given to you in Christ Jesus, that by Him you were enriched in everything — in all speech and all knowledge. In this way, the testimony about Christ was confirmed among you, so that you do not _____ any spiritual gift as you eagerly wait for the revelation of our Lord Jesus Christ." (1 Corinthians 1:5)

The Corinthians were bestowed with all the Spiritual gifts but we also know that they were immature Christians. Spiritual gifts are given by contemplation of the Spirit to each person without regard to their current level of sanctification. The Spirit is wise and knows all things. We may not be operating full-throttle in our Spiritual gifting but that is no excuse to not strive for that goal now.

☙"However, not everyone has this _____." (1 Corinthians 8:7a)

So what is 'this' knowledge? There is one God, the Father. All things are from Him. We exist for Him. There is one Lord, Jesus Christ. All things are through Him. We exist through Him. (v. 6)

An idol is nothing in the world. The passage goes on to say that people are so used to idolatry that if they eat food offered to an idol that their conscious is defiled because they are so weak in the faith. If you believe there is one God and one Lord and an idol is nothing, than anything someone else does regarding their idolatry should not effect you. It is meaningless ~ God has power over all things.

If through our knowledge we know things others do not, let's be mindful and not participate in what we know to be harmless but another person does not. If our actions cause a stumbling block for a weak Christian, we should not sin against them by 'wounding their weak conscience'. How about honoring them instead by either teaching them the knowledge we have or not participating in the activity while around them. Love is the tool that guides manifested knowledge.

ஃ"If I have the gift of prophecy and _____ all mysteries and all _____, and if I have all faith so that I can move mountains but do not have _____, I am _____." (1 Corinthians 13:2)

Love is what guides ALL Spiritual gifts. Love. Love. Love. The love that is spoken about in this verse is the Greek word agapē and is the love that comes from God. God's love. This is a self-sacrificing love. If you operate in the Spiritual gift knowledge but do not lavishly coat it with God's love it is useless to you and anyone else.

ஃ"_____ never ends. But as for prophecies, they will come to an end; as for languages, they will cease; as for _____, it will come to an end. For we know in part, and we prophesy in part. But when the _____ comes, the partial will come to an _____." (1 Corinthians 13:8-10)

Jesus is the perfect. When Jesus returns for His church the gift of knowledge in which we operate in will come to an end. We will have no use for it because the One who has ALL knowledge will be with us.

ஃ"But thanks be to God, who always puts us on _____ in Christ and through us spreads the _____ of the _____ of Him in every place." (2 Corinthians 2:14)

Thank God indeed! He has made us his captives and continues to lead us along in Christ's triumphal procession. Why? So that through us we spread the perfume of the knowledge of Jesus every place we go.

The word 'display' means to make an acclamatory procession; cause to triumph! Because of Christ's triumphal victory, God has allowed US to be the representatives of that victory! We are allowed to walk, head held high because of redemption, and therefore spread the knowledge of Christ every place we are led. As we do so, this knowledge is likened to God as the smell of a sweet perfume. It is our duty to spread the 'sweet smelling' knowledge of Christ to others. Even if it is not received, its ascent will not be hindered as it it rises to the heavens as a sweet, sweet smell because it is the aroma of the Son! Praise God for the honor to do such a thing!

✺"For God who said, "Let _____ shine out of darkness," has shone in our hearts to give the _____ of the _____ of God's glory in the face of Jesus Christ." (2 Corinthians 4:6)

This verse flows so nicely it just seems to be one that must be memorized. God, the Father of lights (James 1:1) created the light to shine upon the earth (Genesis 1:3) and then sent his Son to the be the light of the world (John 8:12) when it became dark again. As God created all light to do, it shines so that all receive. Unless you hide yourself from either the sun or the Son, light indeed penetrates you. As the light of the Son has its intended influence, you are then to shine the light of the gospel to those that have hid themselves. The light of God's knowledge is in Jesus Christ alone.

✺"Now as you excel in everything — faith, speech, knowledge, and in all diligence, and in your love for us — excel also in this grace." (2 Corinthians 8:7)

Someone operating in the Spiritual gift of knowledge will diligently excel in assisting fellow believers with information that prospers their victorious walk with Christ. Excel means to be superior or to surpass. Let's operate in this Spiritual gift of knowledge and in doing so let's excel in grace which manifest itself in love.

✺"We _____ arguments and every _____-_____ thing (pride or any other barrier) that is _____ _____ against the _____ of God, taking every thought _____ (expresses a continuous or repeated action) to obey Christ." (2 Corinthians 10:4-5)

Spiritual warfare requires spiritual weapons. Reliance on worldly knowledge and weapons do not crumble walls of strongholds where spiritual evil resides. Also, we must get into the practice of not accepting every thought that enters our mind as the knowledge of God. Questions should be asked. Did this come from God? Did this come from the enemy? Was this a thought of my natural intellect? Any argument or barrier that cause our eyes to gaze upon – now has our focus. Take those arguments and barriers captive (they are allowed to go nowhere else at this time). Hold them in your mind and put them to the test. Is it in agreement with the Word? Take as many Scriptures as you can and test the argument and barrier. Keep it captive until the question is resolved. If it does not line up with Scripture cast the argument or barrier to the ground and NEVER pick it up again. At this point, the argument or barrier is not allowed to pass to your heart. If it indeed lines up with what Scripture says, you can then allow it to pass from your mind into your heart. Your thoughts must be healthy and good. Take this knowledge, apply it to your own life and teach it to others.

❧"Though _____ in public speaking, I am certainly not untrained in _____. Indeed, we have always made that clear to you in everything." (2 Corinthians 11:6)

Paul may not have been a polished speaker but the knowledge He possessed and graciously shared with others was unmistakable. We do not need to be an orator to share what we have when we operate in the gift of knowledge. If critiques come, they are based on the workings of the flesh and not of the spirit. We welcome all who wish to share knowledge and the criteria shall never be that you have eloquent speech.

❧"For this reason also, since the day we heard this, we haven't stopped praying for you. We are asking that you may be _____ with the _____ of His will in all wisdom and spiritual understanding, so that you may _____ _____ of the Lord, fully pleasing to Him, bearing fruit in every good work and _____ in the _____ of God." (Colossians 1:9-11)

What a glorious thing indeed to receive the new birth! However, it shall not stop there. The intent is that our lives should be continually filled with wisdom and spiritual understanding in the knowledge of God's daily will for us. May you continue growing in God's knowledge and therefore bearing fruit in every good work! I personally loves these verses 9-14. I recommend memorizing it or reading over it several times to receive its fullness. Are you familiar with the knowledge of God's will? Our desire is to walk fully pleasing to Him. Pray for this knowledge to be made manifest in your life and in the life of others.

❧"...and to _____ the Messiah's love that surpasses _____, so you may be filled with all the fullness of God." (Ephesians 3:19)

Do you know the Messiah's love for you? Do you know it surpasses knowledge? Paul's prayers are God's promises. He wants us to have a knowledge of the vast love He has for us. Whatever we think we have figured out about His love it stretches wider and deeper than that. Can you comprehend it? We all need to feel loved. The love we receive even from our closest loved one will never match the love God has for you. Your loved one is not even able to love you with the kind of love your soul desires most because that beloved is a love reserved exclusively to be given by God alone. Do you allow Him to?

❧"More than that, I also consider _____ to be a loss in view of the surpassing value of _____ Christ Jesus my Lord. Because of Him I have suffered the loss of all things and consider them _____, so that I may gain Christ and be found in Him, not having a righteousness of my _____ from the law, but one that is through faith in Christ — the _____ from God based on _____." (Philippians 3:8-9)

Do you consider all things you have worked for a loss in light of knowing Christ? Do you know Christ well enough to be able to make this your testimony? Are you willing to consider all other things to be weightless if weighed on the scale with Christ on the other side? Shall we put more of our time and efforts into things that promote the cause of Christ knowing their value surpasses any other work we can do in the flesh? We gain righteousness based on the work of Jesus and has nothing to do with our own merit. This may lead some to disappointment and some to praise. Which is it for you? Someone operating in the Spiritual gift of knowledge will know this reality and accepts it with full joy. We are blessed indeed.

❧"All the treasures of wisdom and knowledge are hidden in Him." (Colossians 2:3)

A treasure is something you seek and when you find it are overjoyed. Do you seek the knowledge that is found only in Jesus Christ of Nazareth? It is a treasure you will guard because you understand its enormous value.

❧"You are _being_ _renewed_ in _knowledge_ _according_ to the _image_ of your Creator." (Colossians 3:10)

Do you love the picture here? Your new self (if you have been born again, you have new blood – royal blood!) is continually renewed by the knowledge of God. Being renewed means no oldness or decay but a continuous process of taking on the image of your Creator. You must know your Creator through the Word so that you recognize the knowledge you receive is indeed from God. When you receive knowledge, you are compelled to immediately give praise to God because you know He is imparting a part of Him to you! I know you want to raise your hand in praise right now!

☙"_____ what has been _____ to you, _____ irreverent, empty speech and contradictions from the "knowledge" that falsely bears that name." (1 Timothy 6:20)

Natural human knowledge opposes the truth of Scripture and inflates with pride. If anyone thinks he knows anything, he does not yet know it as he ought to know it. But if anyone loves God, he is known by Him (1 Col. 8:1-3) Guard your heart with the words and knowledge of Jesus, from the Book that has been entrusted to you. What are you doing with the knowledge that has been entrusted to you? Are you putting it into action? There is no condemnation in Christ Jesus but let's get busy.

☙"...always learning and _____ _____ to come to a _____ of the _____." (2 Timothy 3:7)

There are people who pose as someone who has learned the truth but in actuality have remained in ignorance. We want no part of this! When we gain God's knowledge it must first be 'chewed' on, then 'digested', and then made to take up its permanent residence in the heart. When we have this knowledge we then impart this knowledge.

☙"For if we _deliberately_ sin after receiving the _____ of the truth, there _no_ _longer_ _____ remains a sacrifice for sins, but a terrifying _____ of _____ and the fury of a fire about to consume the adversaries." (Hebrews 10:26-27)

This is speaking of people who have received the knowledge of the truth (Christianity). If after receiving the knowledge of what God has done in Christ, the person then turns back to their old life and rejects Christ, there remains no sacrifice available for them for their sin. (put together with 2 Peter 2:20-21 below)

☙"Husbands, in the same way, live with your wives with an _____ of their weaker nature, yet showing them _____ as co-heirs of the grace of life, so that your prayers will not be _____." (1 Pe 3:7)

The word knowledge that we have been studying is the Greek word gnōsis. Here the Holman translated it 'understanding'. Many versions do the same with the exception of the King James.

Charisma

This is a sweet verse. In summary, husbands honor your wives and treat your wife with the knowledge you have that she is weaker than you are but an equal partner in God's gift of new life. The final portion of this verse is interesting. Can our prayers be hindered? According to this verse they can. If husbands do not treat their wives honorably, their prayers will be hindered. Wives, let's do our part and make it easy for them to honor us ~ the rest is up to husbands.

☙"For this very reason, make _____ _____ to _____ your faith with goodness, goodness with knowledge, _____ with _____, self-control with endurance, endurance with godliness." (2 Pe 1:5-6)

If you operate in the Spiritual gift of knowledge you will have opportunities to inform others of things they possibly are not in suspense to know. Our gift should be supplemented with self-control. What we may feel anxious to share with another should indeed be told but should be told in love and in a way in which it will be received.

☙"For _____ these qualities are yours and are _____, they will keep you from being _____ or _____ in the _____ of our Lord Jesus Christ. The person who lacks these things is blind and shortsighted and has _____ the cleansing from his past sins." (2 Pe 1:8-9)

This is a continuation of the above verse. If you make every effort to supplement your knowledge with self-control, this verse says it will keep you from being *useless* or *unfruitful*. This certainly would not be helpful. If we operate in a Spiritual gift we want to be useful and fruitful for the cause of Christ. Is this suggesting an arrogance that can come with knowledge? If we forget the cleansing from our own past sins are we thinking we are better than the person we are informing with Spiritual knowledge? We must keep in mind that love is the basis for all Spiritual gifts and is what must be manifest more than any of the gifts. If we operate with love being the foundation we can only build up from there. Let's use the Spiritual gift of knowledge for the building-up of fellow believers and not be blind and shortsighted because of a lack of self-control. In Jesus name we ask and receive.

☙"But _____ in the grace and _____ of our Lord and Savior Jesus Christ. To Him be the glory both now and to the day of eternity., Amen." (2 Pe 3:18)

Why should Peter tell us to grow? Because we have a will that is very able to choose not to. Do you have any more of Christ beauty in your life, any more of His truths, any more of His methods of warfare, any more of His peace, any more of His grace than you did a day ago, a month ago, a year ago, or when you first believed? So many people have barely changed since the time they first were in agreement with Christ. We must grow in knowledge of Jesus. Commune regularly with Christ and walk out your salvation with Him.

🙰"May _____ and _____ be _____ to you through the _____ (full discernment, precise and correct) of God and of Jesus our Lord." (2 Peter 1;2)

Grace and peace is the result of the knowledge of God which causes you to gradually approach nearer and nearer as you deeply contemplate this Source. This kind of knowledge implies love. It contrast the 'knowledge' spoken of in 1 Tim. 6:20 (above) which results in inward pride.

🙰"For if, having _____ the world's _____ through the _____ of our Lord and Savior Jesus Christ, they are again _____ in these things and _____, the last state is worse for them than the first. For it would have been _____ for them not to have _____ the way of righteousness than, _____ knowing it, to _____ _____ from the holy command delivered to them." (2 Peter 2:20-21)

Not accepting the knowledge that Jesus is Lord and Savior is a better state to be in than accepting the knowledge and then turning away. Is it possible then for Christians to lose their salvation? (please read Hebrews 6:4-6, 10:26-27) Yes or No? (please circle) How do you feel about that?

_____

Prayer

Lord, you are the One who teaches us about Your knowledge. Thank you gracious Lord for the anointing I received from the Holy One and the knowledge that has come from You so far. Come Holy Spirit and teach my heart, where true knowledge is manifested. I commit myself to studying the Scripture in order to receive Your further knowledge and to be guarded against false teaching and unbelief. Guide my prayers with knowledge. Please give me a spirit of wisdom and revelation in the knowledge of You. I yield myself to your knowledge and wisdom. Fill me Lord, fill me! You are completely worth it. Amen.

Faith Triumphs

*[handwritten: Jeremiah 29:29 (?)
Faith is in the heart.
Hope is in the mind.
Faith is what allows us to hope.]*

Spiritual faith has its origin in God, not in man. We can experience different types of faith such as natural human faith, faith that saves, faith as a fruit of yielding to the Spirit, and miraculous faith.

We all know and understand natural human faith because it occurs in our daily experiences. This faith we have come to easily rely on because it is revealed to us by our senses concerning our everyday interactions. The faith that originates from God, or supernatural faith, is above our natural senses. In our strength, our faith will never match the faith of God – not ever. We should not base our faith on the experiences or wisdom of man but instead base it on the power of God (1 Corinthians 2:5, 1 Timothy 3:4b).

Let's take a look at three kinds of supernatural faith.

Faith that saves. ❧Romans 10:17 states that _____ comes from what is heard, and what is heard comes through the message about Christ.

When a person hears the spoken word of God and takes it into the heart, faith is received and is the required component needed (on our part) for salvation. It is not a work we do but instead is a gift from God (Ephesians 2:8-9). Saving faith comes to man by the proclamation of God's word.

❧"One believes with the _____, resulting in righteousness, and one _____ with the _____, resulting in salvation. ❧Romans 12:3b says...God has distributed a _____ of _____ to each one." (Romans 10:10)

Since you are doing this bible study, I am confident you have experienced the type of supernatural faith called saving faith. When we have faith for salvation nothing is received that appeals to our senses. We must have faith in God's Word that (1) He indeed delivers and (2) we have indeed received that salvation.

Charisma

Faith as a fruit of yielding to the indwelling Spirit. ☙Galatians 5:22 states, The fruit of the Spirit is _____, _____, _____, _____, _____, _____, _____, _____, and _____.

We receive the Spirit when we confess Jesus Christ as Lord and Savior (John 7:39, 20:22, Gal. 3:2, 3:14). Faith, as a fruit in our lives when yielded to the Spirit, is not the same faith required for salvation. This relates more to the aggregate of traits that form your nature. When a person has faith as a fruit of the Spirit they exhibit faith and trust in God. This type of person typically has no reason for fear, for being melodramatic or for feeling agitated. As you can perceive, this comes by experience and is an endeavor.

Miraculous faith. It is possible in every believer, but unlike the other gifts, becomes more active when the believer is yielded and filled with the Spirit of God. God has all faith and a small portion of His faith is given as a sudden outpouring, usually out of necessity, and generally given as a word to confidently believe without a doubt that as we act or speak in the name of Jesus it shall come to pass. I love the example given in Mark 11:22 when Jesus tells his disciples to "Have the faith of God." One way we exhibit the faith of God is by speaking His word. The word confession is interesting. An example of the word can be found in several verses but one is 2 Corinthians 9:13a. The Greek word for confession is homologia and means to speak the same thing as the Word of God. In speaking (we speak what we believe – period) the Word, we have the faith of God.

Picture this, God is the Creator or Imaginer of all things. Jesus, knowing what God imagines or desires to create, speaks that Word (He is the Word), and the Spirit goes forth in power to accomplish what was spoken.

☙Psalm 33:6 says, "The heavens were made by the _____ of the LORD, and all the stars, by the _____ (spirit) of His mouth."

Can you picture creation coming forth by God's Word and by His Spirit?

☙"In the beginning was the _____, and the Word was _____ God, and the _____ was God. He was with God in the beginning. All things were _____ through Him, and apart from Him not one thing was created that has been created." (John 1:1-3)

Charisma

❧"The _____ became _____ and took up residence among us. We observed His glory, the glory as the _____ from the Father, full of grace and truth." (John 1:14)

I would like to share with you an experience I had with this type of miraculous surge of faith. <u>Fifteen years ago</u> my husband suffered multiple bleeds throughout his brain. A doctor misdiagnosed him which left us bewildered for several days as he suffered. With just a slight move of his head he became dizzy so he constantly endured extreme nausea. He slept for days; probably because he had no other way to escape the situation. Every time he tried to sit up ~ he threw up. Not many days later the things he said became nonsensical. Then, as if it could be any worse, he could not even finish a sentence. We had been in contact with the original doctor and we consistently were told to give it time ~ the nausea was just a reaction to the medication he was taking. One day I realized I could no longer take care of him and I called for another opinion. The person I spoke with was stunned that he had been left in that condition for so long and that he should immediately be taken to the hospital. My first taste of fear set in.

The doctors at the hospital knew immediately there was a serious problem. Multiple tests were ordered. I remember sitting outside in the hall during one procedure. The hall was empty and the lighting was dim. There were no chairs so I had to sit on the cold floor and wait. I never felt so alone. Fear crept back in.

We finally received the news. The doctor was grim as he told us my husband had several bleeds scattered throughout his brain. I remember how the doctor looked at me with such sorrow and pity. There was no offer of hope from him. He gave the diagnosis, said he was sorry, and left the room. Fear reminded me it was still there.

We discovered the hospital he was in was not adequate to handle his condition so he would have to be moved. Because the move was my idea, I had to sign a release to not hold the hospital responsible if he did not make it during transit. No one else stood by me in that decision. The burden was indescribable. Fear stood by me.

It was late at night and forty-five minutes later when the ambulance finally pulled into the hospital. We were in Dallas at the time and I remember seeing people laughing and having fun in the West End. It seemed so odd to me that some people could experience such intense suffering while others could have such happiness. My husband was admitted to the ICU and they informed us that he now had hydrocephalus. About a week later he was scheduled for brain surgery to try to determine the cause and to stop the bleeding. The night before surgery I remember the nurses rolling him out of ICU for us to say

goodbye to him because our one and a half year old daughter was not old enough to go into the ICU area. I remember thinking it seemed insensitive for the staff to suggest we should say our goodbyes but in his situation no one could even offer hope of a positive outcome. Fear was now my constant companion.

Everything we had been through leading up to this moment caused this experience to be more than I could emotionally handle. At this point, I swung the door wide open to fear. Once this happens the only One who can close it is Jesus. Looking back I can say that even during what seemed to be the darkest hours, God's sovereign hand was still involved. I did not recognize His ways at that time so I choose to trust fear.

The surgery went perfectly. Even the surgeons brought in medical students to view his case because it was miraculous, but I remained afraid. Two weeks later he needed another surgery. The surgery again went perfectly. Five months later we were to move to a small town and the only real medical facilities that could handle his condition would be an hour away. Fear was a stronghold now and it was not turning loose.

My husband did not have any real health issues for about the next 8 years, then he had another brain bleed. This time the bleed was in the center of his brain and there was nothing that could be done; surgery would cause too much collateral damage. The doctor said to go home and hope the bleeding would halt. God showed his great mercy to us yet again. It indeed stopped bleeding. Before it did however, the increased pressure in his brain caused his eyes to not work with each other, as both eyes focused in different directions. While he waited six weeks for the blood in his brain to be reabsorbed in his body, he wore an eye patch so that he could at least operate with one working eye.

I have to tell you that for all those years I lived in fear. I always wondered if something would happen. Almost everything gave me cause for concern. Fifteen years ago when this ordeal first surfaced, I knew God for salvation purposes but I did not know His Son who made it all possible. God was a God of the history books for me. I never knew He was approachable or that He even cared. The lack of relationship is what made trusting fear so easy.

Charisma

Not long ago I received a call from my husband and he described symptoms that were extremely similar to symptoms he had 15 years ago. At the time I was surrounded by kids participating in debate presentations, yet all I wanted to do was fall to the floor in a ball of despair. I had to fight the same delusional thoughts as an ostrich. I wondered how this could be happening again?

As the years had past I had not only grown to know the Lord but I also had grown in faith. Fear was trying to make its appearance again so I knew I must seek someone strong in faith who could pray with me. What a blessing indeed to have believers in your midst! I thank the Lord for that every day! As soon as I turned my eyes up I saw that the Lord had arranged for her to be right before my eyes. Together we rebuked fear. By the end of the prayer I was laughing in the face of the crisis because the joy of the Lord had overwhelmed me. My faith became strong again and I could effectively pray.

My husband spent the next several weeks with extreme dizziness (from the blood putting pressure on different parts of his brain) and all the other symptoms that accompany brain bleeds. We had planned a vacation before all this happened and were discussing if we should still go. He decided we would go and he would live with as much life as he could. One night while we were away he told me to look at his eye. One eye was looking straight and the other was off to the side. It was the same thing all over again. This time, however, my reaction was different. I received a surge of faith! I felt no fear at all and no concern over the future. I looked at him (although it seemed as if I was looking at the problem instead) and said with no fear, "Yes. I see that." I turned my face away from him then and quietly said, "And THAT...does...NOT... move me." Finished. Nothing further said and no emotion felt. It was finished. The next morning his eyes were normal again and it was either that day or the next that every symptom of his brain bleed had disappeared. Praise God! I did not allow fear to dictate terms of the trial as it had in the past. Fear and faith do not go hand-in-hand. You choose one or the other. The Lord allowed this crisis to end with a sudden surge of miraculous faith which lead me to confidently believe without a doubt that whatever the outcome, it was under the sovereign control of the Lord our God. Faith triumphed.

Fear did not reign that day as it had so many times in the past regarding a health crisis. I learned when we are bound by fear we become useless. If a crisis calls for prayer we do not call on fear or recount grief. If a situation calls for standing in faith we do so as a warrior in the army of the living God. Fear? Who needs it! Make no mistake – it is your enemy. As a believer you are to rebuke fear and stand in faith. While you are at it, rebuke everything that dares rival

<u>the spot reserved for faith. Remember to stand firm in your faith or you will not stand at all.</u>

With the crisis past, the Lord brought back to my memory my temptation to fall to my knees in fear. The thought that came to my heart was, "I was tempted to bow down to the fear and by the strength of God alone

was I able to resist. Take that overwhelming emotion fear provoked and fall to your knees giving glory to God!" I also sensed that I had grieved the Spirit by being more sensitive to the power of fear than to the power of God. Do not bow down to fear or any other thing your King says you have victory over. If you are tempted to bow down to fear, turn and bow to the King and bring Him glory instead!

Thank you that I can offer a magnificent prayer to the Magnificent! I look to You with the eyes I have for a manifestation of this gift of faith through me. I have faith to expect great things! I look to you Lord to increase my faith. I am no longer satisfied with merely living according to what my senses reveal to me. I desire to walk by faith! I will no longer bow down to fear, stress, or any other emotion that challenges to take the place of faith. Help me Lord in my weakness. I desire to be a warrior in the army of the Living God! Increase my faith!! It is in Jesus name that I ask and believe! Amen.

Please open your Bible and prayerfully consider the verses as you complete the blanks.

As you fill in the blanks indicate which of these verses (and those in the above paragraphs) would best describe 1) faith for salvation (S), 2) faith as a fruit of the Spirit (F), or 3) miraculous faith (M) Indicate with the letter S, F, or M in the line before each verse.

✒(_____) Mark 4:40 Jesus said, "Why are you _____? Do you still have ___ _____?"

Jesus says, "Have faith and do not doubt." (Matthew 21:21) and it should hold top priority in your life today. "Little faith" is also used by the Lord as a gentle rebuke for anxiety in (Matthew 6:30) and for fear in (Matthew 8:26, 14:31, 16:8).

Do you find when fear and faith are in conflict that they duel or does the Spirit step back? There is a requirement on our part in order to operate in faith. One requirement is to have courage (be encouraged) as in Matthew 9:2 and 22. Another is to first believe as in Matthew 9:29. Matthew 15:28 talks about great faith. This great faith happens when we stop exercising confidence in our own faith and ability and start believing for God to work through us in His ability.

ಊ(_____) Mark 11:12-14 Speaks about a time when Jesus was hungry. In the distance he saw a fig tree with leaves. When he came to it He found nothing but leaves, because it was not the season for figs. He cursed the tree. Verses 20 speaks about the disciples later seeing the tree and noticing the tree had withered from the roots up. Verse 21-22

Then Peter remembered and said to Him, "Rabbi, look! The fig tree that You cursed is withered." Jesus replied to them, "Have _____ in God." (literally translated Have God's faith)

One of the things I love about this verse is Peter marveling because Jesus cursed the fig tree and the tree actually withered. But Jesus did not marvel. He had God's faith when he spoke to the tree. His reply was to "Have the faith of God." This implies that we are not to marvel but to have God's faith.

ಊ(_____) "For we _____ by _____ not by _____." (2 Corinthians 5:7)

Let's not always believe what our senses reveal to us but instead live by faith in God's word. Sometimes these things will be drastically different. Believing God over believing what our senses reveal is the conduct that faith inspires.

ಊ(_____) "Now _____ is the _____ of what is _____ for, the proof of what is _____." (Hebrews 11:1)

The bible discusses faith from beginning to end and Hebrews 11:1 gives the definition. Faith is believing before seeing. When your senses reveal what appears to be the truth regarding a situation, faith steps in and believes God's word if the senses are out of line. True faith that comes from God is supernatural, or above the natural senses. Faith is now or it is not at all. Faith does not happen after the fact. Faith stares at the face of "impossible" and says it is "possible"!

ಊ(_____) "Now without _____ it is impossible to _____ God, for the one who _____ to Him must believe that He_____ and rewards those who _____ Him." (Hebrews 11:6)

The author here does not merely say it is difficult to please God; he says it is impossible to please him. The believer must first believe God exists – without it there is no possibility of faith at all. According to James 2:19 the demons can know that sort of faith. Believers must know the nature of God in that He rewards those who earnestly seek him. This is what makes faith possible.

꙳(_____) "By _____ even Sarah herself, when she was unable to have children, received power to conceive offspring, even though she was past the age, since she _____ that the One who had _____ was _____." (Hebrews 11:11)

On the human level, there was no hope, but faith introduced them to the power that brought about the reality.

꙳(_____) "…knowing that the _____ of your _____ produces _____." (James 1:3)

During a trial, if a person has genuine faith, the trial is capable of producing spiritual endurance.

꙳(_____) "But let him ask in _____ without _____. For the doubter is like the _____ sea and _____ by the wind. That person should not expect to receive anything from the Lord. An _____ man is _____ in _____ his ways." (James 1:6-8)

Doubt describes a person who is divided in their mind and waivers between two opinions. Prayer that moves God to respond must be rooted in unwavering faith. Don't be a person who one minute declares "I believe!" and the next declares, "I am not sure!" A person found faithful would be in line with Romans 1:17, "But my righteous one will live by faith."

꙳(_____) "You see that _____ was active together with his _____, _____ was _____." (James 2:22)

Abraham's faith and his actions were working together. James is saying here that the exuberance of faith produces good deeds. We are justified by faith alone and justification is not linked with good works (Galatians 2:16). If faith however, brings about no good deeds, you have to consider whether your faith is genuine.

☙(_____) "For just as the body without the spirit is _____, so also _____ without _____ is dead." (James 2:26)

Verse 26 here and verse 22 above harmonize. Here again it is stated that faith and deeds are entwined. Just as the body is dead without the spirit, so faith is dead without works.

☙(_____) "The prayer of _____ will _____ the sick person, and the Lord will _____ him to health; if he has committed sins, he will be _____." (James 5:15)

This verse gives an assurance that a prayer offered in faith heals the sick person. "If" he has committed sins suggest that someone could be sick because of continual sin (1 Co 11:30). The "if" also indicates that not all sickness is due to sin. A friend recently shared with me the circumstances concerning her mother's death. Her mother had suffered several illnesses in the past and the Lord had been merciful and healed her. The final illness required abdominal surgery and my friend implored the Lord for an encore. She asked if the Lord intended to usher her home to first heal her body so the enemy would not have the victory. If anyone has not known the Lord to be sweet hopefully this will change your mind. Before my friend's mom passed away, the Lord indeed healed her body! The enlarged abdomen went back to normal and the intense heat from the area left her body! She passed away a few days later. Glory and Hallelujah! There would be no gloating here for the enemy! Sweet, sweet Jesus.

☙(_____) "You are being protected by God's _____ through _____ for a salvation that is ready to be revealed in the last time. You rejoice in this, though now for a _____ you have had to _____ in various _____ so that the genuineness of your _____ – more valuable than gold, which perishes though _____ by _____ – may result in _____, _____, and _____ at the revelation of _____." (1 Peter 1:5-7)

You are being continually protected by God while you continually have faith. When gold is refined, its impurities are removed by a fiery process. The gold also softens and becomes pliable for shaping. You are able to withstand fiery trials, because of the genuineness of your faith. Hold your feet to the fire of that trial, sweet thing, desiring that your impurities will be removed and the Lord will find you pliable for shaping into what you are destined for.

Charisma

☙(_____) "Because you are receiving the _____ of your _____, the _____ of your soul." (1 Peter 1:9)

The goal of faith is the salvation of your soul. This verse indicates that even now you are receiving salvation (deliverance, health, preservation). Do you have joy at this present time and joy at what is to be in the coming ages?

☙(_____) "This is the _____ that has _____ the world: our _____." (1 John 5:4b)

Below is a summary of faith found in Scripture and is separated in paragraphs only for ease of reading.

Faith sways Jesus (Matthew 8:10, 9:2, Mark 2:25, Luke 7:9, 18:8). **Faith** changes our situations (Matthew 9:29, 15:28, Mark 5:34, 10:52, Luke 5:20, 7:50, 8:48, 17:19, 18:42). **Faith** cancels out fear (Mark 4:40). We demonstrate our trust in Jesus with our **faith** (Mark 11:22, Luke 8:25). We can ask the Lord to increase our **faith** (Luke 17:5). **Faith** cleanses our hearts (Acts 15:9), sanctifies us (Acts 26:18), justifies us (Romans 3:28, 3:30, 5:1, Galatians 2:16, 3:8, 3:11), and by it we mutually encourage each other (Romans 1:12). We receive God's righteousness through **faith** (Romans 3:22, 4:5, 4:9, 9:30, Galatians 3:24, Philippians 3:9). We obtain access to God by **faith** (Romans 5:2, Ephesians 3:12) and we are called His children (Galatians 3:26). **Faith** comes by hearing the message of Christ (Romans 10:17). **Faith** is not based on the wisdom of man but on the power of God (1 Corinthians 2:5). Stand firm in **faith** (1 Corinthians 16:13, 2 Corinthians 1:24, Colossians 2:5). We should be excelling in **faith** (2 Corinthians 8:7). As your **faith** grows so should your (works, ministry) (2 Corinthians 10:15). We receive the Spirit by hearing the message of Christ by **faith** (Galatians 3:2, 3:14). We are the sons of Abraham by **faith** (Galatians 3:7). **Faith** blesses us (Galatians 3:9) and **faith** frees us from the law (Galatians 3:23). While in the flesh, live by **faith** (Galatians 2:20). **Faith** is a fruit of the Spirit (Galatians 5:22).

Faith is the door through which we receive salvation (Ephesians 2:8). Things that seem impossible are possible through **faith** (Matthew 17:20, 21:21, Luke 17:6). **Faith** has healed people (Matthew 9:22, Mark 5:34, Luke 8:48, 17:19). Have **faith** in the name of Jesus (Acts 3:16, Romans 1:5). Demonstrations of **faith** bring people to the Lord (Acts 6:7, 11:24, 16:5, 24:24). The goal of **faith** is the salvation of our souls (1 Peter 1:9). There will be those who try to lure you away from the **faith** (Acts 13:8). The righteous will live by **faith** (Romans

1:17). God opened a door of **faith** to the Gentiles (Acts 14:27). Have repentance toward God and **faith** in our Lord Jesus (Acts 20:21). Proclaim your **faith** to all who have ears to hear (Romans 1:8, Colossians 1:4, 1 Thessalonians 1:8). We are justified if we have **faith** in Jesus (Romans 3:26). The law of **faith** excludes boasting in ourselves (Romans 3:27). The law is upheld through **faith** (Romans 3:31). The promises are received through the righteousness that comes by **faith** (Romans 4:13) and in the same way we are heirs to this promise (Romans 4:14). The promises of God are based on **faith** and according to grace (Romans 4:16, Galatians 3:22) and they strengthen our **faith** (Romans 4:20).

We can consider various things and still remain strong in **faith** (Romans 4:19, Hebrews 11:11). Righteousness is received only by **faith**, not by works (Romans 9:32). If you have **faith** stand only in awe (Romans 11:20) and persevere (1 Thessalonians 3:6-7). The law is not based on **faith** (Galatians 3:12). We are all a child of God through **faith** in Christ Jesus (Galatians 3:26). There is only one **faith** (Ephesians 4:5). Have joy in the faith (Philippians 1:25). We have been raised with Christ by the powerful working of God who raised Him from the dead (Colossians 2:12). Encourage one another in faith (1 Thessalonians 3:2) and supply to each other what is lacking (1 Thessalonians 3:10). Do not allow the tempter to weaken your faith (1 Thessalonians 3:5) so put on the breastplate of faith (1 Thessalonians 5:8). Allow your faith to grow abundantly (2 Thessalonians 1:3).

Have faith when you are persecuted and afflicted (2 Thessalonians 1:4). We are God's first fruits for salvation because of **belief** in the truth (2 Thessalonians 2:13). God's plan operates by **faith** (1 Timothy 1:4), a sincere faith (1 Timothy 1:5). Grace and **faith** overflow to us (1 Timothy 1:14). Seize hold of eternal life and fight the good fight of **faith** (1 Timothy 6:12). Hold tight to the great doctrine of **faith** in Christ crucified (1 Timothy 6:21) and the pattern of sound teaching (2 Timothy 1:13, 2:18). Pursue **faith** (2 Timothy 2:22). Know the Scriptures which give you wisdom for salvation through **faith** in Jesus (2 Timothy 3:15). Keep the faith (2 Timothy 4:7, Philemon 1:5). Rebuke others if necessary so they may be sound in the **faith** (Titus 1:13). Older men should be healthy in **faith** (Titus 2:2). Servants should demonstrate utter **faithfulness**, to promote the cause of Christ (Titus 2:10). By **faith** we believe the universe was created by the word of God (Hebrews 11:3).

By **faith** Abel was approved by God as righteous and God still speaks through his **faith** (Hebrews 11:4). Enoch pleased God and by **faith** he was taken up so that he did not see death (Hebrews 11:5). Abraham obeyed God when he could not see the entire picture

(Hebrews 11:8). **Faith** conquers kingdoms, brings justice, obtains what is promised, and shuts the mouths of lions (Hebrews 11:33). Imitate your leader's **faith** (Hebrews 13:7). Live out your **faith** showing no favoritism to the brethren (James 2:1). **Faith** is demonstrated through works (James 2:14) or else **faith** is dead (James 2:17, 20, 22, 24, 26). Have **faith** and hope in God (1 Peter 1:21). Resist the enemy, being steadfast in **faith** (1 Peter 5:9). Make every effort by your **faith** to produce virtue and by that virtue, knowledge (2 Peter 1:5). Our **faith** conquers the world (1 John 5:4). Never stop striving in **faith** (Jude 1:3, Revelation 14:12) and build yourselves up in your most holy **faith** (Jude 1:20). Never deny your **faith** (Revelation 2:13). Jesus knows our **faith** (Revelation 2:19). Be **faithful** until the end (Revelation 13:10).

By **faith** Abraham offered up Isaac (Hebrews 11:17), Isaac invoked blessings on Jacob and Esau (11:20), Jacob blessed each of the sons of Joseph (11:21), Joseph mentioned the exodus of the Israelites (11:22), Moses was hidden upon his birth because he was an extraordinary child (11:23), Moses refused to be called the son of Pharaoh's daughter (11:24) and left Egypt as though he saw the One invisible (11:27), he also kept the Passover and the sprinkling of blood (11:28), he crossed the Red Sea (11:29). By **faith** the walls of Jericho fell down (11:30), and Rahab received the spies with peace (11:31). All of this by faith.

❧"Woe to you, _____ and _____, hypocrites! You pay a tenth of mint, dill, and cumin, yet you have _____ the more important _____ of the law — justice, mercy, and faith. These things should have been done _____ neglecting the others." (Matthew 23:23)

Let's not obsess over ritual matter or man-made laws. If we worship the Lord because it is part of our ritual where is the love in that? We worship the Lord in freedom and therefore when our hearts are filled to overflowing what else is there to do but offer praise and worship? If we need a filling of our hearts what better way to accomplish that then through worshipping Him in truth?

Let's not be obsessed with small matters and meanwhile neglect the ones Jesus has identified as important: justice, mercy, and faith.

❧"But I have _____ for you that your _____ may not _____. And you, _____ you have turned back, _____ your brothers." (Luke 22:32)

Oh indeed his faith may show itself to be fragile and insufficient but Jesus prayed that it would not fail. And fail it did not! Jesus has all knowledge and He also knew Peter would play a major role in the church. If you operate in the Spiritual gift of faith you will also strengthen fellow believers in their faith.

🙠"The proposal _____ the whole company. So they chose Stephen, a man full of _____ and the Holy _____..." (Acts 6:5)

If there is a job to do, a person should be full of faith and yielded to the Spirit if we intend to accomplish a work that is pleasing to God.

🙠"_____ the disciples by _____ them to _____ in the _____ and by telling them, "It is _____ to pass through many troubles on our _____ _____ the kingdom of God." (Acts 14:22)

Do we understand that the life we live under the sun is only a vapor? Even as Christ followers we will experience tribulations but we must persist in faith regardless of the difficulty of the trial because as sojourners we are only passing through this life until we enter the kingdom of God. Let's persist in this very important message so that we do not grow weary but remain strong in faith.

🙠"Therefore, having _____ the times of _____, God now _____ all people everywhere to _____, because He has set a day when He is going to _____ the world in _____ by the Man He has appointed. He has provided _____ of this to everyone by _____ Him from the dead." (Acts 17:30-31)

God winked at or overlooked the times when mankind suffered ignorance and idolatry. But now, He commands all people to repent of their imperfections and receive from the extravagant provisions the Cross of Christ provides. If we continue to neglect His offering He will judge indeed and it will be in complete righteousness. Come, beloved and repent and receive. Approach the throne of grace with boldness, He is graciously awaiting your arrival.

🙠"What then? If some did not _____, will their _____ _____ God's faithfulness?" (Romans 3:3)

If we stand in disbelief when we face either a trial or the mercies of God does this render God faithless? Hardly. We have no power whatsoever to change the character of God. Are you thankful for that? If we choose to not believe His promises does this cancel them? Ridiculous. If we are unable to believe there is a resurrection from the dead does this mean it is impossible? Outrageous. Believe God for every single one of His promises He has declared. He remains trustworthy and faithful, even if we are not.

❧"God's _____ through _____ in Jesus Christ, to all who believe, since there is no distinction." (Romans 3:22)

The righteousness of God is *found* through faith in Jesus Christ! This is available to ALL who believe. There is NO distinction. None. This means for all His prophets, teachers, healers, and service providers the same righteousness is provided.

❧"God presented Him as a propitiation, through faith in His blood, to demonstrate His righteousness, because in His restraint God passed over the sins previously committed." (Romans 3:25)

Jesus Christ is God's atonement (or mercy seat) for the sins you and I and every other repentant Believer make. God made the Messiah, who did not know sin, take our sin so that we could take His righteousness. Does that fall fresh on you as a knee-bending revelation? God loved us before we chose to love Him. He did not send Jesus when we decided to receive the Message but before. We were defiant rebels and He released His Son of mercy, grace, and love into the hands of our disbelief. For the time being, God continues to have enormous patience with sin. Therefore, let's have the faith of God and pray for the salvation of the lost. Someone did the same for you once.

❧"For by the _____ given to me, I tell _____ among you not to think of himself more _____ than he should think. Instead, think _____, as God has distributed a _____ of _____ to each one." (Romans 12:3)

God, through the Spirit has distributed a measure of faith to each one. Let's not think too highly of ourselves even when we give counsel to another. We will always benefit from remembering the pit Jesus removed us from when we are privileged to advise others and edify them with the truth of the Word.

❧"Accept anyone who is _____ in _____, but _____ argue about doubtful issues." (Romans 14:1)

We are going to accept everyone who is weaker in faith than we are. (Everyone should be striving to run the race and not sitting on the sidelines.) In accepting even those weak in faith it does not mean we are to argue about their personal opinions. Let's stay busy teaching and speaking the truth of the gospel and leave the rest alone.

❧"Do you have a _____? Keep it to _____ before God. The man who does not _____ himself by what he _____ is blessed. But whoever _____ stands condemned if he eats, because his eating is not from a _____, and everything that is not from a conviction is _____." (Romans 14:22-23)

Do you experience freedom to worship the Lord in a way that another believer does not? Let's not let our freedom cause a stumbling block to someone else because they consider it scandalous. If, for example, someone translates the meaning of Ephesians 5:19, "singing and making music from your heart to the Lord to mean no instruments should accompany your singing when worship God, is there any harm in reserving your freedom of listening to your instrumental worship music to a time when they are not around? I see it as an opportunity for reasoning together regarding the verse as opposed to having a door shut due to offense.

Can we edify one another while bickering? Do you feel blessed because you have no reason to condemn yourself for what you approve? Do not doubt but be convinced by your faith.

❧"Now to Him who has power to _____ you according to my _____ and the _____ about Jesus Christ, according to the _____ of the mystery kept silent for long ages but now _____ and made known through the prophetic _____, according to the _____ of the _____ God to advance the obedience of _____, among all nations."
(Romans 16:25-26).

The Lord has the power to strengthen you according to:
1)   the *proclamation* of the gospel of Jesus Christ
2)   the *revelation* of the birth, crucification, and ascension
3)   the *command* of God to *advance* the *obedience* of faith

Fellow Believers, our obedient faith should be advancing. Not only our own faith but we should be testifying to others as to the power of our faith and the transformation it has powerfully manifested in our lives. This testimony should be so powerful that it is envied and therefore desired by others to such an extent they seek it out for their own. All for the glory of God.

❧"Now these three _____: _____, _____, and _____. But the greatest of these is love." (1 Corinthians 13:13)

Charisma

The Lord has all faith and all hope. We are given a measure of these things from Him in order to victoriously walk a life that is pleasing to Him and to serve and minister to Him and His people. When He returns there will no longer be a need for a faith and a hope because they will both be made manifest in Jesus and we will behold Him right before our very fleshly eyes. The love spoken of here is agapē love which is God's love poured into us. The is a self-sacrificing love that readily demonstrates. This love is poured into us, will never end, and therefore is the greatest of the three.

🕮"But if there is no _____ of the dead, then Christ has not been raised; and if Christ has not been raised, then our proclamation is without _____, and so is your _____." "And if Christ has not been raised, your _____ is worthless; you are still in your _____." (1 Corinthians 15:14, 17)

One of the powerful foundational pieces of our faith is the Resurrection. Where is our faith if God did not resurrect Christ? Our faith is then empty. Believers we *know* this to not be true! Christ has indeed been raised and we proclaim this truth and all it's benefits in full throttle faith to all who have an ear to hear!

🕮"And since we have the same spirit of _____ in keeping with what is written, I _____, therefore I _____, we _____ believe, and therefore _____." (2 Corinthians 4:13)

When we are filled to overflowing with faith, our faith can do nothing else but manifest with the spoken word. The beauty is then when we hear ourselves speak our faith is built up all the more (Romans 10:17)!

🕮"For we _____ by _____, _____ by sight." (2 Corinthians 5:7)

Oh Believers, our senses indeed reveal what is going on in this world. But we navigate our faithful life NOT by what our senses reveal to us but by what our faith tells us is true. If you operate in the Spiritual gift of faith you will be lead to encourage other believers to not be discouraged at what the senses reveal but to be encouraged by the Word and your personal relationship with Jesus Christ of Nazareth. Your compass should always point to eternal things!

🕮"Test _____ to see if you are in the _____. _____ yourselves. Or do you yourselves not recognize that Jesus Christ is _____ you? — unless you fail the test. And I hope you will recognize that we do not fail the test. Now we pray to God that you do nothing _____ — not that we may appear to _____ the test, but that you may do what is right, even though we may appear to fail." (2 Corinthians 13:5-7)

The Lord may present trials to determine the steadfastness of your faith but have you ever considered testing yourself to to settle if you are living in the faith you profess? What would this look like in your life?

___

If Christ is currently actively working in you? If you know this to be true because of a need of repentance, for a desire to speak to others about the gospel of the Messiah, or for sharing of the marvelous workings of Christ in your own life then this would be one way to determine Christ is currently actively working in your life. Do you have any other examples?

___

꙳"So then, does God _____ you with the Spirit and _____ miracles among you by the works of the law or by _____ with _____?" (Galatians 3:5)

I love this! God supplies us with His Spirit and works miracles among us because we hear His truth by *faith*. Amen! It is not a work we do at all. I love this because God supplies us with everything we need to lead a life that is pleasing to Him in the Spirit. Our part? Yield to the Spirit He gave. God works miracles among us when we hear His truth with faith. An knee-bending, eye-popping, revelation of the Lord Himself! Miraculous indeed.

꙳"For _____ the Spirit, by _____, we _____ wait for the hope of _____. For in Christ Jesus _____ circumcision nor uncircumcision _____ anything; what matters is _____ working through _____." (Galatians 5:5-6)

Believers, living by faith through the Spirit of the Living God is powerful! We want nothing short of this. We are considered to be in right standing with God when we stand strong in faith knowing *He* sanctifies us and makes us righteous! Faith is the essence of our Christian walk. Through a love relationship with Jesus Christ, we are enabled to continue our faith journey divinely inspired and victoriously anointed. Amen.

Charisma

☙"This is why, since I _____ about your _____ in the Lord Jesus and your _____ for all the saints, I never stop giving thanks for you as I remember you in my prayers." (Ephesians 1:15-16)

Believers, let's make it a priority to never stop praying and giving thanks for those who have faith in the Lord Jesus! What a privilege indeed! (This verse is similar to Colossians 1:4.) What does our faith do? In short, it preserves and increases daily. We see the faithfulness of our Lord today and as a result our faith tomorrow will exceed yesterday's faith because it builds on the revealed faith He has shown towards us. Therefore, our faith boldly and audaciously increases daily. If you operate in the Spiritual gift of faith you will see this manifest in your own life and the fruit produced will be powerful and transforming in the lives of others that choose to sample this profound fruit.

☙"I _____ that He may grant you, according to the _____ of His glory, to be _____ with _____ in the inner man through His Spirit, and that the Messiah may _____ in your hearts through _____." (Ephesians 3:16-17a)

Shall we pray this over ourselves and others? Grant me Lord Jesus, according to the riches of Your glory to be internally strengthened with power through Your Spirit, and may the Messiah dwell in my heart through bold faith!

Oh indeed that we allow the Messiah to settle down and abide in our hearts. That we may allow Him to sit upon His throne there and never usurp Him! In this we will be strengthened due to His permanent residency and may be always have the power to yield to His prompting and counsel because He is faithful.

☙"For the _____ of the saints in the work of _____, to _____ ___ the body of Christ, until we ____ reach _____ in the _____ and in the _____ of God's Son, growing into a _____ man with a stature measured by Christ's _____." (Ephesians 4:13)

The Lord personally gave apostles, prophets, evangelist, pastors, and teachers. This verse will be found throughout this study. Why were we provided the gifting of these five roles in the church? So that, the saints will be trained for ministry and so that the body of Christ will be built up. This will continue, beloved, until we all reach unity in the faith and in the knowledge of God's Son. We are intended to grow into mature people measured not by the maturity of other leaders in the church but measured by the fullness of Christ. We are fully able to work toward this goal engaged in all out faith.

🙢"In _____ situation _____ the shield of _____, and with it you will be able to _____ all the flaming _____ of the _____ one." (Ephesians 6:16)

This is a defensive and an offensive position. Let's break this down into all its pieces. First, we must pick up the shield of faith that is provided us by God Himself. Second, it must be used in every situation our day presents to us. Thirdly, without a doubt it has the power to perform if you have faith to pick it up and faith to use it. Lastly, it absolutely *extinguishes* ALL the flaming arrows the evil one chooses to hurl your way.

The type of shield this verse is referring to is something like a door. This concept is similar to a person planting the buffer in the ground and then standing firm in full faith and assurance behind the protection. When you take the bold step of wearing the breast plate (representing faith) and then putting yourself behind the buffer you not only have a sort of double protection but you are putting your faith in the hands of a mighty faithful God who provides these buffers for you.

🙢"_____ to the brothers, and _____ with _____, from God the Father and the Lord Jesus Christ. _____ be with all who have _____ love for our Lord Jesus Christ" (Ephesians 6:23-24)

We shall always pray faithful prayers for fellow Believers and especially for those who are vigorously ministering for the cause of Christ. Peace to the sojourners, with endless love and resolute faith.

🙢"Just one thing: _____ your life in a manner _____ of the gospel of Christ. Then, whether I come and see you or am absent, I will hear about you that you are standing _____ in one spirit, with one mind, working side by side for the _____ that comes from the gospel, not being _____ in any way by your opponents. This is a sign of destruction for them, but of your _____ — and this is from God." (Philippians 1:27-28)

Fellow sojourners, make it a point in your life to stand firm together with one spirit and a unified mind that desires to work in faith side by side with others. We shall not be dazed when trials come, when worldly distractions appear, and when the enemy puff himself up like a cobra hoping to make us back down. In fearless faith based only in the name of Jesus, we will boldly press forward in this life.

Charisma

☙"But now He has _____ you by His physical _____ through His death, to _____ you _____, _____, and _____ before Him — if indeed you _____ shifted away from the _____ of the gospel that you _____." (Colossians 1:22-23a)

What does remaining grounded and steadfast in the faith deliver to us? We are presented holy, faultless, and blameless before Him. Beloved, there is no other way you want to stand before Him. Thank Him from the depths of your heart for this outrageous gift of mercy. Do you see the condition? IF you remain grounded and steadfast in the faith AND are not shifted away from the hope of the gospel you heard. Trust and have faith in Him. He is beyond worth it.

☙"Therefore, as you have _____ Christ Jesus the Lord, _____ in Him, _____ and _____ _____ in Him and _____ in the _____, just as you were _____ _____ with gratitude." (Colossians 2:6-7)

This exhortation is something that we should prepare ourselves to do continually. We want our vessels to be filled to overflowing with faith in the Lord which results in overflowing gratitude for His love towards us. Have you ever met someone with this overflowing gratitude? If you are like me, when you are around a gracious believer you can't help but be moved with the same spirit of gratitude and allow your own gratitude to also overflow. Praise God.

☙"We recall, in the _____ of our God and Father, your _____ of _____, labor of _____, and endurance of _____ in our Lord Jesus Christ, knowing your election, brothers _____ by God." (1 Thessalonians 1:3-4)

Here again we see our vital elements: faith, hope, and love. When we go to the Lord in prayer let's remember the work of our fellow sojourners. Those who labor in faith, excel in a ministry prompted by love, and possess an endurance which influenced by a never-ending hope in Christ.

☙"And in view of this, we always pray for you that our God will _____ you worthy of His calling, and will, by His power, _____ every _____ for goodness and the work of _____, so that the name of our Lord Jesus will be _____ by you, and you by Him, _____ to the grace of our God and the Lord Jesus Christ." (2 Thessalonians 1:11-12)

We are unable to please the Lord in our faithful walk or ministry if we intend to do this strictly from a work of the flesh. We serve, minister,

Charisma

and live victoriously by operating from and yielding to His Spirit that He made available to us. Let's pray for ourselves and others, asking God to empower us to live this life worthy of His calling beseeching Him to bestow the power necessary to accomplish all the good things our faith prompts us to do in faithful service to Him.

❧"Timothy, my son, I am giving you this instruction in keeping with the prophecies previously made about you, so that by them you may strongly _____ in battle, having _____ and a good _____ shipwreck of their _____." (1 Timothy 1:18-19)

This was given as a direction to Timothy from Paul but let's also heed that same instruction. By faith and the powerful work of the Spirit in us we shall boldly engage in spiritual battles, never losing faith and standing strong in excellent morals. If you operate in the Spiritual gift of faith, encourage others in their divine calling. Desiring all to be edified in faith, unified in truth, and empowered to strive for the fullness of Christ stature.

❧"Deacons, likewise, should be _____ of respect, not _____ not drinking a _____ of wine, not _____ for money, holding the mystery of the _____ with a clear conscience." "For those who have served well as deacons acquire a good standing for themselves, and great _____ in the _____ that is in Christ Jesus." (1 Timothy 3:9, 13)

Deacons in the church are leaders and should be worthy of respect and should also receive our respect. When teaching others the powerful gospel message it should not be done as a hypocrite. What is spoken and taught to others should be the same teaching we abide in for our own life. The mystery of faith can be thought of as the revealed truth of Christianity. We benefit greatly when deacons speak with great boldness in the faith that is found in Christ Jesus. This boldness comes from a firm foundation of faith.

If we operate in the Spiritual gift of faith let's have bold assured confidence in our Lord and not allow an ounce of fear to creep in to this holy temple.

❧"Now the Spirit _____ says that in later times some will _____ from the _____, paying attention to _____ spirits and the teachings of _____, through the hypocrisy of _____ whose consciences are seared." (1 Timothy 4:1)

In the preceding verses we are spoken to as the "church of the living God, the pillar and foundation of the truth." With this expectation we are expected to then proceed faithfully in teaching the gospel message in truth. Our faith is "He was manifested in the flesh, vindicated in the Spirit, seen by angels, preached among nations, believed on in the word, and taken up in glory." (1 Timothy 3:15b-16) Some will depart from this faith and allow themselves to be entertained with another sort of teaching done by demons. What will this look like? God knows. Let's focus on what we do know and heed the warning we are given. Let's advance the cause of Christ, full of faith and in the sound teaching we were given. We shall not deny what is true and not tolerate additions that are false.

&"If you _____ these things out to the brothers, you will be a good _____ of Christ Jesus, _____ by the words of the _____ and the good teaching that you have _____" (1 Timothy 4:6)

What things are to be pointed out? Deceitful spirits and demons will "forbid marriage and demand abstinence from foods that God created to be received with gratitude by those who believe and know the truth. For everything created by God is good, and nothing should be rejected if it is received with thanksgiving, since it is sanctified by the word of God and by prayer." (verse 3-5)

I love the phrase "nourished by the words of faith". Think of it as educating and forming your mind around the truth of the Word.

&"Let no one _____ your youth; instead, you should be an _____ to the believers in _____ in _____, in _____, in _____, in _____." (1 Timothy 4:12)

Do you see these five examples going from the most discernible which is speech and then the next visible which is conduct? The following three traits also seem to follow a progression; love, faith, and purity. Why do you think this is?

_____

We shall not be deceived in thinking a young person is unable to make an impact for the cause of Christ! Who would ever be prideful enough to decide at what age God would call someone for His eternal purposes! Are we wise enough to judge? Hardly.

&"But if anyone does not _____ for his own, that is his own household, he has _____ the _____ and is worse than an _____" (1 Timothy 5:8)

Charisma

What is it about the faith we are denying? Philippians 1:27 says to "Live your life in a manner worthy of the gospel of Christ." We are also instructed to have grace, mercy, peace, and love. What characteristic regarding an unbeliever do you think would lead them to not provide for their own household?

_____

&"For the love of _____ is a _____ of all kinds of evil, and by _____ it, some have _____ away from the _____ and _____ themselves with many _____. But you, man of God, _____ from these things, and _____ righteousness, godliness, faith, love, endurance, and gentleness." (1 Timothy 6:10-11)

I am sure you have heard plenty of times that money itself is not evil. Evil arises when it becomes your love; when you crave it. We don't really even crave money but we certainly crave what we can do with the money. Do you crave things of this world more than you crave a strong faith? We have a stern warning here that informs us that when we crave things of this world we will be pierced by these cravings and torture our soul with sorrows. May we crave only what nurtures our souls, Jesus Christ Himself.

&"For we also have _____ the good news _____ as they did; but the message they heard did not _____ them, since they were not _____ with those who heard it in _____" (Hebrews 4:2)

We can hear a message and be joined with those who have no faith and the message will not avail us. We can also hear the same message and be joined together with those of faith and receive the benefit of the Word. When was a time you experienced this phenomenon. What was your account of what happened?

_____

_____

&"Therefore, _____ the elementary message about the Messiah, let us go on to _____, not laying _____ the _____ of repentance from dead works, faith in God." (Hebrews 6:1)

Milk versus meat. The elementary message of repentance from sin and faith in God is milk. Our bodies thirst for this milk indeed but once we have tasted the milk, it is time to move on to the meat of the

Charisma

message and the maturity that is expected and required in order to chew on the meat and digest it.

🕮 "Now we want each of you to _____ the same _____ for the final realization of your hope, so that you won't become _____ but will be _____ of those who inherit the promises through _____ and _____" (Hebrews 6:11-12)

We must make every effort to not become slothful or sluggish to accomplish what is required to run the race that has been appointed to us. What are the fruits of a life that preservers in faith? We can all begin a 'race' with good intentions. What is difficult is the middle and final lap of the course. Unfortunately, good intentions don't carry us through to the end. We must determine before the difficulty presents itself that we will stand strong, come what may. Let's not be naive and think just because we have given ourself to the Christian life that we will be immune to trials. The word clearly tells us trials are what bring up the 'dross' in order to be skimmed away so that all that remains is pure gold. If there is no skimming, there is no dross removal and therefore no purity. No matter how difficult, let's swing our gates wide and allow the only One that can sanctify us full access to our mind, heart, and soul. You can trust Him.

🕮 "But My righteous one will _____ by _____; and if he draws _____, I have no _____ in him. But we are not those who draw back and are _____, but those who have _____ and obtain life." (Hebrews 10:38-39)

Thank you Lord for this truth. There is no labor on our part that needs to be accomplished in order to be declared righteous by God! Faith pleases God. Drawing back from faith displeases God. Which will you choose? What does *living* by faith look like to you? What is required of you to maintain your daily life in the flesh?

_____

What do you think is required to daily live a life of faith?

_____

🕮 "Now _____ is the reality of what is _____ for, the _____ of what is not seen." (Hebrews 11:1)

Are you familiar with the 'hall of faith' in Hebrews 11? Some of the believers that without a doubt believed God, did not witness the fulfillment of His promises with their fleshly eyes.

Living a life of faith will mean there will never be conclusive proof that God is the Creator. This is what faith is all about. Have you ever considered it takes more faith to believe most elements of the theory of evolution than to believe God as Creator?

☙"Now without _____ it is _____ to please God, for the one who draws near to Him must believe that He _____ and _____ those who seek Him." (Hebrews 11:6)

Here again we see faith pleases God. Oh beloved, don't you desire to draw near to God and receive what He intends to give you to overflowing? God set up the system of reward. As parents, we enjoy rewarding our children to encourage their behavior. Seek God and the Creator of the universe will reward you. Can you even imagine?

☙"By _____ Noah, after he was warned about what was not yet seen and motivated by godly _____, built an ark to _____ his family. By _____ he condemned the world and became an heir of the righteousness that comes by _____." (Hebrews 11:7)

The unbelieving world would suffer condemnation. What did they think when they carried on with life's busyness while observing Noah's ark being built in the background? Noah's righteousness was manifested as obedience and was clearly motivated by the fear of God as opposed to the fear of man. If God instructs you to symbolically build your 'ark' will you obey in faith or let the world talk you out of it?

What steps are you willing to take, if needed, to be delivered?

_____

☙"Let us run with _____ the race that lies before us, keeping our eyes on Jesus, the _____ and _____ of our _____, who for the _____ that lay before Him _____ a cross and despised the shame and has sat down at the right hand of God's throne." (Hebrews 12:1b-2)

The author and perfecter of our faith. Jesus modeled how He intended for us to run the race under the sun. We are to continue the race in full throttle faith until we are in His presence and He declares our striving is finished.

☙"Consider it a great _____, my brothers, whenever you experience various _____, knowing that the _____ of your _____ produces _____" (James 1:2-3)

Charisma

Count it all joy Believers! Why? Because when our faith is tested it produces patience. We live in a world that teaches us we must have things now. What does this type of teaching produce? Impatience. Not only do we learn impatience but we strive for things this world has to offer as opposed to waiting for eternal rewards. Trials can also be considered temptations. In the heat of a trial are we tempted to find the easy way out? Or, do we keep our feet to the holy fire expecting to be refined through His sovereign sanctification process?

🙠"But let him ask in _____ without _____. For the doubter is like the surging sea, _____ and _____ by the wind." (James 1:6)

Know the holy Scriptures. When you know what God's heart and desire is, which is found in His Word, you can then ask in full faith without doubting His will is regarding your petition. We know God is pleased when we demonstrate faith in Him so why would we ever want to be driven and tossed by the winds of uncertainty? This doubting outcome only churns up muck.

🙠"The prayer of _____ will save the sick person, and the Lord will _____ him to health; if he has committed sins, he will be _____." (James 5:15)

So what is a prayer of faith? A prayer offered in full throttle faith trusting that the One you are petitioning not only hears you but in His sovereignty is well able to do the impossible.

🙠"Simeon Peter, a slave and an apostle of Jesus Christ: To those who have _____ a _____ of equal _____ with ours through the _____ of our God and Savior Jesus Christ." (2 Peter 1:1)

This is remarkable to me. Have you ever considered that those such as Paul, Peter, James, John, and whomever else has received a faith in Jesus Christ of Nazareth is of equal privilege with ours? _____ (insert your name) has equal privilege! We have no less of a faith or a privilege to serve. Mind blowing.

Now engage your faith, consider it a privilege, honor the work of the Messiah, count yourself worthy among the brethren and live out your full throttle faith never looking back but looking straight ahead at the wondrous Author and Perfecter of your faith.

Prayer

Thank you Lord for the faith you have given me in order to possess momentous confidence in Your great power and faithful promises. Increase my faith even more! I desire for you to use my faith and enable me to stand boldly for the cause of Christ. I know you respond to Your people's prayer by Your sovereign grace and mercy. I don't require evidence to continue daily prayers to the Magnificent! I stand in faith knowing that as I forgive others you will also forgive me. I choose to not allow any hinderance to halt my prayers. Infuse me with Your faith to a greater extent than I have ever known. I thank you in advance for what You will do in and through my life because I faithfully believe Your promises. I pray and receive all You have for me in the faithful and mighty name of Jesus. Amen.

The Compassion of Healing

Have you ever considered of the gift of healing as Jesus' compassionate ministry to a people in need? Almost all of Jesus' recorded time was spent healing the suffering. His first instruction to His disciples was, "Heal the sick!" (Matthew 10:8) Gifts of healing is probably the most widely accepted of the nine gifts of the Spirit today. Why? Because most people see a need for supernatural healing which restores people to wholeness. Healing can be manifested when there is an atmosphere for healing in which many are made whole at the same time or at the individual level as the Spirit guides. The Spiritual gift of healing iama seems to be closely related to the gift of faith.

You might have wondered what the Father's will is regarding your healing. "For I am Yahweh who heals you." (Exodus 15:25) "I will remove illnesses from you." (Exodus 23:24) "He heals all your diseases." (Psalm 103:3) His will is for you to be made whole. This may require a process in getting there – but it is His will. Jesus is our deliverer and only does the will of the Father. There are three scenarios in which we will experience His deliverance. (1) He will deliver us from the illness and we will escape the trial. (2) He will deliver us through the illness. In this case, we walk through the trial but are healed in the process because of his sovereign plan to strengthen us (or someone around us that He plans to strengthen by observing us). The last scenario (3) is that he will deliver us into the Kingdom.

Healing comes through faith in the Lord. (Matthew 9:22, 29) Sometimes the illness is too great and the person is too weak to exercise their own faith for healing. When this happens a person can be healed through another's faith. (Mark 2:3-5) Healing can also come from the combined faith of the sick person and the one offering a prayer by faith in the name of Jesus. (Mark 5:25-35) Jesus Christ is the same yesterday, today, and forever (Hebrews 13:8) Whatever He taught yesterday, He teaches today and will continue to teach. The words He speaks are eternal.

Charisma

Years ago when I first began attending bible study I listened to a leader speak of an experience they were a part of a short time earlier. They shared that towards the end of their bible study gathering there was a call for prayer requests. A blind man was in attendance and he asked for prayer for healing. The group prayed for him and his sight was restored. Praise God! As I listened to the story my heart started beating faster. The account was amazing and I praised God quietly at the edge of my seat! Stunningly, the person communicating the story spoke as if the healing was not the highlight of the narrative. As they continued, however, the person did begin to get excited. Apparently during weekend services at their church, the restored man was allowed to present himself as healed and speak to the congregation. As a result of this opportunity, many confessed Jesus and received salvation! As I sat and listened I understood why the person had an abundance of enthusiasm for the those who received salvation but I still did not understand why there was no expressed emotion for the man's recovered sight (indeed they were excited for the man but the bigger picture was the multitude who had received). It was some time later I thought about the incident again and realized when Jesus is involved there is always more than one person who benefits! It indeed was a wondrous healing for the man to have his eyesight restored! But, what a grander thing indeed that through this manifestation of healing many others received an eternal gift of salvation ~ Hallelujah indeed!

How about another account of someone miraculously receiving their sight? As Jesus left the temple complex he past by a man who had been blind since birth. Jesus told the disciples that the man did not have his sight so that the works of God may be glorified. He spit on the ground, made some mud from the saliva and then spread the mud on the blind eye. "Go, He told him, wash in the pool of Siloam (which means "Sent"). So he left, washed, and came back seeing." (John 9:7)

Some years ago I had a pointy bone protruding under my ankle bone. I was evaluated by a specialist who informed me there was absolutely nothing that could be done about the bone aside from surgery. No medication was available and it would not heal on its own. Since surgery would not be immediately required, I decided I would lay my hand on the bone every morning and ask for healing from the Lord. As the days turned into weeks, my faith increased concerning the healing. As the days progressed I actually wondered if the protruding bone was getting smaller. One morning I put my hand on the bone, as I had done for weeks, and it was gone! In my confusion I thought, "was it the other ankle?" I searched the other and could not find any difference between both ankles. Thank you Lord! About six months later however, the bone began to protrude from my ankle again. I looked at the bone and thought, "I don't think so. If you can be prayed away once you can be prayed away again." I immediately began to pray for healing over my ankle and again the protrusion slowly began to disappear. Praise God and to this day it has not returned! Hallelujah!

Please open your Bible and prayerfully consider the following verses as you complete the following blanks:

☙"I have seen his ways, but I will _____ him; I will _____ him and restore comfort to him and his mourners, _____ words of praise. The Lord says, Peace, peace to the one who is far or near, and I will _____ him. But the wicked are like the storm-tossed sea, for it cannot be still, and its waters churn up mire and muck. There is no peace for the wicked, says my God." (Isaiah 57:18-21)

God, through His grace promises to heal. Do you find it interesting that the Lord says He will heal His people and give them peace but then right afterwards He says the wicked are like the storm-tossed sea, they cannot be still, they churn up undesirable things, and they have no peace? Do you ever feel storm-tossed on the inside? Do you long for peace and healing? Jesus rebuked the wind and said to the sea, "Silence! Be still!" and what followed was a great calm. Follow the Master and rebuke what is churning your insides and expect a great calm! (See also Psalm 107:29-30, James 1:6, Mark 4:39) Healing and peace. We need them Lord in this storm-tossed world!

☙"_____ me, Lord, and I will be _____; save me, and I will be saved, for You are my praise." (Jeremiah 17:14)

Shall we all be driven to plead for the Lord's help because we know He is faithful? Only the Lord can heal and save. Do you pray with the confidence of Jeremiah? Heal me Lord and I WILL be healed! He is worthy of our abundant reverence and praise.

☙"But for you who _____ My name, the sun of righteousness will rise with _____ in its wings, and you will go out and playfully _____ like calves from the stall. (Malachi 4:2)

What about the 'Son" of righteousness? When the sun shines at the highest point in the sky does not all of creation receive the warmth and light? Unless you make efforts to hide yourself, the sun's rays are available for everyone. The same is true of the Son. In His rays are healing and salvation indeed. Only those that choose to hide themselves from the Son are the ones who do not receive freely from His provision. Just as we need the sun's rays for survival we also need the rays from the Son's light to bring us joy, peace, and healing. Once you have received

YOU WILL go out boldly, playfully jumping in freedom because you have been set free from the 'stall' Amen!

There are three Greek words used in the New Testament in regards to healing:

Sozo ~ to deliver out of danger and into safety (salvation), used principally of God rescuing believers from the penalty and power of sin. To save a suffering one (from perishing), to save one suffering from disease; to make well, heal, restore to health, can also include spiritual healing. To save from the evils which obstruct the reception of the Messianic judgment. (THAYER'S GREEK LEXICON, Electronic Database biblehub.com) Restoring spirit, soul, and body.

Therapeuo ~ *therapeía* – healing, focusing on the reversal of the physical condition (illness, disease) itself carrying the responsibility of fully serving the Lord through it. (*therapeuō*). (HELPS Word-studies, biblehub.com) Someone who provides service to another. Therapeuo can include miraculous healing and casting out demons.

Iaomai ~ healing, particularly as supernatural and bringing attention to the Lord Himself as the Great Physician; the supernatural Healer, i.e. beyond the physical healing itself and its benefits. (HELPS Word-studies, biblehub.com) to cure (i.e. by curing to free) one from a disease. To make whole i.e. to free form errors and sins (THAYER'S GREEK LEXICON, Electronic Database biblehub.com) This is instantaneous miraculous healing and can be associated with casting out demons. When the kingdom of God is manifested the forces of darkness are ousted.

The following is a summary of the instances where the Greek word sozo is used in the New Testament. The paragraphs are separated simply for ease in reading:

Jesus will **save** people from their sins (Matthew 1:21). The disciples were afraid and asked Jesus to **save** them from the storm (Matthew 8:25). A woman merely touched Jesus' garment knowing she would be made **whole** (Matthew 9:21, Mark 5:28). Fatih made the woman **whole** at the very hour Jesus pronounced her **wholeness** (Matthew 9:22, Mark 5:34). The one that endures for the sake of Jesus shall be **saved** (Matthew 10:22, 24:13, Mark 13:13). When fear began to overtake Peter he called out to Jesus to **save** him (Matthew 14:30). Jesus came to **save** the lost (Matthew 18:11). Jesus can **save** even when it seems impossible (Matthew 19:25, Mark 10:26, Luke 18:26). The days of the Tribulation will be shorted on account of having the elect **survive** (Matthew 24:22, Mark 13:20). Jesus confronted the Pharisees regarding the truth of **saving** a life (Mark 3:4, Luke 6:9). Jairus knew Jesus had the power to lay His hands on his daughter and she would be **healed** (Mark 5:23).

Everywhere Jesus traveled people came to Him and begged to just touch the tassels of His robe, knowing they would be made **whole** (Mark 6:56). Whoever is willing to lead a crucified life on account of Jesus and the gospel will ultimately **save** their life (Matthew 16:25, Mark 8:35, Luke 9:24, 17:33). Faith has the power to make someone **whole** (Mark 10:52, Luke 17:19, 18:42, Acts 14:9). The faithful that believe in Jesus and are baptized will be **saved** (Mark 16:16). A woman's faith **saved** her (Luke 7:50, Luke 8:48). Do not allow the Devil to take away the word from your heart. Guard it so you can believe and be **saved** (Luke 8:12). The demon-possessed can be **delivered** (Luke 8:36). Do not fear but only believe and you will be made **whole** (Luke 8:50). Jesus did not come to destroy your life but to **save** it (Luke 9:56, John 3:17, John 12:47). Jesus seeks and **saves** the lost (Luke 19:10). Jesus speaks truth so we can be **saved** (John 5:34). Jesus is the door which allows you to be **saved** and to receive things you need in this life (John 10:9).

Jesus cried out to His Father during His trial to **save** Him, knowing He would be obedient in all things (John 12:27). Whoever calls on the name of the Lord will be **saved** (Acts 2:21, Acts 16:31). We must **save** ourselves from this corrupt generation (Acts 2:40). Those who are to be **saved**, Jesus will add them to His church (Acts 2:47). It is by Jesus Christ of Nazareth that a good deed was done causing a man to be made **whole** (Acts 4:9). Jesus is the only way to receive **salvation** (Acts 4:12). Hearing Christ's message by faith has the power to **save** (Acts 11:14). Grace through Jesus Christ alone is what **saves** us (Acts 15:11). Just because all hope seems lost does not mean you will not be **saved** (Acts 27:20). We have been declared righteous by His blood and reconciled to God and will also be **saved** through Him (Romans 5:9-10). A remnant of Israel will be **saved** (Romans 9:27, 11:26). Confess with your mouth Jesus is Lord and believe in your heart God raised Him from the dead and you shall be **saved** (Romans 10:9,13).

We can make people jealous to also know the Lord and be **saved** (Romans 11:14). The cross is the power of God to those who are **saved** (1 Corinthians 1:18). It pleased God to **save** those who believe the 'foolishness' of the gospel message (1 Corinthians 1:21).

Make certain your work in life will be considered worthy by the Lord; you will still be **saved** if it is not but your reward will be lost (1 Corinthians 3:15). Understand it is better to suffer trials on earth if it brings repentance so that we will be **saved** (1 Corinthians 5:5). Live in peace, we do not know if by our example we will save our unbelieving spouse (1 Corinthians 7:16). Strive to reach unbelievers where they are so that some may be **saved** (1 Corinthians 9:22). Seek not your own profit but the profit of many so they may be **saved** (1 Corinthians 10:33). Always remember the message you heard so that you will be saved by it (1 Corinthians 15:2). To God, we are the sweet smell of Christ to those that are **saved** and those that are not (2 Corinthians 2:15). We are **saved** by grace (Ephesians 2:5, 8). Accept the love of the truth in order to be **saved** (2 Thessalonians 2:10). We are **saved** only by His mercy not by anything we do (Titus 3:5). He is always able to **save** those who come to God through Him (Hebrews 7:25).

The implanted word is able to **save** your soul (James 1:21). Faith with works **saves** us (James 2:14). God desires all to be **saved** and come to the knowledge of the truth (1 Timothy 2:4). Persevere in your life and teaching for by doing this you will **save** both yourself and your hearers (1 Timothy 4:16). The Lord will bring us **safely** into His heavenly kingdom (2 Timothy 4:18). Only one judge is able to **save** and destroy (James 4:12). The prayer of faith will **save** the sick person (James 5:15). If you convert a sinner you have **saved** his soul from death and cover a multitude of sins (James 5:20). Baptism **saves** you (1 Peter 3:21). Believe and be **saved** (Jude 1:5). **Save** others by snatching them from the fire (Jude 1:23).

"Jesus was going all over Galilee, _____ in their synagogues, _____ the good news of the kingdom, and _____ (therapeuō) _____ disease and sickness among the people. Then the news about Him spread throughout Syria. So they brought to Him _____ those who were _____, those suffering from various _____ and intense _____, the _____ - possessed, the epileptics, and the paralytics. And He _____ (therapeuō) them." (Matthew 4:23-24)

NO ailment is beyond Jesus' power to heal! No matter how stubborn or impossible it seems! For His child, *nothing* is beyond His reach. "Lift up your heads, you gates! Rise up, ancient doors! Then the King of glory will come in. Who is this King of Glory? The LORD, strong and mighty, the LORD, mighty in battle." (Psalm 24:7-8) Thank you Lord. This is a terrific prayer of edification.

What do you think of our God and King that can heal diseases by a word from His mouth? Diseases for which there are no cure! Diseases in which medicine does not seem to touch! That, my friend, is a God that can not be put into a box and labeled. A God that cannot be described with human words. A God that is bigger than what you can imagine. A God that is bigger than you have ever experienced. Look to the skies, look to creation all around you. How big does God have to be to even imagine the intricacies of this entire creation? And when it fails to operate how He intended we shall not be deceived, He is the only One who can reconcile it. We praise you Lord! You ALONE are worthy of glory and praise and honor!

❧"When He entered Capernaum, a centurion came to Him, _____ with Him, Lord, my servant is lying at home paralyzed, in terrible agony! I will come and _____ (therapeuō) him, He told him. Lord, the centurion replied, I am not worthy to have You come under my roof. But only say the _____, and my servant will be _____ (iaomai). Then Jesus told the centurion, Go. As you have _____, let it be done for you. And his servant was _____ (iaomai) that very moment." (Matthew 8:5-8, 13)

Jesus is the Mighty Physician that makes house calls. Will you swing your gate wide and allow the Mighty Physician into your home? He has the final say over every other physician on this planet. He is the One that supplies physicians with wisdom and strength. Go to the Source first for your healing and then seek secondary sources.

❧"When evening came, they brought to Him _____ who were demon-possessed. He drove out the spirits with a _____ and _____ (therapeuō) all who were sick, so that what was spoken through the prophet Isaiah might be fulfilled: He Himself _____ our weaknesses and _____ our diseases." (Matthew 8:16-17)

Jesus cast out the harassing spirits with a word and healed all who were miserable.

❧"Then Jesus went to all the towns and villages, _____ in their synagogues, _____ the good news of the kingdom, and _____ (therapeuō) every disease and every sickness." (Matthew 9:35)

The authority Jesus has over every disease and sickness is the **same** authority He gave His disciples to declare in Matthew 10:1 (also seen in Mark 6:7 and Luke 9:1).

Charisma

🕮 "Summoning His 12 disciples, He gave them _____ over unclean spirits, to drive them _____ and to _____ (therapeuō) every disease and sickness." (Matthew 10:1) "As you go, announce this: 'The _____ of heaven has come _____.' _____ (therapeuō) the sick, _____ the dead, _____ those with skin diseases, _____ _____ demons." (Matthew 10:7-8a, also seen in Luke 10:9)

Announcing the 'kingdom of heaven has come near' should prick the hearts and souls of those with eyes to see and ears to hear the truth of the Message. After that, they were told to therapeuō the lost sheep of the house of Israel.

🕮 "Moving on from there, He entered their synagogue. There He saw a man who had a paralyzed hand. And in order to accuse Him they asked Him, "Is it lawful to _____ (therapeuō) on the Sabbath?" But He said to them, "What man among you, if he had a sheep that fell into a _____ on the Sabbath, wouldn't take _____ of it and lift it out? A man is worth _____ _____ than a sheep, so it _____ lawful to do what is _____ on the Sabbath." (Matthew 12:9-12 also seen in Luke 6:6-9)

Do you recall where you were when you first heard the magnificent Word spoken to you and the power it displayed in that person's life that you wanted to experience the revolutionary transformation for yourself? Well sweet thing, the baton has been passed to you and the beauty of the Lord radiating throughout your life is being observed by a multitude. Keep looking for someone to pass sweet Jesus to. The word made flesh met you right where you were in that season of your life and has had a lasting impact on you. Let's not expect people to come where we are and hope Jesus to meet them there. Jesus goes to the depths of each hurting person's soul and meets them right where they are. We experience different trials and journey at different paces. Forgive us Lord for being so prideful that we expect everyone to be right where we are and judging them as less because they are not at our level. We recall the depths from which you have pulled us and we will honor the faith walk of others as they are pulled from their depths at Your own sweet precious time. Let's go to the trenches sweet things and retrieve some hurting souls. Why? Because Jesus gladly goes to the trenches and pits regularly to retrieve His lost sheep. Are you willing to go ahead of Him and shine His light in those dark places?

Sabbath or not, Jesus is not hindered by anything this world throws at Him. I am grateful for that.

☙"Then a demon-possessed man who was blind and unable to speak was brought to Him. He _____ (therapeuō) him, so that the man could both speak and see." (Matthew 12:22)

Amen.

☙"For this people's _____ has grown callous; their ears are hard of hearing, and they have shut their eyes; otherwise they might _____ with their eyes and _____ with their ears, _____ with their hearts and turn back — and I would cure (iaomai) them. (Matthew 13:15)

Jesus is the fulfillment of Isaiah 6:9-10. Let's boldly bring some people to Jesus so He can cure them.

☙"As He stepped ashore, He saw a huge crowd, felt _____ for them, and _____ (therapeuō) their sick." (Matthew 14:14 see also Matthew 19:2)

Even though Jesus was trying to escape the crowds in order to be alone, the crowd could not help but follow Him. Instead of feeling frustrated, He had compassion on them and healed their sick.

☙"Then Jesus replied to her, Woman, your _____ is _____. Let it be done for you as you want. And from that _____ her daughter was _____ (iaomai). Moving on from there, Jesus passed along the Sea of Galilee. He went up on a mountain and sat there, and large crowds came to Him, having with them the lame, the blind, the deformed, those unable to speak, and many others. They put them at His _____, and He _____ (therapeuō) them. So the crowd was _____ when they saw those unable to speak talking, the deformed restored, the lame walking, and the blind seeing. And they _____ glory to the God of Israel." (Matthew 15:28-31)

I absolutely love how the people brought their loved ones to the *feet* of Jesus. Allow yourself to completely picture this scene. Not only were they humbly seeking Jesus to meet their most desperate need but I also see them offering a sacrifice to Him; indicating that the end of their striving they are on their knees and at His feet. Glory to God indeed.

☙"Then Jesus replied to her, Woman, your _____ is _____. Let it be done for you as you want. And from that moment her daughter was _____ (iaomai)." (Matthew 15:28)

Charisma

Regardless of how the woman felt upon questioning, her faith remained strong. She stood courageously in her unwavering faith. Mark adds an interesting component to this story: "Then He told her, Because of this reply, you may go. The demon has gone out of your daughter. When she went back to her home, she found her child lying on the bed, and the demon was gone."

We must stand in the kind of relentless faith that has the power to change choking despair into a full throttle assurance of hope.

❧"Then Jesus _____ the _____, and it came out of him, and from that _____ the boy was _____ (therapeuō)." (Matthew 17:18)

Mark 9:25 gives a us a little more insight. "He rebuked the unclean spirit, saying to it, You mute and deaf spirit, I command you: come out of him and never enter him again!" Jesus' authority allows Him to speak a commanding word and all must obey. Amen.

❧"The blind and the lame came to Him in the temple complex, and He _____ (therapeuō) them." (Matthew 21:14)

This was the place where people came to worship. In the proceeding verse Jesus rebuked the community because they were making the 'house of prayer' a 'den of thieves'. As New Testament believers we are the temple in which the Spirit of the living God resides. Will Jesus find 'your' temple a 'house of prayer' or a temple practicing unsuitable things? Swing wide the gate of 'your temple' and allow the King and Mighty Physician *full* access.

❧"When evening came, after the sun had set, they began _____ to Him all those who were _____ and those who were _____ - _____ The _____ town was assembled at the door, and He _____ (therapeuō) many who were sick with various diseases and drove out many demons. But He would not permit the demons to speak, because they knew Him." (Mark 1:32-34, Luke 4:40-41)

Jesus has a compassionate ministry. He heals people with various conditions not only because He loves us but so that we are then free to victoriously serve Him and His church.

❧"In order to _____ Him, they were watching Him _____ to see whether He would _____ (therapeuō) him on the Sabbath." (Mark 3:2)

The band of Scribes and Pharisees, following the precepts of Mosaic law were so unyielding to the mercy and grace that flowed from Jesus that they were hostilely bent on finding fault in Him. Believers, we may be quick to say we would not behave as a Scribe or Pharisee but let's also not be so intransigent that we put the Miraculous in a box and expect to see His healing.

🕭"Since He had _____ (therapeuō) many, all who had diseases were _____ toward Him to touch Him. Whenever the _____ spirits _____ Him, those possessed _____ down before Him and cried out, You are the Son of God!" (Mark 3:10-11)

If you need the healing touch of Jesus do you 'press' in to pray and meditate on His Word?

🕭"For she said, if I can just _____ His robes, I'll be made _____!(sōzō) _____ her flow of blood ceased, and she sensed in her body that she was _____ (iaomai) of her affliction. At once Jesus realized in Himself that power had gone out from Him. He turned around in the crowd and said, Who touched My robes? So He was looking around to see who had done this. Then the woman, knowing what had happened to her, came with fear and trembling, _____ _____ before Him, and told Him the whole _____. Daughter, He said to her, your faith has made you _____ (sōzō). Go in peace and be _____, from your affliction." (Mark 5:28-34 also found in Luke 8:43-47)

We have all suffered trials of illnesses; some people more intensely than others. You know what it is like to carry the burden of the trial, do you also know what it is like to be released and feel the peace? If so, praise Him! If not, ask Him!

Here is something interesting to think about. Prior the twentieth century many Americans regarded the real estate or land tax as immoral because it violated the teaching of Scripture. The understanding was that the earth is the Lord's therefore property taxes were considered to be anti family, God and private property. Interesting? Americans did not realize that the power to tax a piece of property dictated who was ultimately in control of the property. This example makes me think of our bodies. The earth is the Lord's but as a Believer aren't our bodies also His? If we do not allow the Word of God to infiltrate our minds and souls what then is it that we are allow to infiltrate? We were purchased with a price and were set free from the dominion of sin and Satan. Let's get in line with what the Word of God says regarding our healing and let the Mighty Physician take over; come what may. (Not implying I agree or disagree with the tax, only using it as an example.)

🕭"So He was not able to do any _____, there, except that He laid His hands on a few sick people and _____ (therapeuō) them. And He was _____ at their unbelief." (Mark 6:5-6)

Anyone who received any sort of healing by Jesus I am sure did not think it was anything short of a miracle. However, Jesus was hindered in performing the miracles He could have because of their amazing unbelief.

🕭"So they went out and _____ that people should _____. And they were driving out many _____, anointing many sick people with olive oil, and _____ (therapeuō) them." (Mark 6:12-13 also seen in Acts 8:7)

The disciples were commissioned by Jesus to go out with His authority and perform these miracles to those in need. As disciples of Christ we have the same authority in His name. The anointing oil is symbolic of the Holy Spirit. They anointed with oil and offered a prayer in faith to the One who has the power to heal.

🕭"Then He said to them, ____ _____ you will quote this proverb to Me: Doctor, _____ (therapeuō) yourself. So all we've heard that took place in Capernaum, do here in Your hometown also." (Luke 4:23)

Elijah and Elisha who were compelled to work miracles among people outside of Israel because they were not accepted by their own nation. Generally, God's anointed teacher is not as readily accepted by those he knows as compared to strangers. The malice of his household or friends brings his ministry into contempt and they are therefore unable to accept that one that once considered an equal is now doing something beyond them.

🕭"But the news about Him _____ even more, and large _____ would come together to hear Him and to be _____ (therapeuō) of their sicknesses. Yet He often withdrew to _____ places and _____. On one of those days while He was teaching, Pharisees and teachers of the law were sitting there who had come from every village of Galilee and Judea, and also from Jerusalem. And the Lord's power to _____ (iaomai) was in Him." (Luke 5:15-17)

The fame of Jesus cannot be kept quiet. His withdrawing to private places indicates His need to 'draw' from the Father for His equipping. How much more do we need to have our time with the Lord to receive our equipping? The Lord's power was present to heal but did the Pharisees and teachers of the law have the faith to receive?

ꙮ"They came to _____ Him and to be _____ (iaomai) of their diseases; and those _____ by unclean spirits were made well. The whole crowd was trying to touch Him, because _____ was coming out from Him and _____ (iaomai) them all." (Luke 6:18-19)

Can you imagine the freedom and joy that was experienced in this crowd?

ꙮ"That is why I didn't even consider myself _____ to come to You. But say the word, and my servant will be _____ (iaomai)." (Luke 7:7)

The centurion had faith to understand the only thing required was a word spoken by Him, nothing else. Jesus commended the centurion's faith. So great was the power of God that nothing stands between or hinders His healing power when He orchestrates it to happen.

ꙮ"At that time Jesus _____ (therapeuō) many people of diseases, plagues, and evil spirits, and He _____ sight to many blind people." (Luke 7:21)

Not only does Jesus have the authority to teach, and forgive sins, but He also has in Him the power to heal!

ꙮ"The Twelve were with Him, and also some women who had been _____ (therapeuō) of _____ spirits and _____: Mary, called Magdalene (seven _____ had come out of her)." (Luke 8:2)

Do you believe that typically those who have received the most from Jesus have an acute awareness of the pit from which they have been retrieved and therefore find it harder to take Him for granted?

ꙮ"Summoning the Twelve, He _____ them _____ and _____ over _____ the _____, and power to _____ (therapeuō) _____. Then He sent them to _____ the kingdom of God and to _____ (iaomai) the sick." (Luke 9:1-2) "So they went out and traveled from village to village, proclaiming the good news and _____ (therapeuō) everywhere." (Luke 9:6)

The disciples were given power and authority over ALL the demons as well as given power and authority over disease. All creation is subject to Christ's authority regardless of the ambassador who speaks it. Christ desires that we are free from Satan's bondage! If we speak the gospel message with love and truth and it is still rejected and disdained, it leaves the listener with no excuse.

🞲"When the apostles returned, they _____ to Jesus all that they had done. He took them along and withdrew _____ to a town called Bethsaida. When the _____ found out, they _____ Him. He _____ them, spoke to them about the kingdom of God, and _____ (iaomai) those who needed _____ (therapeuō)." (Luke 9:10-11).

Even when Jesus needed time alone, He did not turn away those who searched and found Him. Jesus continually meets our need. Search for Jesus with all your heart, He can be found and will not turn you away.

🞲"I _____ Your disciples to drive it out, but they _____. Jesus replied, You _____ and _____ generation! How long will I be _____ you and put _____ with you? Bring your son here. As the boy was still approaching, the _____ knocked him down and _____ him into severe convulsions. But Jesus _____ the unclean spirit, _____ (iaomai) the boy, and gave him back to his father. And they were all _____ at the greatness of God." (Luke 9:40-42)

Are these the 9 disciples (the other 3 were witnessing the transfiguration) or were these the disciples from the larger group? If they were from the larger group or just the onlookers, the rebuke about them being unbelieving and rebellious might make sense. In any case, <u>if you operate in the Spiritual gift of healing, faith and obedience to God is a must</u>.

🞲"When Jesus saw her, He called out to her, " Woman, you are _____ of your _____." Then He laid His _____ on her, and _____ she was _____ and began to _____ God. But the leader of the synagogue, indignant because Jesus had healed on the Sabbath, responded by telling the crowd, There are six days when work should be done; therefore come on those days and be _____ (therapeuō) and not on the Sabbath day." (Luke 13:12-14)

Are we mostly concerned with the rules of what we deem appropriate or are we more willing to be astonished at the greatness of God! Let's not ever be accused of trying to make Jesus behave.

🞲"One Sabbath, when He went to eat at the house of one of the leading Pharisees, they were _____ Him _____. There in front of Him was a man whose body was _____ with fluid. In response, Jesus asked the law experts and the Pharisees, Is it lawful to _____ (iaomai) on the Sabbath or not? But they kept

Charisma

silent. He took the man, _____ (iaomai) him, and sent him away. And to them, He said,

Which of you whose son or ox falls into a well, will not _____ pull him _____ on the Sabbath day? To this they could find no answer." (Luke 14:1-6)

Are you seeing a pattern here of the offense people took when Jesus healed on the Sabbath? God initially set the rules in place of what should and what should not happen on the Sabbath. His Son was now present among them and attempting to show them a new Way which was being placed before them but they refused to accept the life offered in Jesus. Instead they rebelliously chose to cling to death.

➢"As He entered a village, 10 men with serious skin diseases met Him. They stood at a _____ and raised their voices, saying, Jesus, Master, have _____ on us! When He saw them, He told them, Go and _____ yourselves to the _____. And while they were going, they were _____ (katharizō). But one of them, seeing that he was _____ (iaomai), returned and, with a loud voice, gave _____ to God. He fell facedown at His _____, thanking Him. And he was a Samaritan." (Luke 17:12-16)

In other words, you ought to know better. The reason they stood at a distance is because they were contagious and were not allowed to approach people. Jesus instructed them to show themselves to the priest in accordance to their law (ex: Leviticus 14:11, 24). In this way Jesus was indicating He did not come to destroy the law but to fulfill it.

The verse said while they were going they received healing. Was it as soon as they acted in obedience to Jesus by leaving to show themselves to the priest? Oh but as soon as the one noticed his healing he could not contain his gratitude for a second and ran back to His Lord thanking Him and giving profuse glory to God!

➢"But Jesus responded, "No more of this!" And _____ his ear, He _____ (iaomai) him." (Luke 22:51)

Here are two possible scenarios. Jesus is either saying, "No more of this" to 1) His captors to release His arms so that He may heal the man, or 2) His disciples so there would be no more violence and to let things take their course. What we know is Jesus is peaceful and He could have been stating "No more this" because there would have been no need for resistance.

❧"Then He went _____ to Cana of Galilee, where He had turned the water into wine. There was a certain royal official whose son was ill at Capernaum. When this man _____ that Jesus had come from Judea into Galilee, he went to Him and _____ with Him to come down and _____ (iaomai) his son, for he was about to die." (John 4:46-47)

Have you ever been in a situation in which you were desperate for help, not knowing which way to turn and then heard of someone just close enough and just seeming to be what you need? I have. When I learned of the help it consumed by thoughts and quickened my pace for the opportunity to receive what they were willing to offer. I imagine when the royal official learned of Jesus' visit his heart beat and his feet marched double time to the One who could heal.

❧"By the Sheep Gate in Jerusalem there is a pool, called Bethesda in Hebrew, which has five colonnades. Within these lay a large number of the sick — blind, lame, and paralyzed (waiting for the moving of the water, because an angel would go down into the pool from time to time and stir up the water. Then the _____ one who got in after the water was stirred up recovered from whatever ailment he had). One man was there who had been sick for 38 _years_. When Jesus saw him lying there and knew he had already been there a _____ time, He said to him, Do you _____ to get well? Sir, the sick man answered, I don't _____ a man to put me into the pool when the water is stirred up, but while I'm coming, someone goes down ahead of me. Get _____, Jesus told him, pick _____ your mat and _____! Instantly the man got well, picked up his mat, and started to walk. Now that day was the Sabbath, so the Jews said to the man who had been _____ (therapeuō), This is the Sabbath! It's _____ for you to pick up your mat. He replied, The man who made me well told me, Pick up your mat and walk." (John 5:2-11)

Being sick for 38 years is a long time. Would you agree? The man had probably become comfortable with his condition. It was his way of life, his 'normal'. Can you relate? When Jesus sees us He sees through our facade and straight to the heart of the matter. When Jesus spoke I suppose He also got straight to the point. When he asked the man, "Do you want to get well?", He already knew the true condition of the man. The answer was, "Sir……" can you hear the impatience? Can you sense the tone of "Why else do you think I am here?" Just like this man, after your long years of discouragement, comfort with your condition, the predictable habit of your days, "Do you really want to get well?" Does your will need to be challenged and encouraged to be different? The man here was waiting for someone else to do the work, to make the first move for him. How about you? Jesus can heal the

Charisma

heart and emotions just as easily as He can heal the physical ailments. If you were asked today, "Do you want to get well?" how would you respond?

_____

ᴥ"But the man who was _____ (iaomai) did not know who it was, because Jesus had slipped away into the crowd that was there. After this, Jesus found him in the temple complex and said to him, See, you are well. Do not _____ anymore, so that something _____ doesn't happen to you." (John 5:13-14)

These words connect the man's past suffering with sin. Is every illness connected with sin? No, but some illnesses apparently are. If someone is operating in the Spiritual gift of healing, wisdom might direct you to ask questions regarding the need for repentance.

ᴥ"He has _____ their eyes and _____ their hearts, so that they would not _____ with their eyes or _____ with their hearts, and be _____, and I would _____ (iaomai) them." (John 12:40)

Believers, let's face the truth of Scripture with eyes and hearts wide open! We might be able to understand why an unbeliever might not have eyes to see and ears to hear but let's make absolutely sure we do not operate in this way. When our eyes and hearts are completely open to Jesus then we can teach others the truth that has been revealed to our hearts.

ᴥ"A large group came together from the towns surrounding Jerusalem, _____ sick people and those who were t_____ by unclean spirits, and they were all _____ (therapeuō)." (Acts 5:16)

Jesus is for us! Let's gather our sick and those tormented by unclean spirits and bring them to Jesus ~ the Mighty Physician.

ᴥ"Peter _____ to him, Aeneas, Jesus Christ _____ (iaomai) you. Get _____ and make your bed, and _____ he got up. So all who lived in Lydda and Sharon saw him and _____ to the Lord." (Acts 9:34-35)

Peter SAID Jesus Christ *heals you*. Amen! When someone operating in the Spiritual gift of healing is filled with bold faith to speak that kind of proclamation expect to be swept off your feet!

❧"God _____ Jesus of Nazareth with the Holy Spirit and with power, and how He went about doing good and _____ (iaomai) all who were under the _____ of the Devil, because God was with Him." (Acts 10:38)

Amen and Amen. Jesus is the same today as He was yesterday. He is anointed with power to deliver you from the stronghold of the enemy. Period.

❧"In Lystra a man without _____ in his feet, lame from birth, and who had _____ walked, sat and heard Paul speaking. After observing him closely and seeing that he had _____ to be _____ (sōzō), Paul said in a loud voice, "Stand upright on your feet!" And he _____ up and started to walk around." (Acts 14:8-10)

Are you seeing a pattern here with 'jumping'? We do not receive and collapse or decline, we 'jump' with the power of the Majesty! Paul, after first observing the man indeed had faith to be healed, he then spoke a word of healing to him. The man with no strength in his legs (because he had never walked) then 'jumped' up and started 'walking' around! The man had faith to believe for healing, heard the word and was immediately healed. There was no contemplation, no wondering if it was real, and no thought of 'was it for him'. Do you suppose he cared what his neighbor thought as he responded to Jesus' command to "Stand!" Jesus Himself spoke many words to us through the Scriptures. Do you take His words as a command just like this man did? I believe we would see more healing in our midst if we copied this lame man and stood strong.

❧"Publius's father was in bed _____ from fever and dysentery. Paul went to him, and _____ and laying his _____ on him, he _____ (iaomai) him. After this, the rest of those on the island who had diseases also came and were _____ (therapeuō). So they _____ many honors on us, and when we sailed, they _____ us what we needed." (Acts 28:8-10)

What love and grace Paul showed to someone with a fever and dysentery. He laid his hands on the sick man showing Jesus' compassion. Also, the laying on of hands frequently accompanied miraculous cures. Beautiful.

❧"For the _____ of these people have grown _____, their ears are hard of _____, and they have _____ their eyes; otherwise they might _____ with their eyes and _____ with their ears, _____ with their heart, and be

Charisma

_____, and I would _____ (iaomai) them." (Acts 28:27)

This verse was quoted by Paul from the book of Isaiah. Have you made sure your heart is soft, your hears can hear, and your eyes can see? Looks to me like this is a promise. "They might see with their eyes, hear with their ears, understand with their heart, and be converted (repent and turn away from evil), and I would heal them." Shall today be your day to respond and receive?

⋆"And if the Spirit of Him who _____ Jesus from the dead lives in you, then He who raised Christ from the _____ will also bring your mortal bodies to _____ through His Spirit who lives in you." (Romans 8:11)

The indwelling Spirit in the life of the believer is a mark of Christ's ownership. Let that sink in deep. Past your brain….into your heart. As His possession, does it make sense that He would not want you sick? Every work or trial in our life is to bring about further sanctification. If you are currently sick, prayerfully seek the Lord to determine what He desires to bring about in you through this sickness. The Spirit provides life and righteousness. God receives glory through the health of his people. (Psalm 30:9) Hallelujah!

⋆"No _____ seems enjoyable at the time, but _____. Later on, however, it yields the fruit of _____ and _____ to those who have been _____ by it. Therefore strengthen your tired hands and weakened knees, and make straight paths for your feet, so that what is lame may not be dislocated but _____ (iaomai) instead." (Hebrews 12:11-13)

This to me is a prayer of exhortation we can entreat for ourselves and others. "My tired hands will be strengthened and my knees will be steady as I make my paths straight for walking so that what is lame may not be dislocated but healed in the name of Jesus!"

⋆"Is anyone among you _in trouble_? He should call for the elders of the church, and they should _pray_ over him after anointing him with olive oil in the name of the Lord. The prayer of _faith_ will _heal_ the sick person, and the Lord will _raise_ him to health; if he has committed sins, he will be _forgiven_. Therefore, confess your sins to one another and pray for one another, so that you may be _healed_ (iaomai). The urgent request of a righteous person is very _powerful_ in its effect." (James 5:14-16)

Some time ago when I came across this verse in James 5:13-16. I read it continually and I was fascinated by every word. I wondered if there was a specific "prayer of faith"? It was odd, but I asked every person I came across whom I thought could explain it to me but no one seemed to be able to. So, I took it to the Lord (which was probably His intent anyway) and asked, "What is the prayer of faith?" Several days later my small children were playing with a neighbor's new puppy. After coming inside I noticed every one of them had itched their eyes and now they were read and puffy. I lined them up and washed each of their eyes with saline. My youngest was last and as I looked at her eyes I noticed a dark mark across the sclera that appeared to be a splinter. I panicked and thought "I can not handle any more illness and disease." I plainly told the Lord "This is something you must handle." As I held my daughter's face in my hands I looked into her eyes and said, "Heal her eye Lord". I put her back in line and went back to the first child to apply another round of saline. When I got to the youngest again I took a deep breath, looked into her eyes and saw that the 'splinter' was gone! Immediately I knew the Lord had taught me what the prayer of faith was! Simply, it is any prayer offered in faith. Whatever had been in her eye was gone and I knew it would never return – in Jesus name it would not!

Another interesting point in verse 14 is that we are to call for leaders in the congregation to pray over us if we are sick. I think what James meant here is that elders, or church leaders (if in their correct walk with the Lord) should, without question have great faith. If a person is unable to pray with assurance and faith for the sick, they should wait until they can or seek someone else that can pray. Someone who prays without faith can either quench the Spirit or quench the faith in the sick person.

The person who feels led to pray for the sick should first ask the Lord how the prayer should proceed. It would not be surprising if other gifts of the Spirit such as a word of knowledge and a word of wisdom should manifest in this scenario. Knowledge and wisdom is beneficial here if there is something in the sick person's life that needs to be addressed in order to swing the gates wide for healing.

> "He _____ bore our sins in His body on the tree, so that, having died to sins, we might live for _____; you have been _____ (iaomai) by His wounds." (1 Peter 2:24)

These words come from Isaiah 53:5. By Jesus' death we are spiritually healed. The Greek word translated healing here is iaomai. Looking back at the definition and after prayerful consideration how does this verse speak to your spirit?

_____

Charisma

Prayer

Thank you Lord for Your great compassion towards me. Thank you for sacrificing yourself so that I may be saved. You settled all accounts when I was purchased out of the hand of the enemy by Your own blood, therefore I am your treasured possession. Teach me everything you desire for me to know about your great compassion of healing. If you desire for me to pray for the healing of someone in need give me Your faith and the courage to not pass them by. Show me if I need to address something in my own life to receive healing. I desire to do anything You have called me to do in this life. I am your child and choose to walk in no one else's footsteps but yours. You alone are worthy of great praise and honor and I choose to serve your other treasured possessions through the power of your Holy Spirt! Amen.

Miracles ~ God's Miraculous Power

Have you ever yearned for a miracle? Pleading with God for you or someone you know to be the beneficiary of His powerful outstretched hand, producing results only He is capable of? Lord, we need Your miraculous intervention in our lives! Do you know that even accepting Jesus Christ as Savior of your soul is a miracle? It is only by the work of the Holy Spirit, brilliantly revealing the truth of the Word to an unbeliever that reveals the powerful work of the Cross to them (Matthew 16:17, John 6:44). How about when we deny the pride of the flesh and serve God's people strictly out of love? That also is a miracle.

The Greek word for the Spiritual gift of miracles is dynamis. Strong's defines dynamis as a force, miraculous power (usually implied as a miracle), ability, abundance, worker of miracles, power, strength, mighty wonderful work. (biblehub.com)

Do you recall when Elisha asked for a "double portion" of the Spirit that had rested on Elijah? As Elijah was taken up into heaven his mantle (symbolic of his anointing) fell off. Elisha 'picked it up' and performed a miracle by parting the waters (2 Kings 2:9-14). The Scripture records that Elisha's request was honored because through him, twice as many miracles were seen! What is also fascinating is Jesus said we would do the works He does and will do even greater works (John 14:12). We SHALL do greater works than Jesus! Do you ever consider the weightiness of that? He did not say we would receive a double portion because no limit was set! Shall you 'pick up' where Jesus left off?

Let's expect to see great miracles in this day! We have been given full power of the Spirit. Remember Moses had difficulty leading God's people and he asked for assistance? God took 'some of the Spirit that was on Moses and placed the Spirit on the 70 elders' (Numbers 11:25). He took only 'some of the Spirit'. The portion He took from Moses was enough to spread around to 70 others while Moses still retained some! The 70 others could then operate with the power of the Spirit. What is interesting to keep in mind is the measure taken from Moses was enough to supply 70! Moses had plenty of the anointing of the Spirit that some could be taken and he was obviously still left with plenty. He had the ability to operate in tremendous power! As believers yielded to the Spirit, that same divinely powerful Spirit is available to us. Would you agree we operate shamefully below our potential? How often do you feel you operate full throttle in the Spirit?

A couple of years ago I was doing bible study with a beloved friend and her precious mom. I frequently prayed for both of them but on this day I had been praying exclusively for the mom. I prayed as I was driving that day and I experienced a strong feeling of love (agape) for her. I continued praying as the Spirit led and as I was praying, my arms and legs began shaking so dramatically I could no longer drive the car. I pulled into a parking lot and my body continued to shake as I prayed. I was filled with joy for her and knew without a doubt something miraculous was about to take place in her life. I phoned her daughter and asked her to relay to her mom that she would soon receive "the joy of her salvation." Speaking became difficult because it seemed my entire body was shaking uncontrollably and so were my vocal cords. When our flesh is overcome by the influence of the Spirit it does not maintain the status quo! My friend contacted her mom and as best she could, relayed the message I had given. A few days later I got word that my friend's mom had been praying and attempting to explain to her husband the message I had given her. As she asked the Lord to help her, she began shaking uncontrollably just as I had a couple of days earlier. As she spoke on the phone her vocal cords were also shaking so her speech was difficult for her, just as it had been for me. The power of the Holy Spirit had fallen on her. By His sovereign wisdom, He allowed us to share the same experience. By her own account, she received the joy of her salvation and has never been the same since. A miraculous intercession indeed. Praise God!

Here are some recorded examples of Jesus' miracles (There were more not even recorded John 21:25). When Jesus performed the miracles they were either to a believing crowd or to those needing encouragement to believe. Some of His miracles include asking Peter to retrieve tax money from the mouth of a fish (Matthew 17:27), feeding the multitude (Mark 6:38-44, 8:1-9), walking on water (Matthew 14:25-33), rebuking a storm (Mark 6:45-52), turning water into wine (John 2:1-11), and suggesting a perfect fishing spot (John 21:5-12). The power that was in Jesus came out from Him to heal others (Mark 5:30, Luke 8:46, Luke 6:19). Following Pentecost, there are times when believers received miracles. Some examples are when the believers were set free from prison (Acts 5:17-25, 12:1-17, 16:25-40), and when Phillip was bodily transported in Acts 8:39-40.

When Jesus returns He will come with power and great glory (Matthew 24:30, Mark 9:1, 13:26, Luke 21:27) and we will see Him seated at the right hand of Power (Matthew 26:64, Mark 14:62, Luke 22:69). Unbelief has hindered God's miraculous powers (Matthew 13:58, Mark 6:2,5).

What to watch out for with this gift:

❊ All power and All glory belong to God ~ we share NONE ❊
❊ God intervenes in situations the way He sees fit ~
not how we do ❊
❊ Pride has no place when serving God ❊
❊ Disappointment ❊
❊ Impatience ❊

Here is a summary of some places in Scripture that speak of miracles (dynamis):

The **power** of the Most High overshadowed Mary and Jesus would be born (Luke 1:35). God raises up rulers to display His **power** in them so that His name is proclaimed (Romans 9:17)! Someone performing a **miracle** by the name of Jesus can only bless His name (Mark 9:39)! As Jesus taught and loved the crowds **power** came out from Him and healed them all (Luke 6:19). Jesus gave the Twelve **power** over demons and **power** to heal diseases (Luke 9:1). Jesus the Nazarene performed **miracles**, wonders, and signs through God (Acts 2:22). Peter and John performed **miracles** by speaking in the name of Jesus Christ the Nazarene (Acts 4:7). People were astounded when they observed Jesus' great **miracles** (Acts 8:13). **Powerful** angels will take vengeance on those who don't know God and on those who don't obey the gospel of Jesus (2 Thessalonians 1:7-8). God's **power** to heal is in Jesus (Luke 5:17). The apostles gave testimony regarding Jesus' resurrection with great **power** and grace was on all of them (Acts 4:33). The **power** of the Spirit fills us with hope, joy, and peace to overflowing (Romans 15:13). God anointed Jesus of Nazareth with **power** and He healed all who were under the tyranny of the Devil (Acts 10:38). To those saved, the message of the cross is God's **power** (1 Corinthians 1:18). God's kingdom is not a matter of talk but of **power** (1 Corinthians 4:20). The Apostles performed **miracles** (2 Corinthians 12:12) and God confirms His message by various **miracles** (Hebrews 2:4). In the resurrection, we will be raised in **power**! (1 Corinthians 15:43) We may be weak in the flesh but when yielded to God we live with Him in **power**. (2 Corinthians

13:4) Jesus sustains all things by His **powerful** word (Hebrews1:3). Have you tasted God's good word and the **powers** of the coming age (Hebrews 6:5)? Jesus is at God's right had and all earthly and demonic **powers** are subject to Him (1 Peter 3:22). Jesus is returning and He is coming in **power** (2 Peter 1:16). Angels, who are greater in might and **power** than people are, do not slander anyone (2 Peter 2:11) why should we?

Recently I heard someone make a comment regarding God not performing any more miracles based on Matthew 12:39-40. However, Mark 16:17 (please read) says something different. As always, it is a matter of the heart; if you require a sign to believe then where is your faith? The recorded miracles of the Old and New Testament show God intervening to meet the needs of His people and to demonstrate His sovereignty. Always having the same character, (Hebrews 13:8) we can still expect to see the miraculous in His perfect sovereignty. Are we witnessing the same occurrences as in the church in Acts? No. Does this mean God has ceased providing this gift today? No. I do not see Scriptural evidence that God has taken away this gift. There is not always a clear line between the gift of healing and the gift of miracles. The gift of healing is *usually* associated with a curing of illness or disease while other experiences could be classified as a gift of miracles. Let's expect God to reveal Himself to us anyway His sovereign way chooses.

Please open your bible and prayerfully consider the following verses as you complete the following blanks:

"On that day many will say to Me, Lord, _____, didn't we prophesy in Your name, drive out demons in Your name, and do many _____ in Your name? Then I will announce to them, I never knew you! Depart from Me, you lawbreakers!" (Matthew 7:22-23)

It is not about demonstrating the miraculous, it is about a life transformed by a relationship with Jesus Christ of Nazareth. Demons can counterfeit miracles to ultimately draw attention away from God. The miraculous is not exclusively about the seemingly impossible being made possible but about a heart willing to burst at the seams for the cause of Christ.

"Then He proceeded to denounce the towns where most of His _____ were done, because they did not repent: "Woe to you, Chorazin! Woe to you, Bethsaida! For if the _____ that were done in you had been done in Tyre and Sidon, they would have

Charisma

_____ in sackcloth and ashes long ago!" "And you, Capernaum, will you be exalted to heaven? You will go down to Hades. For if the _____ that were done in you had been done in Sodom, it would have _____ until today." (Matthew 11:20-21, 23)

Some translations render 'denounce' with 'unbraid'. Jesus began to unbraid the towns. Wow. We don't want Jesus to feel like He has to unbraid anything we are associated with - Amen? This unbraiding was done because people desired to partake of Jesus' miracles but would not allow Him further access to their hearts which would have resulted in repentance.

✎"He went to His hometown and began to _____ them in their synagogue, so that they were _____ and said, "How did this wisdom and these _____ come to Him?" (Matthew 13:54)

You have heard of the principle of cause and effect, which God created. God, in the miraculous, works outside of cause and effect – things outside explanation. The wondrous. The things beyond our imagination.

✎"And He did not do many _____ there because of their _____." (Matthew 13:58)

Unbelief is a great obstacle to receiving from Christ. Many people have difficulty accepting miracles as a possibility because they do not accept God and His nature. God is a god of the miraculous. He created the universe from nothing and He created you and I out of the dust of the ground which He also created. A person operating in the Spiritual gift of miracles has no problem believing God can do what He says he can do and that He is who He says He is. Period.

✎"Jesus answered them, "You are _____, because you don't know the _____ or the _____ of God." (Matthew 22:29, Mark 12:24)

I think it is knee-slapping and jaw-dropping the way Jesus responds to His critics. He is explaining to the Sadducees that in the resurrection there is no need for the saints to have children because they are eternal. Because the Sadducees referred only to the Genesis - Deuteronomy teaching, Jesus referred to Himself as the *current* God of Abraham (to show Abraham was alive in Heaven) so they would understand in their context. Brilliant!

◆"To one he gave five talents; to another, two; and to another, one — to each _____ to his own _____. Then he went on a journey." (Matthew 25:15)

The word translated 'ability' is the Greek word dynamis. God distributes a measure of faith to each one of us (Romans 12:3) and gifts are also distributed to us according to what the Spirit determines is appropriate.

The word 'talents' here is referring to a large sum of money. Someone given less of a 'talent' than another has still been entrusted with a *substantial* gift. Is it interesting to think that we use the word 'talents' in our everyday language to describe things we are humanly gifted at? God knows our human abilities and gives us Spiritual gifts to match our capabilities. Also keep in mind that when we operate in our 'comfort zone' that usually is an indication we are operating in the flesh and not stepping out in faith and trusting the Spirit to work beyond our natural capabilities. Let's not put the 'talents' we have been entrusted with on a shelf and wonder about their usefulness. We must work faithfully so that when the Master returns he tells us, "Well done!"

◆"You have said it, Jesus told him. But I tell you, in the future you will see the Son of Man _____ at the right hand of the _____ and coming on the clouds of heaven." (Matthew 26:64, Mark 14:62, Luke 21:27)

Do you find it interesting that the high priest informed Jesus, "By the living God" he was placing him "under oath to tell them if He was the Messiah"? By the living God? Indeed! Jesus told them they were right and furthermore they would see Him in the highest position in heaven. Sitting at the right hand of Power (God) is the chief place of honor.

◆"At once Jesus realized in Himself that _____ had gone out from Him. He turned around in the crowd and said, Who touched My robes?" (Mark 5:30, Luke 8:46)

Many may attempt to 'rub shoulders' with Jesus and it will be of no deep personal avail to them but the one who reaches out to Him with profound faith is the one that receives the powerful transformation that is found in Him alone.

◆"And he will go before Him in the spirit and _____ of Elijah, to turn the hearts of fathers to their children, and the disobedient to the understanding of the righteous, to make ready for the Lord a prepared people." (Luke 1:17)

Charisma

This was the prophecy spoken by Gabriel to Zechariah concerning his son John. John would have more than a typical measure and power of the Spirit in order to accomplish God's purposes. He would be powerfully transformed by Jesus and speak the truth of God with the power that converts lost souls.

🙵"Then Jesus returned to Galilee in the _____ of the Spirit, and news about Him spread throughout the entire vicinity. He was _____ in their synagogues, being _____ by everyone." (Luke 4:14-15)

This is the Son of God. The One with God when all of creation was conceived and established. He was the Word with God from the beginning. Because He was the Word that took on flesh (John 1:14) He must rely on the Spirit just as we do. Even though He was the powerful Son of God He still was led into the wilderness to fast for 40 days. The Devil tempted Him in His weakened condition but was woefully unsuccessful. Jesus then returned to Galilee in the power of the Spirit and well equipped for ministry.

This verse recently has caused me to pause. Jesus stepped out of glory and took on flesh. He therefore spent significant time alone with God learning how to ignore the demands of the flesh in order to be yielded to the Spirit. How *much more* are we required to be aware of yielding to the Spirit and ignoring the demands of the flesh in order to live a divinely victorious Christian life? Do we do this?

🙵"_____ came over them all, and they kept saying to one another, "What is this _____? For He commands the unclean spirits with authority and _____, and they come out!" And news about Him began to go out to every place in the vicinity." (Luke 4:36-37)

Do we want to be astonished by His Word? We must not be deceived by not knowing the power that awaits us in the Scriptures.

While in the synagogue Jesus cast out an unclean demonic spirit that was harassing a man with a word of rebuke, "Be quiet and come out of him!" (Luke 4:35) The people mused about His authoritative power over the demonic world. The people might not have understood but the demos have nothing to think through. They are well familiar with Jesus and His powerful authority. Rumors began to spread wildly about His power over the spiritual realm. Are you also spreading His fame?

🙵"_____ to you, Chorazin! Woe to you, Bethsaida! For if the _____ that were done in you had been done in Tyre and

Sidon, they would have _____ long ago, sitting in sackcloth and ashes!" (Luke 10:13)

Chorazin and Bethsaida were cities near Capernaum where Jesus mainly resided during His Galilean ministry and He most likely frequented these cities. If you are a recipient or witness to the miracles of Jesus is your soul more aware of its wretched depravity and know nothing more but to bend the knee in repentance? Jesus' miraculous interventions in our lives should prick our hearts to realize how far sin has taken us away from holiness. If you operate in the Spiritual gift of miracles, teaching the power of the Cross and of His great mercy and grace is foundational.

"Look, I have given you the _____ to trample on snakes and scorpions and over all the _____ of the enemy; nothing will ever harm you. However, don't rejoice that the spirits _____ to you, but rejoice that your names are _____ in heaven." (Luke 10:19-20)

We are victoriously anointed in the name of Jesus. All of our victories over the enemy are based upon the finished work of Jesus Christ of Nazareth. By the power of His name we have authority over the influence of the Devil. Rejoice in this truth and invoke the name of Jesus over your conflicts while all the more rejoicing that your name is written in heaven. If you operate in the Spiritual gift of miracles you will also teach this truth with powerful conviction to other believers in need.

"Now He came near the path down the Mount of Olives, and the whole _____ of the disciples began to _____ God _____ with a loud voice for all the _____ they had seen: The King who comes in the name of the Lord, is the blessed One. Peace in heaven and glory in the highest heaven!" (Luke 19:37-38)

Now this is a crowd quiet different than the one we saw in Luke 10:13. These people were transformed by His miraculous works and responded with loud, joyful praise! They worshiped Him and blessed His name. Under the power influence of Jesus we will never seek the miracles more than we seek the miracle Worker!

"And look, I am _____ you what My Father promised. As for you, stay in the city until you are _____, from on high." (Luke 24:49)

The disciples were rejoicing about Christ's resurrection which is one of the foundational truths of the gospel message. While Jesus was in their midst He, 1) opened their minds to understand the Scriptures and 2) He sent the Spirit for their empowerment. If you have accepted Jesus as Lord you have also received the Spirit. Never forget the Spirit comes in power! A marvelous prayer might be for Him to "open my mind to understand the Scriptures!"

👉"But you will receive _____ when the Holy Spirit has come on you, and you _____ _____ My witnesses in Jerusalem, in all Judea and Samaria, and to the ends of the earth." (Acts 1:8)

We should not be amazed at the miracles God allows to be preformed through us. God IS a God of miracles, why do we marvel? God created the heavens and the earth and man from the dust of the ground. This is a miracle indeed. If we believe these things why do we marvel at other things?

The power of the Cross and Resurrection is a where our faith lies. When we testify to the power of these truths we should not marvel at what great works of God will follow. It is nothing but an honor to spread the fame of Jesus.

👉"Stephen, full of grace and _____, was performing great wonders and signs among the people." (Acts 6:8)

Stephen was one of the first deacons. He spoke body about God and the message he spoke was accompanied by powerful signs and wonders which unsurprisingly led to many people being converted to the faith.

👉"God was performing _____ _____ by Paul's hands, so that even facecloths or work aprons that had touched his skin were brought to the sick, and the diseases left them, and the evil spirits came out of them. Then some of the itinerant Jewish exorcists _____ to pronounce the _____ of the Lord Jesus _____ those who had evil spirits, saying, "I command you by the _____ that Paul _____!" (Acts 19:11-13)

God is not common and neither are the miracles that are demonstrated when a powerful move of the Spirit is manifested. If you operate in the Spiritual gift of miracles every powerful act is meant for a confirmation of His word, to bring Him glory, and to demonstrate His supreme authority. In this case, even those that were not disciples witnessed the power of His authority over the demonic world and also used His name.

👉"His Son, Jesus Christ our Lord, who was a _____ of David, according to the _____ and who has been _____ to be the

Charisma

_____ Son of God by the _____ from the dead according to the _____ of holiness." (Romans 1:3-4)

Jesus was a descendant of David through the flesh but according to the Spirit He is the powerful Son of God. The Spirit of holiness raised Jesus from the dead exhibiting victory over death and He now reigns with all power and authority which was given to Him by God!

❧"For I am not _____ of the gospel, because it is God's _____ for salvation to everyone who believes, first to the Jew, and also to the Greek. For in it God's _____ is revealed from

faith to faith, just as it is written: The _____ will _____ by _____." (Romans 1:16-17)

Ashamed of the gospel? Do you boldly speak the message of Christ when opportunities are presented to you? You are an ambassador for Christ *pray* that you "might be bold enough in Him to speak" as you should. (Ephesians 6:20) God's righteousness is revealed through His powerful message! Do you see the depth in the words 'the righteous will live by faith'? You are in right standing with God if you live not by what your fleshly eyes and heart reveal but by what your faith reveals to your soul. God's power is made manifest in this kind of faith!

❧"For His invisible attributes, that is, His eternal _____ and _____ nature, have been clearly seen since the creation of the world, being _____ through what He has _____." (Romans 1:20)

This verse regards how creation clearly bears witness to God the Creator. Through that revelation, understanding brings a conclusion to your intellect about who God is. Lets also consider that miraculous power is one of His attributes (a characteristic of Himself, like the color or shape of your eye is one of your characteristics). It is an attribute that testifies as to who He is. When God is invited into your circumstances, He brings all the workings of His attributes with him! Hallelujah! Matthew 26:62 speaks of Jesus being seated at the right hand of the Power. God is called the Power (dynamis). Mark 9:1 describes the Kingdom of God as power (dynamis). That is why in Luke 21:27 (above) He will be coming in power and glory! The Kingdom is coming! Are you and those entrusted to your influence ready?

❧"For I am persuaded that not even death or life, angels or rulers, things present or things to come, hostile powers, height or depth, or any other created thing will have the _____ to _____

Charisma

us from the _____ of God that is in Christ _____ our Lord!" (Romans 8:38-39)

Believe in God – be filled with all joy and peace. This is not just an exhortation to believe God exists but to believe what He says He can do. Believe God! The Spirit miraculously fills you with hope and with this kind of powerful believing! Do you believe it ~ come what may? Do you also communicate this truth to anyone else with an ear to hear?

☙"For I would not dare say anything except what Christ has accomplished through me to make the Gentiles obedient by word and deed, by the power of miraculous signs and wonders, and by the power of God's Spirit. As a result, I have fully proclaimed the good news about the Messiah from Jerusalem all the way around to Illyricum." (Romans 15:18-19)

Have you ever humbly considered that Christ would use any of us (in light of our sin) to promote the cause of Christ? We are sanctified and considered righteous through Jesus Christ alone and He equips us for what He calls us to do. We have no cause to boast in ourselves but our powerful boast is in what Christ has accomplished in our lives and through the lives of others.

☙"For the _____ of the _____ is foolishness to those who are perishing, but it is God's _____ to us who are being saved." (1 Corinthians 1:18)

See notes on Romans 1:16 above.

God rejects human wisdom's attempts to acquire salvation apart from God as well as man-made precepts and the empty mouthed words of salvation (please read Isaiah 29:13-14). However, to those with humble hearts turned towards the Lord, the cross of Christ is miraculous power made available to us on a continual basis.

☙"Yet to those who are _____, both Jews and Greeks, _____ is God's _____ and God's wisdom, because God's foolishness is wiser than human wisdom, and God's weakness is _____ than human strength." (1 Corinthians 1:24-25)

Divine power is found in Christ. God's own Darling of heaven is brimming with the love of His Father and God shares His glory with Him. Does man's wisdom think he has it all figured out and needs no one else but himself? Foolishness. There is nothing that compares or even dares to share the stature of His power and wisdom. I am thankful for that. Can you express why you are thankful that no human can match God's wisdom and strength?

_____

🕭"My speech and my proclamation were not with persuasive words of wisdom but with a _____ demonstration by the _____, so that your faith might not be based on _____ wisdom but on God's _____." (1 Corinthians 2:4-5)

This type of powerful teaching has the ability to convict the soul of man. Someone operating in the Spiritual gift of miracles can also teach someone the powerful truth of Scripture and the impact of God's message along with the working of the Spirit. This can powerfully transform hearts and minds.

🕭"When you are _____ in the name of our Lord _____ with my spirit and with the _____ of our Lord Jesus, turn that one over to Satan for the destruction of the _____, so that his _____ may be _____ in the Day of the Lord." (1 Corinthians 5:4-5)

Do we expect during our assemblies to be supernaturally forged together by the power of the Spirit? Those assembled and filled with the Spirit of God will be directed *in love* to allow someone, if necessary, to be confronted with their sin having repentance and salvation as the priority goal.

Every generation has their jargon and what seems to be in vogue right now is a casual laugh and shrug accompanied with a "don't judge me" comment. The problem with this 'leave me alone in my ideas and actions' mentality is when there is a need to bring something to a person's attention (when only done in love) but we are already heeding their warning to keep quiet. Decide in advance if you are willing to speak the truth *in love* to people in order to bring about repentance, even at the risk of being rejected.

🕭"God raised up the _____ and will also raise _____ up by His _____. Don't you know that your bodies are a part of Christ's body?" (1 Corinthians 6:14-15)

By the same miraculous power God used to raise His son from the tomb, He will also raise His people from the grave. The grave could not hold Jesus and it will not hold the Christian believer either. Hallelujah!

☙"Therefore, if I do not know the _____ of the language, I will be a foreigner to the speaker, and the speaker will be a foreigner to me." (1 Corinthians 14:11)

The word translated 'meaning' in this verse is the same Greek word dynamis we are studying. There is power in the spoken word. The demons understand it and if we desire to effectively communicate the gospel message to others we must also speak in a way that is powerfully received.

☙"Then comes the end, when He hands over the kingdom to God the Father, when He abolishes all rule and all authority and _____." (1 Corinthians 15:24)

All rule and authority that man implemented in his limited wisdom will be abolished. The government of God will be established and His divine kingdom will be faithfully and powerfully established on His earth. We will see the Lord and His throne will be set in place among us. God's kingdom will come and His will indeed will be done through Christ Jesus. He will reign victoriously for one thousand years exactly as He sovereignly planned it.

☙"For we don't want you to be unaware, brothers, of our affliction that took place in Asia: we were completely overwhelmed — beyond our strength — so that we even despaired of life. Indeed, we personally had a death sentence within ourselves, so that we would not trust in ourselves but in God who raises the dead." (2 Corinthians 1:8-9)

Living by faith and the unsurpassed power of the living God is foundational victorious living.

☙"Now we have this _____ in clay jars, so that this extraordinary _____ may be from God and not from us." (2 Corinthians 4:7)

The treasure we have is the Holy Spirit. The clay jar is our body. We were formed from the dust (clay) of the ground. The miraculous power will be evidence to others of God at work in our lives by manifestations of the Spirit as well as a extraordinarily transformed life.

☙"But as God's _____, we commend ourselves in everything: by great endurance, by afflictions, by hardship, by difficulties, by beatings, by imprisonments, by riots, by labors, by sleepless nights, by times of hunger, by purity, by knowledge, by patience, by kindness, by the Holy Spirit, by sincere love, by the message of truth, by the _____ of God; through weapons of righteousness on the right hand and the left..." (2 Corinthians 6:4-7)

No one ever promised a Christ follower's life would be free from pain and suffering or free from trial. Paul committed himself to endure such suffering for the pinnacle purpose of advancing the cause of Christ. He allowed the transforming power of God to strengthen Him, equip Him, and confirm His message.

☙"I testify that, on their own, according to their _____ and _____ their _____, they _____ us insistently for the _____ of sharing in the ministry to the saints, and not just as we had hoped. Instead, they gave _____ especially to the Lord, then to us by God's will." (2 Corinthians 8:3-5)

What praise! Not only did they desire to share in the privilege of ministry based on their own ability but they were also motivated by their Spiritual ability to do some good! These people gave themselves to the Lord.

Beautiful indeed. <u>If you operate in the Spiritual gift of miracles you will also have an intense desire to love God's people and minister to them out of the overflow of what God has poured into you.</u>

☙"But He said to me, "My grace is sufficient for you, for _____, is perfected in weakness." Therefore, I will most gladly _____ all the more about my _____, so that Christ's _____ may reside in me." (2 Corinthians 12:9)

Paul asked God to remove the 'thorn' he was suffering and God's response is recorded above. Even though the 'thorn' would remain, God promised Paul would never lack ample grace to conquer it. According to verse 8, Paul asked for the 'thorn' to be removed three times. Have you ever prayed hoping for a particular response but the answer you received was not what you hoped for? Paul did. The answer to his prayer did not come as he expected but he received an answer nonetheless. His affliction would not be leaving any time soon but he found reason to rejoice in the provision God provided! The grace Paul received was sufficient for him because miraculous power is perfected in human weakness. The greater the believer confesses human weakness, the more conspicuous Christ's empowering strength will be. How will you choose to respond today?

Are we ashamed of our weaknesses or do we boast in them knowing full well that the things we do are only because of Christ's power that resides in us. Do you have any examples?

"So then, does God supply you with the Spirit and work miracles among you by the works of the law or by hearing with faith?" (Galatians 3:5)

☙"I pray that the _____ of your mind may be _____ so you may know what is the hope of His _____, what are the glorious _____ of His _____ among the saints, and what is the immeasurable greatness of His _____ to us who _____, according to the working of His vast strength. God's Power in Christ He _____ this _____ in the Messiah by raising Him from the dead and seating Him at His right hand in the heavens — far _____ every ruler and authority, power and dominion, and every title given,, not only in this age but also in the one to come." (Ephesians 1:19-21)

Do you see how this can also tie in with 2 Corinthians 12:9 above?

'Far above' in this verse is not speaking of dimension but superiority. We may be tempted by the powers of rulers and authorities to think of ourselves as unworthy or unable but that is a lie straight from the pit of hell authored by non other than the enemy of your soul. Let's not be deceived to think the enemy does not possess power, but Christ's power trumps all power the enemy can pull together. Don't be tempted to think anything else.

Dwell on the words "the immeasurable greatness of His power to those who believe". What action words are most powerful to you? Why?

_____

☙"I was made a _____ of this gospel by the gift of God's grace that was given to me by the _____ of His _____." (Ephesians 3:7)

God's power enables us to serve in a way that pleases Him by teaching and spreading His Good News. Don't neglect the gift entrusted to you. It was given to you to fulfill a purpose.

☙"I pray that He may _____ you, according to the riches of His glory, to be _____ with _____ in the inner man through His _____, and that the Messiah may _____ in your hearts through _____. I pray that you, being _____ and _____ established in _____, may

Charisma

be able to comprehend with all the saints what is the length and width, height and depth of God's love, and to know the Messiah's love that _____ knowledge, so you may be _____ with all the fullness of God. Now to Him who is able to do _____ and _____ all that we ask or think according to the power that works in us — to Him be glory in the church and in Christ Jesus to all generations, forever and ever. Amen." (Ephesians 3:16-20)

We have divine resources through the Spirit because of Christ's redemptive work of the Cross. We shall rebuke discouragement and be strengthened by the miraculous power that God made available to us through His Spirit. Even though our outer man is being wasted away our inner man should be getting stronger and healthier by the working of the Spirit through our faith. Are you insuring your 'inner man' is getting stronger and healthier as a top priority?

The word 'able' is also a form of the Greek word we are looking at for power. This verse is considered to be a doxology – an outpouring of praise and worship to God. The word 'above' (exceedingly abundantly) and 'beyond' is the same word for the abundant grace of God in Romans

5:20. According to the power that works in us, Wuests translates: in the measure of the power which is operative in us. Strongs indicates it can be used with the connotation of "distribution". (both from biblehub.com) He is going to do this superabundantly more than we can ask or think in the measure of the power that is distributed from us. How much are you yielded to the Spirit and how much of the Spirit is distributed from you? Do you ever think He will do above and beyond all that we ask or think according to the miraculous power of the Spirit that is distributed from us? Why or why not?

_____

⋆"My _____ is to know Him and the _____ of His resurrection and the fellowship of His sufferings, being conformed to His death, assuming that I will somehow reach the resurrection from among the dead." (Philippines 3:10)

Shall we not only know the miraculous power that raised Christ from the dead but also that same miraculous power that resides in us? Do you know Christ well enough to identify with Him and put to death your previous way of life and walk continually in the miraculous power made available to you by Christ's resurrected life?

🕮 "He will _____ the body of our humble condition into the likeness of His glorious body, by the _____ that enables Him to subject everything to Himself." (Philippines 3:21)

The humble condition is referring to lowness. As you know, your body is weak and vulnerable to oppression, disease, sinful desires, and death. At the return of Christ your body will be transformed into a glorious representation of who you are in Christ Jesus and the weaknesses of the flesh will pass away. Thank you Lord. How does this happen? By the miraculous power that enables Him to bring all things under the subjection of His authority. Hallelujah!

🕮 "May you be _____ with all _____, according to His glorious might, for all _____ and _____, with joy giving thanks to the Father, who has _____ you to share in the saints' inheritance in the light." (Colossians 1:11)

Amen! May we be strengthened with all God's power! Christians are engaged in righteous conflict with the powers of this fallen world and nothing short of divine empowerment will enable us stand. You are strengthened WITH ALL POWER, according to His glorious MIGHT (vigor, strength, dominion). Do you think you have been able to stand any other way? Look to the Father to enable you EVEN MORE with His miraculous strength. Stare down your moral conflict with the eyes of faith and stand strong in HIS strength!

🕮 "We _____ Him, _____ and teaching everyone with all wisdom, so that we may present everyone _____ in Christ. I labor for this, striving with His strength that works _____ in me." (Colossians 1:28-29)

Fellow Believers, our labor should consist of striving done in HIS strength. Yielding to HIS Spirit so that it works powerfully *through* you. The goal in our proclamations, teachings, and warnings should be that everyone is mature in Christ! This can not be accomplished by a work in our flesh but by a yielding of our flesh to His powerful Spirit. We do the yielding and leave the details to Him. He is more than able to accomplish His purposes through His yielded child.

🕮 "For our gospel did not come to you in word _____, but also in _____, in the Holy Spirit, and with much assurance. You know what kind of men we were among you for your benefit, and you became imitators of us and of the Lord when, ___ _____ _____ severe persecution, you _____ the message with joy from the Holy Spirit." (1 Thessalonians 1:5-6)

Charisma

The gospel committed to them was not only heard as a revelation but demonstrated in power!

🕮 "And in view of this, we always pray for you that our God will consider you _____ of His calling, and will, by His _____, fulfill every desire for goodness and the work of faith, so that the name of our Lord Jesus will be _____ by you, and you by Him, according to the grace of our God and the Lord Jesus Christ." (2 Thessalonians 1:11-12)

Shall we edify each other and build up the fainthearted? Even in the certainty of God's plan we shall continue to pray for its fulfillment! (Please read Phil. 2:13) The prayer given by Paul is for the fulfillment of your every good purpose and act which is prompted by your faith. (Please read James 2:26) The realization of which will only be known by God's power.

🕮 "The coming of the lawless one is _____ _____ Satan's working, with all kinds of false _____, signs, and wonders, and with every unrighteous deception among those who are perishing. They perish because they did not _____ the love of the truth in order to be saved." (2 Thessalonians 2:9-10)

We must have discernment to recognize the authentic from the corrupt.

🕮 "For God has _____ given us a spirit of fearfulness, but one of _____, love, and sound judgment. So don't be ashamed of the testimony about our Lord, or of me His prisoner. Instead, share in suffering for the gospel, _____ on the _____ of God." (2 Timothy 1:7-8)

In order to be effective in your service to Christ you must receive the power that is provided by the Spirit (see Acts 1:8). The Spirit enables you to operate in love, power and self-discipline. Fear does not originate with the Spirt of God. Fear is deadly and one of its symptoms is paralysis. We are given God's love (Romans 5:5). We are given a sound mind (1 Co 2:16). We are given power.

Paul is speaking to Timothy from prison and desired to strengthen his courage. It is easy enough to boldly proclaim the gospel of Christ when there are no threats to your life or even your faith. How bold is your proclamation when your loved one is dying, when the dam burst that has been holding back all your sorrows, when you receive a diagnosis, when there seems to be no end in sight for your suffering, or when a fellow believer suffers for the sake of the Gospel? This verse is exhorting (1) don't be ashamed, (2) share in the suffering and, (3) rely on the power. Don't be tempted to shrink back in fear or hesitation.

🕭"holding to the _____ of godliness but _____ its _____. Avoid these people!" (2 Timothy 3:5)

What 'form' of godliness or religious standards do people follow? Church goers? Prayer reciters? Followers of habits or traditions? If you deny the power of the Cross you have an empty religion. Let it not be so! Why do you think the command is given to 'avoid these people'?

_____

🕭"By _____ even Sarah herself, when she was unable to have children, received _____ to conceive offspring, even though she was past the age, since she _____ that the One who had promised was _____." (Hebrews 11:11)

She was past the age to have a child under natural human conditions but she was not beyond the miraculous reach of God! What was her part? Her faith *considered* the miraculous One that had *promised*. Does your faith consider the powerful Word in the face of your difficult trial?

Here is an example of individuals who by faith relied on the power of God. "And what more can I say? Time is too short for me to tell about Gideon, Barak, Samson, Jephthah, David, Samuel, and the prophets, who *by faith* conquered kingdoms, administered justice, obtained promises, shut the mouths of lions, quenched the raging of fire, escaped the edge of the sword, gained strength after being weak, became mighty in battle, and put foreign armies to flight." (Hebrews 11:32-34)

🕭"You are being _____ by God's _____ through _____ for a salvation that is ready to be revealed in the last time." (1 Peter 1:5)

You are protected by God's miraculous power! Hallelujah! Our part in the arrangement is that it is done 'through faith'. God is continually protecting you. Do you have the kind of faith that is *continually* operating?

"His divine _____ has given us everything required for _____ and _____ through the knowledge of Him who called us by His own glory and goodness. By these He has given us very great and precious _____, so that through them you may _____ in the divine _____, escaping the _____ that is in the world because of evil _____." (2 Peter 1:3-4)

The Word of God contains everything we need for salvation, and for trusting and obeying Him perfectly. His Holy Spirit and the cross of Christ is the divine power at work in us. Are you allowing the miraculous power of the cross to transform your life? Make the exchange today. Lay your burdens and stubborn places of sin at the cross. Since the cross is the place of exchange, you release your burdens and sins and 'exchange' them with the Lord's forgiveness and peace. Whatever you lay down at the cross you then make the exchange for the Lord's provision in that area. Don't leave that place of exchange until you have received. (If you have not received then you have not yet released what you are trying to lay down.)

"I know your works. Because you have limited strength, have kept My word, and have not denied My name, look, I have placed before you an open door that no one is able to close." (Revelation 3:8, 5:12)

Even though we operate in the power of God it is still limited. Despite those limitations, there will be some that will keep His Word and will not deny His name. Will this be you?

These verses in Revelation speak of the power of God:

"Our Lord and God, You are worthy to receive glory and honor and power, because You have created all things, and because of Your will they exist and were created." (Revelation 4:11)

"All the angels stood around the throne, the elders, and the four living creatures, and they fell facedown before the throne and worshiped God, saying: Amen! Blessing and glory and wisdom and thanksgiving and honor and power and strength be to our God forever and ever. Amen." (Revelation 7:12)

"The 24 elders, who were seated before God on their thrones, fell facedown and worshiped God, saying: We thank You, Lord God, the Almighty, who is and who was, because You have taken Your great power and have begun to reign." (Revelation 11:17)

"Then I heard a loud voice in heaven say: The salvation and the power and the kingdom of our God and the authority of His Messiah have now come, because the accuser of our brothers has been thrown out: the one who accuses them before our God day and night." (Revelation 12:10)

"Then the sanctuary was filled with smoke from God's glory and from His power, and no one could enter the sanctuary until the seven plagues of the seven angels were completed." (Revelation 15:8)

"After this I heard something like the loud voice of a vast multitude in heaven, saying: Hallelujah! Salvation, glory, and power belong to our God." (Revelation 19:1)

Prayer

You are the God who performs miracles; displaying your power among Your people. You perform wonders that cannot be fathomed and miracles that cannot be counted. We learn from Your word that in some places you visited you were unable to do many miracles because of the lack of faith. Let it not be so in my life! Bring your gift of miracles into the church! I yield completely to the Spirit and I am ready to represent your hands and voice for a work of miracles whenever you see fit. Display your power in me so that your name is proclaimed in all the earth! You ARE the God of miracles! I thank you in advance for all that you will do through me for your believers, all in Your name Jesus. Amen!

The Brilliance of God's Discernment

[handwritten note, left:] Discernment is all about a relationship with God.

[handwritten note, right:] Pray & study to increase discernment.

Christians and non-Christians alike possess natural discernment. This is the discernment that allows us to judge and understand people and situations. This judgment is learned and can be a product of our environment and the culture we live in. As is evident in these times, human morality varies from culture to culture and from generation to generation which makes this natural discernment unstable. What we perceive or encounter gets weighed in our scales that we call balanced and the result is what we discern to be acceptable or unacceptable. What was favorable two generations ago might not be discerned as favorable in this generation. As time progresses the current generation seems to discern more and more leniency towards their own thinking and behavior as it best fits their ideals and lifestyles. There must be something better; something more consistent.

An example of this natural discernment can be witnessed in how one culture views the appropriate treatment of women and children versus another culture viewing it as inappropriate. Insist your heart be forever thankful if you happened to be born in a culture that favors honorable treatment of people. So easily the privileges we claim can be shamelessly taken for granted. The discernment in some hard line religiously dominated areas see the treatment of some people as a means to their own gain (without even a remote regard for their others' well-being) while imagining it is cloaked in worship. Lord, help us see that natural discernment alone is poverty and we desperately need Your true discernment to guide us in this difficult age. Your word says people without Your discernment are doomed. (Hosea 4:14) Help us to thrive Lord and be blessed!

The source of true discernment does not come from our world leaders, cultural acceptance, norms, habits, or even the majority. The source is God alone. As we pray and study the Word, this true discernment grows. As our 'mind of Christ' (1 Cor. 2:16) matures, it comes in agreement with the Scripture and with the Spirit. We must renew our minds so we are able to recognize when we hear strange teaching or see shifts in morality that does not line up with what we know about Christ and His word.

Luke 10:18

When we have true discernment we know not to fear events in the world. We discern the enemy's influence on people and situations but we know Jesus has conquered the world so we choose thanksgiving and prayer in the face of uncertainty. We will discern that in our trials, God desires to sanctify us and we will choose to look up during the trial and discern God's love for us. The peace He gives will transcends every thought. God is perfect order. When we try to discern in the natural mixed with the supernatural there can be chaos in our thinking. We establish order by yielding to the Spirit of God then seeking His perfect discernment. We then discern where our strife is – and it is not with flesh and blood. Discern the battle you are fighting as significant for your growth as well as having kingdom significance as opposed to seeing it merely as another struggle to endure. That is empowerment for turning what the enemy would have has your stumbling block into what God would have for your advantage!

Discerning of spirits (diakrisis) is one of the gifts spoken of in 1 Corinthians 12. This gift enables a believer to know the underlying motivation of a person or situation. A believer operating in this gift will be able to discern whether the person is operating under the inspiration of the Spirt or if they are merely expressing their own thoughts, feelings, or desires or even if they are speaking from the influence of an oppressive spirt. One way a believer can discern spiritual influence is by the 'feeling' the spirit brings. The Spirit of God brings love, joy, and peace. A wrong spirit brings feelings of heaviness and agitation. A person influenced by a wrong spirt can bring heaviness with them into a meeting and draw all attention to themselves in an attempt to manipulate the gathering. A discerning person will recognize the problem and pray for wisdom to know how to proceed. There could be a hesitation on the part of the person due to concern of coming across as insensitive or uncaring – but be strong in the Lord! The source of this gift is God and is given under the Spirit's control. It originates from a place of power not fear! People search for a power that is beyond them. There are demons of witchcraft among people around us – even in the church. If they do not seek the power that resides with God for righteousness, they WILL seek it elsewhere and find it with wrong spirits. Lord, give us true discernment when we come together in Your name. If there is a spirit with a desire to hijack what You would have for us, guide us in Your orderly ways. (Note: Discerning of spirits has nothing to do with spiritualism (belief that the dead communicate with the living). Wrong spirits are the 'rulers of the darkness of the world' – fallen angels or demons. Matthew 10:8, Ephesians 6:12)

Charisma

We should always make an effort to discern the Spirit when we meet with other believers because our aim is to follow His guidance. We never want to miss what the Spirit would like to do on our behalf. Lord, teach us to lay aside our human plans as needed when we sense Your movement in our gatherings. We welcome Your presence and desire your direction!

An example of true discernment is found in Acts 16:17. Paul and Silas were on their way to a prayer meeting when a slave girl (who made a large profit for her owners by fortune telling) continued to cry out for days, "These men, who are proclaiming to you the way of salvation, are the slaves of the Most High God." Paul was aggravated and turned to the spirit (is it interesting it says the spirit and not the girl?) saying, "I command you in the name of Jesus Christ to come out of her!" And it came out right away. Even though the girl was proclaiming truth regarding Paul and Silas, Paul discerned she was speaking under the influence of the enemy and the proclamation was meant to bring disruption instead of glory. Oh the brilliance of God's discernment!

Another example is found in 2 Kings 5. Naaman, a captain in the Syrian army was a leper. He went to the prophet Elisha and he instructed him to wash seven times in the Jordan to receive his healing. When he did this, his skin was restored to health and he went back to Elisha to offer him a gift. Elisha, however, would not accept the gift. When Naaman left, Gehazi, (Elisha's attendant) sought Naaman to deceitfully persuade him that Elisha now wanted the gift and he would bring it to him. Gehazi then stored the gift in his home. When Elisha asked Gehazi what he had been up to Gehazi did not tell him. Elisha not only discerned Gehazi's dishonest spirit but also what he had done. Elisha operated in power and with a sound mind to discern the things of God and to speak out. Therefore, he was not held back by fear of reprisal because of the confrontation. Elisha had the fear of the Lord and was not moved by the fear of man.

Please open your Bible and prayerfully consider these verses as you complete the blanks:

❧"So give Your servant an obedient heart to judge Your people and to _____ between _____ and _____." (1 Kings 3:9)

For who is able to judge this great people of Yours?" Solomon asked for a heart obedient to the word of God so that he could serve His people with discernment. How about you? Let's have an obedient heart to God at all times. A heart that does not waiver but is steadfast! In this way, we will be able to discern what is pleasing to God and serve His people in truth. Amen!

🔸"Teach me good judgment and _____, for I rely on Your commands." (Psalm 119:66)

Loving and relying the magnificent Word of God leads to good judgment and discernment. Do you love the Word? Do you find your life in the Word? If we are to discern we must start from a solid foundation of the powerful Word.

🔸"Do not be conformed to this age, but be _____ by the _____ of your mind, so that you may _____ what is the _____, _____, and _____ will of God." (Romans 12:2)

Do you discern that you must be vigilant in order to maintain your commitment to serve the Lord? Do you also discern that the world tries to charm your heart away from the things of the Lord? Being transformed leads to discernment and discernment leads to knowing the perfect will of God.

"_____ anyone who is _____ in faith, but don't _____ about doubtful issues." (Romans 14:1)

The word translated 'argue' is the Greek word diakrisis which we are looking at concerning 'discernment'. Immature Christians have a more difficult time relating to truths that more fully established Christians can understand. The goal is for all Christians to be unified in the faith. Building peace and kindness coupled with faithful teaching is key as opposed to a teaching peppered with harshness and criticism because someone is weak in the faith.

🔸"And I pray this: that your love will keep on growing in _____ and every kind of _____, so that you can _____ the things that are _____ and can be pure and blameless in the day of Christ, filled with the _____ of righteousness that comes through Jesus Christ to the _____ and _____ of God." (Philippians 1:9)

Bishop Wordsworth (biblehub.com) says, "that delicate tact and instinct, which almost intuitively perceives what is right, and almost unconsciously shrinks from what is wrong." It cannot exist without love. With God's love (agape) comes the spiritual insight we need to live and serve in ways that please Him.

🕊"Watch out that no one _____ you. For many will come in My name, saying, 'I am the Messiah,' and they will _____ many." (Matthew 24:4-5)

In the last days more deceiving spirits will be unleashed so we must be prepared to discern the counterfeit. We build ourselves up by reading the Word and with prayer.

🕊"Many false prophets will _____ _____ and _____ many." (Matthew 24:11)

This verse is speaking about those who have turned away from the faith and are then deceived. Maintain the love of God in your heart. Do you discern that to maintain something it requires effort? We must have true discernment to recognize a false prophet. How would you discern a false prophet or teacher in your midst?

_____

🕊"Then I saw another beast coming up out of the earth; he had two horns like a lamb, but he sounded like a dragon. He exercises all the authority of the first beast on his behalf and compels the earth and those who live on it to worship the first beast, whose fatal wound was healed. He also performs great signs, even causing fire to come down from heaven to earth in front of people. He _____ those who live on the earth because of the _____ that he is _____ to perform on behalf of the beast telling those who live on the earth to make an _____ of the beast who had the sword wound and yet lived." (Revelation 13:11-14)

If you do not want to be deceived you must be able to discern. In this scenario, having natural discernment will not enable you to discern the truth of what is happening. Because of the powerful signs he is allowed to manifest, people will be deceived. Father, give us discernment to see through the enemy's endeavors both now and in his "great fury". Give us wisdom to know he is the ultimate false prophet, with an unholy gospel, and counterfeit signs.

The next five scriptures are examples when Jesus used discernment:

~John 1:47 "Then Jesus saw Nathanael coming toward Him and said about him, Here is a true Israelite; no deceit is in him. Jesus discerns the inner motive and heart."

~John 2:23-25 "While He was in Jerusalem at the Passover Festival, many trusted in His name when they saw the signs He was doing. Jesus, however, would not entrust Himself to them, since He knew them all and because He did not need anyone to testify about man; for He Himself knew what was in man. Jesus discerned the people's superficial faith because they witnessed His miraculous works. He did not trust himself to those who made a profession based solely on a witnessed miracle. Our profession of faith must go deeper. It is always a matter of the heart. We must not marvel at the miraculous and follow Him because our eyes have had a feast. A true confession is based on a heart that is certain of the reality of who and what Jesus represents."

~Mark 9:17-27 "Out of the crowd, one man said, Teacher, I brought my son to You. He has a spirit that makes him unable to speak. Whenever it seized him, it throws him down, and he foams at the mouth, grinds his teeth, and becomes rigid. So I asked Your disciples to drive it out, but they couldn't. Jesus replied, Bring him to Me. When the spirit saw Him, it immediately convulsed the boy. He fell to the ground and rolled around, foaming at the mouth. How long has this been happening to him? Jesus asked his father. From childhood, he said. And many times it has thrown him into fire or water to destroy him. Jesus rebuked the unclean spirit, saying to it, You mute and deaf spirit, I command you: come out of him and never enter him again! Then it came out, shrieking and convulsing him violently. Jesus, took him by the hand, raised him, and he stood up. Jesus discerned it was a spirit by asking questions."

~Matthew 16:15-17 "Jesus asked, But you, who do you say that I am? Simon Peter answered, You are the Messiah, the Son of the Living God! And Jesus responded, Simon son of Johan, you are blessed because flesh and blood did not reveal this to you, but My Father in heaven. Jesus discerned the source of Simon Peter's wisdom".

~Luke 9:54-55 When the disciples James and John saw this (while on the way to Jerusalem the Samaritans in a village did not welcome Jesus), they said, "Lord do You want us to call down fire from heaven to consume them?" But He turned and rebuked them. In our natural discernment would we have such harsh words for someone that would reject the Gospel of Christ? If Jesus would not have his disciples say such a thing, He would have the same word for you and I when we come across someone who rejects Jesus. Lord, help us to discern the reason for the rejection, and wisdom and knowledge to then know what You would have us do.

When others discerned:

~"In Lystra a man without strength in his feet, lame from birth, and who had never walked, sat and heard Paul speaking. After observing him closely and seeing that he had faith to be healed, Paul said in a loud voice, Stand upright on your feet! And he jumped up and started to walk around." (Acts 14:8-10)

Paul first observed the man and then discerned the spirit of faith in him.

~"The next day John saw Jesus coming toward him and said, Here is the Lamb of God, who takes away the sin of the world! John discerned Jesus. Later in verses 31-33 John says, I didn't know Him, but I came baptizing with water so He might be revealed to Israel. And John testified, I watched the Spirit descending from heaven like a dove, and He rested on Him. I didn't know Him, but He who sent me to baptize with water told me, The One you see the Spirit descending and resting on – He is the One who baptizes with the Holy Spirit." (John 1:29)

John discerned Jesus (and His mission) by revelation of the Spirit. By introducing Him as the Lamb of God, John discerned the many aspects of Jesus' mission and His sacrificial character.

More Scripture references regarding discernment:

⚜"Wisdom is found on the lips of the _____." (Proverbs 10:13)

Lord, give me wisdom to discern the words that bring comfort and edification to your people!

⚜"For the _____ the path of life leads upward." (Proverbs 15:24)

The one that discerns Your ways find themselves are on the path of life. Set your mind on what is above, not what is on earth. (Col. 3:2)

⚜"Anyone with a _____ heart is called _____." (Proverbs 16:21)

From the overflow of the heart the mouth speaks. It speaks with discernment and is able to edify and influence others.

🕮 "Even a fool is considered _____ when he keeps silent, _____ when he seals his lips." (Proverbs 17:28)

Wisdom indeed! Have you ever spoken careless words and then wished you could take it all back? True discernment from God comes when you step away from needing to defend yourself and choose instead to leave room for your Defender. Lord, help me to discern when to 'seal my lips'. I am not a fool. I have discernment from the Giver of all good gifts! Praise God! Shall we have discernment and honor the Father with our good gifts?

🕮 "The mind of the _____ acquires knowledge." (Proverbs 18:15)

Let's we be wise and search the Scripture, learning to discern the path of life and even assisting a fellow sojourner along the way! Thank you Lord for such an incredible honor that is beyond words.

🕮 "Two or three prophets should speak, and the others should _____." (1 Corinthians 14:29 ties in with 1 John 4:1)

🕮 "For you were once darkness, but now _____ _____ light – for the _____ of the light results in _____ goodness, righteousness, and truth – _____ what is _____ to the Lord." (Ephesians 5:8-10)

Shall we discern through our walk with Christ was is pleasing to Him, rejecting what is not and holding steadfast to what is? This requires full-throttle faith in action. Are you willing? Discern what is good, right, and true and walk in it. You can do it by the *power* of God when fully yielded to the Spirit.

This verse is interesting to me because of the wording 'you were once darkness but now are light'. Do you you ever think of yourself as 'light'? As a Christian receiving the new birth you are light. It makes me think of the verse that instructs us that Satan disguises *himself* as an angel of light. (2 Corinthians 11:14) What do you imagine it would be like if you came across him?

🕮 "But solid food is for the mature – for those whose senses have been trained to _____ between good and evil." (Hebrews 5:14)

This tells us discernment can be cultivated. If God has given us discernment shall we operate in the provision He has given? In order to discern between good and evil we must train ourselves by studying the Word. Practicing spiritual discernment helps keep us from doing the wrong thing. This discernment will empower our Christian service. Praise God!

⚜"Dear friends, do not believe every spirit, but _____ the spirits to _____ if they are _____ God, because _____ false prophets have gone out into the world." (1 John 4:1 tying in with 1 Corinthians 14:29 here)

True discernment is needed when someone comes forth with a word, with a manifestation of the Spirit, or when we hear a teaching or preaching. We must first have received discernment from God. Let's work beyond our flesh to gain God's understanding. There may be a time when someone approaches you with a 'word'. You should discern whether or not it is from the pureness of the Spirit and the person did not add any of their thoughts or emotions to the 'word'. Remembering the Spirit operates through imperfect people with varying degrees of sanctification. This is also true if you have a 'word' for another believer. You should always test the spirits to determine if the 'word' was indeed from God and was not from the influence of a different spirt or even your own thoughts. Discernment can also say wait. The Lord will reveal the time when a 'word' should be spoken. Sometimes the 'word' given was meant only for prayer. Discernment is a must!

⚜The Pharisees and Sadducees approached (Jesus), and as a test, asked Him to show them a sign from heaven. He answered them: "When evening comes you say, It will be good weather because the sky is red. And in the morning, Today will be stormy because the sky is red and threatening. You know how to _____ the appearance of the sky, but you can't _____ the _____ of the _____." (Matthew 16:1-3)

Jesus told them they can read the 'signs' to predict the weather yet they can't look to the heavens for a 'sign' of the times. Discerning the weather was not as valuable as discerning that Jesus was indeed the darling of heaven (it was a disruption to their thinking). We must also put aside our natural discernment and look to the scriptures for discerning the 'sign' of the times we are in. (Please read more for indications of signs of the times. Hosea 3:5, 2 Tim. 3:1-5, Acts 2:17-21, Matthew 24: 6-8, 2 Peter 3:3)

Prayer

Father, You have all discernment. I desperately need Your impartation to serve You better. Thank you Father that You have given me everything I need for holiness in my life. I turn away from relying on my inferior natural discernment and I ask to be filled with Your brilliance. I desire to discern good from evil, Your Spirit from the world's spirit, and Your truth from a lie. I ask to discern the work of the enemy in my life and by Your glorious power I am sprung from his trap! Thank you for allowing me to see the greatness of Your power available to all believers that are yielded to Your Spirit. Your thoughts are higher than my thoughts and Your ways are superior to the world's ways. Teach me what You desire me to know. Your servant is listening! I pray and believe in the name of the Darling of heaven, Jesus Christ. Amen.

The Relevance of Speaking in Tongues and Giving Interpretation

Someone operating in the Spiritual gift of languages (tongues) or the interpretation of languages is speaking or interpreting in a language (glossa) different than their own and in one not learned. Strongs (biblehub.com) speaks about the Spiritual gift of languages in this way: "The Greek word glossa has traditionally been translated as "tongue" because the Greek word is used for the organ of speech as well as for a language. Some see glossolalia as having a specialized meaning: either ecstatic speech or heavenly languages."

Revelation 7:9-10 tell us, "After this I looked, and there was a vast multitude from every nation, tribe, people, and language, which no one could number, standing before the throne and before the Lamb. They were robed in white with palm branches in their hands. And they cried out in a loud voice: Salvation belongs to our God, who is seated on the throne, and to the Lamb!" This was a gathering of people from every nation, tribe, and language. Were they all speaking the same language? I would guess they are. They are speaking the same thing, in the same language, all in one accord. The intention of the Spiritual gifts of tongues is to glorify God and the interpretation unifies those that hear it and allows it to be tested by Scripture.

Interpretation of the language (hermēneia) is utilizing the ability given by the Spirit to provide the meaning of the words spoken in the unknown language. The interpretation does not have to come as an exact translation. How do you know if you are to give an interpretation after someone speaks in an unknown language or tongue? Perhaps you will have words of Scripture that 'must be spoken' or perceive a picture. Go ahead and provide the interpretation you were given and see what else shall follow. Even though these two gifts are supplied by the Spirit, it is always under your control as to whether or not you will speak them.

One point I think is particularly important to take note of is the different kind of tongues. One is for personal spiritual edification (1)

Corinthians 14:5, 26-27) and the other is for public ministry. As stated in 1 Corinthians 12:28, not all believers have a public ministry of tongues (A language or tongue for personal spiritual edification is not what is spoken about here in this verse) as is also true for gifts of healing, miracles, or teaching. Yielded, baptized-in-the-Spirit believers (Acts 11:15-17, 1 Corinthians 12:13) have the *ability* to speak in tongues for personal spiritual edification. We receive the Spirit when we receive Jesus in our hearts. There are biblical references for those receiving the Spirit at that moment and there are instances when they received at baptism. All who have Jesus and are baptized also have the Spirit. Believers who are yielded to the Spirit will have manifestations of the Spirit's influence in a variety of ways in their lives.

Have you ever wondered what would be the purpose of speaking in another language or tongue? I think of 1 Corinthians 2:13-15. "We also speak these things, not in words taught by human wisdom, but in those taught by the Spirit, explaining spiritual things to spiritual people. But the unbeliever does not welcome what comes from God's Spirit, because it is foolishness to him; he is not able to understand it since it is evaluated spiritually". If the Spirit is speaking to us it will be communicated for our understanding. Do you think He will at times speak to us in a heavenly language? His Spirit to our spirit. When we are filled and yielded to the Spirit then we are influenced by the Spirit. Have you ever pondered the idea that if we speak things taught by the Spirit then we can also use the Spirit's language at times?

According to the Linguistic Society of America, "much pioneering work in documenting the languages of the world has been done by missionary organizations (such as the Summer Institute of Linguistics, now known as SIL International) with an interest in translating the Christian Bible. As of 2009, at least a portion of the bible had been translated into 2,508 different languages, still a long way short of full coverage". (www.linguisticsociety.org) How amazing! Did you know there are about 6800 to 6900 distinct languages in the modern world? Have you ever thought of the Spirit's ability to speak intimately to believers in these vast number of languages? Through the Spirit, we are able to manifest what is beneficial to His people such as a message of wisdom and knowledge, faith, gifts of healing, working of miracles, prophecy, distinguishing between spirits, different kinds of languages and interpretation of languages. Would you be willing to be yielded to the Spirit if He desired to reach someone in our midst by a word spoken through us in an unknown language? How incredible! Lord, I desire to look beyond my present understanding and set my eyes on things that have eternal purposes.

Please retrieve your bible and prayerfully consider these verses as you complete the blanks.

❧"And these _____ will accompany those who _____: In My _____ they will drive out demons; they will speak in _____ _____." (Mark 16:17)

These five things Jesus spoke about were regarding the Great Commission to His disciples. All gifts given are for unity of the body of Christ. The following verse (Acts 2:1-8 below) demonstrates the new tongues that Christ told them they would speak with in this verse. Jesus spoke with the Eleven and gave them instructions to go into all the world and preach the gospel. He informed them that one of the signs that accompanied believers would be speaking in new languages (tongues).

❧"When the day of Pentecost had arrived, they were all together in one place. Suddenly a _____ like that of a violent rushing _____ came from _____, and it _____ the whole house where they were staying. And _____, like flames of _____ that were divided, appeared to them and _____ on each one of them. Then they were all _____ with the _____ _____ and began to _____ in different _____, as the Spirit gave them _____ for speech." (Acts 2:1-8)

There were Jews living in Jerusalem, devout men from every nation under heaven. When this sound occurred, a crowd came together and they were confused because each one heard someone speak in his own language. They were astounded and amazed saying, "Look, aren't all these who are speaking Galileans? How is it that each of us can hear in our own native language? In Jewish tradition there were three signs of the Spirit's coming – wind, fire, and inspired speech. (This alone could justify an entire study) What were they speaking? The magnificent acts of God! Shall we be so filled with the Spirit that there is nothing more to say? Glory to God that it be so! May our lives be so filled with the Spirit that what impacts our heart and therefore overflows from our mouths are the magnificent acts of God. Verse 11 even says, "...we hear them speaking the magnificent acts of God in our own languages." God is magnificent and His ways are beyond our reasoning skills. Let's stop trying to put God in a box and make Him all neat and tidy. God behaves in ways we can not explain.

❧"The circumcised believers who had come with Peter were astounded because the gift of the Holy Spirit had been poured out on the Gentiles also. For they heard them _____ in other

_____ and _____ the greatness of God." (Acts 10:45-46)

The Spirit will fall whenever and on whomever as God sees fit. Who are we to evaluate the manifestation of the Spirit? One thing is for certain, when the Spirit manifest it will be for the magnification of Jesus and nothing else.

❧"When they heard this, they were _____ in the name of the Lord Jesus. And when Paul had laid his hands on them, the Holy Spirit came on them, and they began to speak in other _____ and to _____." (Acts 19:5-6)

❧"And God has placed these in the church: first apostles, second prophets, third teachers, next miracles, then gifts of healing, helping, managing, various kinds of _languages_. Are all apostles? Are all prophets? Are all teachers? Do all do miracles? Do all have gifts of healing? Do all speak in other languages? Do all interpret?" (1 Corinthians 12:28-30)

Paul is speaking of ministering gifts that God has set in the church. Since believers operate as a body (Each with different functions that are meant to work together effectively. There is no need for all to operate in the same gift.) If everyone ministered to the congregation in a different tongue who would be present to manifest God's healing? If everyone taught then who would listen? And why would everyone be used to manifest God's miracles all at once? God is one of order not disorder. As His child we are to act in the exact manner. We do not do anything impulsively. If you sense the Spirit giving a witness to your spirit, pray quietly and ask if you are to share. If you are, then by all means do so! Never speak out by interrupting or steamrolling but mention the Lord has brought something to you and you would like to share.

God does not use everyone to spontaneously speak out in an assembly with an unknown language. This is what Paul meant when he said not all speak in tongues. Likewise, God does not use everyone in the gift of interpretation of tongues. As with all things we desire to learn about God, we must use the entire council of the Word He has given us. Those with the gift of tongues that are not for use in the congregation can use them at any time they desire as you may already know. There are believers who speak in tongues as the Spirit wills for purposes of bringing glory to God and edifying the church and there are those who speak in tongues for private prayer. The church spoken of here is an assembly of Christian gatherers and not referring to someone speaking in tongues for private prayer.

Charisma

🕮"If I speak human or angelic _____ but do not have _____, I am a sounding gong or a clanging cymbal." (1 Corinthians 13:1)

The tongues of men are human languages and angelic languages are those of supreme utterance. If any of these languages are spoken but love is not foundational what have we accomplished? Is it nothing more than a prideful discourse that elevates the flesh? If this is the case are we no better than instruments unbearably out of harmony and only useful for producing noise?

🕮"Love never _fails_. But as for prophecies, they will come to an end; as for _tongues_, they will _end_; as for knowledge, it will come to an end. For we know in part, and we prophesy in part. But when the _perfect_ comes, the _imperfections_ will come to an end." (1 Corinthians 13:8-10)

==The gifts of the Spirit are advantageous in accomplishing the purposes of God until Jesus (the perfect) returns. Jesus has not returned therefore the gifts have not come to an end.== Yes, the Bible is complete but people are still coming to Christ and as Paul said, a powerful demonstration of the Spirit establishes people's faith based on God's power and not on man's persuasive words. (1 Corinthians 2:4-5)

🕮"For the person who speaks in another _language_ is _____ speaking to men but to _____, since no one _____ him; however, he speaks _____ in the _____." (1 Corinthians 14:2)

This verse is describing a time when a person is in private communion with God using a (devotional) language for personal edification and therefore needs no interpretation.

🕮"The person who speaks in another _language_ builds _himself_ up, but he who prophesies builds up the church. I wish all of you spoke in other _____, but even more that you prophesied. The person who prophesies is greater than the person who speaks in _____, unless he interprets so that the church may be built up. But now, brothers, if I come to you speaking in other _languages_, how will I benefit you unless I speak to you with a revelation or knowledge or prophecy or teaching? Even inanimate things that produce sounds — whether flute or harp — if they don't make a distinction in the notes, how will what is played on the flute or harp be recognized? In fact, if the _trumpet_ makes an unclear sound, who will prepare for __battle__? In the same way, unless you use your tongue for intelligible speech, how will what is spoken be known? For you will be speaking into the air. There are doubtless many different kinds of languages in the world, and all have meaning. Therefore, if I do not know the meaning of the language, I will be a __foreigner__ to the speaker, and the speaker will be a foreigner to me. So also you — since you are zealous for spiritual gifts, seek to __excell__ in building up the church. Therefore the person who speaks in another __language__ should pray that he can __interpret__." (1 Corinthians 14:4-13)

The gift of tongues is manifested when a believer, baptized in the Spirit is inspired to speak in tongues while assembled with others. This type of language is for the edification of the church and not for individual edification. If speaking in a tongue is done in an assembly, the interpretation of the tongue should follow.

When speaking in a language for private prayer there is no indication here that the person must understand the language or tongue. The word 'builds up' is interesting. The Greek word refers to a house builder, embolden, to build from the foundation, to restore by building, to rebuild or repair. Metaphorically it speaks of promoting growth in Christian wisdom, affection, grace, virtue, holiness, and blessedness. (biblehub.com) So a person who speaks in another language or tongue for personal spiritual edification is like a person building a house beginning with a solid foundation of impeccable Christian values. Does it get any better?

"Therefore the person who speaks in another language should _____ that he can _____. For if I _____ in another _____, my spirit _____, but my understanding is _____. What then? I will _____ with the _____, and I will also _____ with my _____. I will _____ with the _____, and I will also _____ with my _____. I thank God that I speak in other _____ more than all of you; yet in the _____ I would rather speak five words with my understanding, in order to _____ others also, than 10,000 words in another language." (1 Corinthians 14:13-19)

Otherwise, if you praise with the spirit, how will the uninformed person say " Amen" at your giving of thanks, since he does not know what you are saying? For you may very well be giving thanks, but the other person is not being built up. ==The sole intention of gifts is for edification, comfort, and encouragement.== If you have been given a gift of the Spirit and it is meant for your edification, keep it for a private time. If, however, it is meant for edification, comfort, or encouragement of other believers then it should be brought forth. In these verses, Paul is speaking of the importance of edification of others. In the preceding verses, He explains how we should desire to be close to each other and not be so distant that we cause a separation between believers. If someone speaks in a tongue and there is no interpretation no one benefits and the result is fruitless. Verse 13 says the person who speaks in another language should pray that he can interpret. If Scripture instructs us to pray for something, why not do it? Let us all pray to interpret.

Paul could responsibly speak in other languages more than the others. Here he is speaking not of tongues for personal edification but for ministry in the church. If a tongue is brought forth but no interpretation is offered than the tongue does not bring edification to the church and is therefore not helpful.

☙"It follows that speaking in other _____ is _____ as a _____, not for believers but for _____." (1 Corinthians 14:22)

This is a language spoken that needs interpretation. If an unbeliever hears a tongue and the interpretation convicts them of sin, it is meant as a sign inspiring them to turn to Jesus.

☙"What then is the conclusion, brothers? Whenever you come together, each one has a psalm, a teaching, a revelation, another _____, or an interpretation. All things must be done for edification. If _____ person speaks in another _____, there should be _____ two, or at the _____ three, each in _____, and someone must _____. But if there is _____ _____, that person should _____ _____ in the _____ and speak to _____ and to _____." (1 Corinthians 14:26-28)

If believers are assembled with unbelievers or an uninstructed believer, this should not be used unless an explanation is given. 1 Corinthians 12:23 explains: "Therefore, if the whole church assembles together and all are speaking in other languages and people who are uninformed or unbelievers come in, will they not say that you are out of your minds?"

☙"Therefore, my brothers, be eager to prophesy, and do not _____ speaking in other _____. But everything must be done _____ and in order." (1 Co 14:39-40)
From Genesis to Revelation all evidence points toward God acting orderly. If we operate in a gift of the Spirit order accompanies it

Charisma

because no one under the influence of the Spirt will behave in a disorderly fashion. If you witness someone behaving oddly and out of sink with what you know about God, there is an excellent chance there is a different spirit involved. When the Spirit manifest it is to point toward Jesus and not to a person. If a person is behaving in a way that makes you uncomfortable or brings an odd amount of attention to themselves it most likely means there is another spirit involved.

👉"So too, though the _____ is a small part of the body, it _____ great things. Consider how large a forest a small fire ignites. And the tongue is a _____. The tongue, a world of _____, is placed among the parts of our bodies. It _____ the whole body, sets the course of life on fire, and is set on fire by _____. Every sea creature, reptile, bird, or animal is tamed and has been tamed by man, but ____ _____ can _____ the tongue. It is a _____ evil, full of deadly _____. We _____ our Lord and Father with it, and we _____ men who are made in God's _____ with it. Praising and cursing come out of the same mouth. My brothers, these things should _____ be this way. Does a spring pour out sweet and bitter water from the same opening? Can a fig tree produce olives, my brothers, or a grapevine produce figs? Neither can a saltwater spring _____ fresh water." (James 3:5-11, something similar found in 1 Peter 3:10)

What have we learned so far about boasting?

_____

The tongue can speak marvelous truths about God and can also wreck havoc on our testimonies. Let's be fully aware of this restless potential for evil and keep a guard over our mouths. Our tongues should at all times be used for bringing glory to God. At the same time, since we know the tongue is an untamable restless evil let's be quick to forgive when someone else errs by the same evil. Help us Lord to honor you with full-throttle forgiveness.

The next four verses are not directly related to tongues or the interpretation but are beneficial for maturity and deserve notice.

👉"No _unwholesome_ language is to come from your mouth, but only what is good for _building_ up someone in need, so that it gives _benefit_ to those who hear." (Ephesians 4:29)

Charisma

If we are to be so graced by the words God desires to come forth from us, why would we ever want to pollute our mouth with foul language? We should avoid this type of behavior and go on to maturity! Lay aside the behaviors and thoughts of unbelievers and stand out from among them. Let us move on to maturity!

"If anyone thinks he is religious without <u>controlling</u> his <u>tongue</u>, then his religion is useless and he deceives himself." (James 1:26)

Sanctification by the Spirit changes our hearts, minds, and souls. Let's purposefully show the manifestation of this evidence by controlling what comes out of our mouth.

" <u>Praise</u> and <u>Cursing</u> come out of the <u>same</u> mouth. My brothers, these things _____ _____ _____ this way. Does a _____ pour out _____ and _____ water from the same opening?" (James 3:10-12)

Fresh water is what we crave. Let's operate in wisdom and not demonstrate our immaturity by behaving with a lack of self-control. We live intentionally and are able to do so by the power of the Spirit. Let's also admit that we will make mistakes along the way and be quick to correct them.

"But now you must also _____ _____ all the following: _____, _____, malice, slander, and filthy _____ from your mouth." (Colossians 3:8)

(Also consider James 3:4-6) If we anticipate the words of the Spirit of God to come forth from our mouths why would we ever allow holy things to pass through such pollution? What union can there be between God's sanctuary (which is what you are) and things we allow to pollute that sanctuary? From the overflow of the heart the mouth speaks. What are we allowing to penetrate our hearts? It is wrong for believers to join in the ways of the wicked and profane. Let's accept nothing less but a powerful progression towards maturity!

Have you ever heard someone speak careless words about another? We must not propagate that folly by repeating them to someone else even if it is because we are shocked! If we were shocked because they came from someone else's mouth why should we be less shocked when they come out of ours! While you are at it, don't even allow the words to tumble through your mind.

Thank you Lord for the exhortation from 1 Peter 4:7-11. How about praying this as your own proclamation:

Now the end of all things is near; therefore, be serious and disciplined for prayer. Above all, maintain an intense love for each other, since love covers a multitude of sins. Be hospitable to one another without complaining. Based on the gift each one has received, use it to serve others, as good managers of the varied grace of God. **If anyone speaks, it should be as one who speaks God's words**; if anyone serves, it should be from the strength God provides, so that God may be glorified through Jesus Christ in everything. To Him belong the glory and the power forever and ever. Amen.

If God's love can conquer you whereby leading you to submit yourself completely to God, you can serve Him in ways you never imagined. Peace results when your will is dethroned in your heart and the Lord is allowed to reign. If this has not been settled, inner turmoil is created as a result of your desires relentlessly devising ways to usurp the King. Shall we cast aside immaturity once and for all and demand our will pledge its loyalty to the King? Bow your heart not just your knees at the throne of grace. Now stand alongside the Darling of heaven wearing your new Kingdom clothing, the robe of righteousness. Grieving the Sprit of God by lessening His ability to manifest Himself through you is a thing of the past. Rise purchased child, and live your remaining days on this earth fully yielded to the Spirit and thereby fulfilling your calling.

Prayer

Father, I repent of beliefs I have held that do not line up with Your word and demolish barriers that have kept me from Your best. Forgive me Lord if I have held steadfast to notions that have caused my mind to think less than what you really are. Give me spiritual eyes so I can see things that have eternal purposes instead of my main focus being rooted in things of this earth. I hunger for my spiritual awareness to be weightier than the common awareness of things my senses reveal. I desire to yield to Your Spirit and to be Your instrument to reach Your people in whatever way You choose. I ask the Spirit to teach me things of Himself and I will be open to learning Spiritual things that my intellect may have rejected in the past. My desire is to live in-step with the Spirit, however that may look. I ask and receive in the name of Jesus in which all things are possible. Amen.

The Mission of the Apostle

The Spiritual gift of apostle (apostolos) is defined as a messenger, envoy, delegate, one commissioned by another to represent him in some way, especially a man sent out by Jesus Christ Himself to preach the Gospel. (Strongs. biblehub.com) Someone operating the Spiritual gift of apostleship does not seem to work exclusively within a local assembly but based on the definition is one who is sent out on a mission.

Paul instructs the church that if anyone considers themselves a prophet or spiritual (meaning they are given an inspired word from the Spirit to the body of Christ) that he should recognize that what he writes are commands of the Lord and should not deviate in any way from that. (1 Corinthians 14:37-38) The remaining discussion on apostleship will be included with the following Scriptures.

Galatians 1:6-10

Characteristics of an apostle (same for prophet):

❈ To lay the foundation of the gospel of Jesus Christ (Ephesians 2:20) ❈
❈ To receive and declare the revelation of God's Word (Acts 11:28, 21:10-11, Ephesians 3:5) ❈
❈ To give confirmation of the declared word with signs and wonders and miracles (2 Corinthians 12:12, Acts 8:6-7, Hebrews 2:3-4) ❈
❈ Sent from the body to plant churches or be missionaries ❈
❈ To equip the church with right doctrine ❈

Please retrieve your bible and prayerfully consider these verses as you complete the following blanks.

❧"He also appointed 12 — He also named them _____, — to be with Him, to _____ _____ out to preach, and to have authority to _____ _____ demons." (Mark 3:14-15, Luke 6:13)

Many people were gathered around Jesus. He left the crowd, went up the mountain, and called for those He wanted. He named those He summoned apostles, as they were to go out on missions He would assign them. The apostles would be with Jesus for training, then He would send them to preach and to drive out demons. Jesus wanted them to recognize the spiritual world and that He indeed came to destroy the works of the devil. Someone operating in this gift will preach the gospel as well as drive out demons in the name of Jesus.

The twelve disciples/apostles were: Simon (Peter), Andrew, James, John, Philip, Bartholomew, Thomas, Matthew, James, Thaddaeus, Simon (Zealot), and Judas. (Matthew 10:2-4) Judas betrayed Jesus and was replaced by Matthias.

The following servants of Christ were apostles but were not part of the original twelve: 1) Paul and Barnabas, 2) Most likely Silas and Timothy and maybe even Apollos and James, Jesus' brother, 4) In Romans 16:7 Paul introduces Andronicus and Junia as "noteworthy in the eyes of the apostles." It is not clear if this indicates they actually were apostles. 5) In Philippians 2:25, Paul introduces Epaphroditus who might also be an apostle. Because there appeared to be different kinds (different roles) of apostles, a precise list of names might not be possible.

❧"The _apostles_ gathered around Jesus and reported to Him all that they had _had_ and _taught_." (Mark 6:30, similar to Luke 9:10)

It is interesting to note the apostles returned to Jesus and spoke of the miracles first and then the teaching of the gospel. Being new apostles were they more enthralled with the miracles than the teaching His message? We do not know their hearts but we must know our own. We must keep a check on our hearts to never allow them to be confused with the desire to know the healing more than we know the Healer.

❧"Because of this, the wisdom of God said, 'I will send them prophets and _____, and _____ of them they will kill and _____." (Luke 11:49)

The earthly reward of God's prophets and apostles should not be assumed to be glittery esteem but most likely will be hatred and persecution by some unbelievers. The message they speak does not line up with the world's message of uplifting self but that of crucifying self to bring all glory to the Lord they serve. If you operate in the Spiritual gift of apostle your paramount desire will be to promote the cause of Christ even if it results in worldly loss.

Charisma

🕮"The _____ said to the Lord, "Increase our _____." (Luke 17:5)

The apostles knew they needed assistance in doing the extremely difficult things such as overcoming all the obstacles of temptation. The desire to have their will in line with the will of their Teacher was obvious to them. Yes, their words would also be accompanied by a powerful demonstration of the Spirit but what they personally needed was a mighty disruption in their thinking so that they would wholeheartedly rely on their Lord.

🕮"I assure you: A slave is _____ greater than his master, and a _____ is _____ greater than the one who _____ him." (John 13:16)

The word messenger here is the same Greek word apostolos. This saying is also repeated with somewhat different examples in Matthew 10:24, Luke 6:40, and John 15:20. How can you see this relating to:

Pride:_____

Expectations: _____

🕮"I wrote the first narrative, Theophilus, about all that Jesus began to do and teach until the day He was taken up, after He had given orders through the Holy Spirit to the _____ He had chosen." (Acts 1:2)

Jesus taught His apostles during His earthly tenure. After His ascension, the Spirit would teach His apostles what they needed to know to continue victoriously in the mission He gave them. Let's keep in mind that the Spirit teaches *all* who call Jesus lord!

🕮"When they heard this, they came under deep conviction and said to Peter and the rest of the *apostles*: "Brothers, what must we do?" "*Repent*," Peter said to them, "and be *baptized*, each of you, in the name of Jesus Christ for the forgiveness of your sins, and you will *receive* the gift of the Holy Spirit." (Acts 2:37-38)

When the people submitted themselves to Peter's teaching, their hearts were pricked with remorse at the depravity committed which resulted in the Crucifixion. As a result of this, they desired to know what they must do to escape the penalty of such a sin involved in the heart-breaking dismissal of the Messiah.

Charisma

Because of the conviction in our own hearts, it drives us to also share the foundational Gospel message with all who have an ear to hear and teach them to repent, be baptized, and receive the Spirit.

🙢"And they __devoted__ themselves to the __fellowship__ teaching, to the fellowship, to the breaking of bread, and to the prayers. __Then__ fear came over everyone, and many wonders and signs were being performed through the apostles." (Acts 2:42-43)

It is interesting to note there were one hundred and twenty Jesus followers on the morning of Pentecost and before the close of the day there were over three thousand converts. These new converts 1) devoted themselves to the apostles' teaching, 2) to fellowship, 3) to communion, and 4) to the prayers. Someone operating in the Spiritual gift of apostle will teach and instruct others to follow this same design. However, does this pattern hold fast in the lives of professing Christians? They may think of themselves as a 'good' Christian but do they devote themselves to the gospel teaching, to fellowship with other believers, to communion, and to prayer? An apostle can teach these matters but it is up to the believer to make it a steadfast longing in their own heart.

The final portion of this section says, **then** fear (reverence for the Lord) came over everyone, and wonders and signs were performed. First the converts bowed their hearts and were obedient and *then* signs and wonders were manifest. Are you willing to obey this pattern in your own life?

🙢"And the __apostles__ were giving testimony with __great__ power to the resurrection of the Lord Jesus, and great _____ was on all of them. For there was _____ a needy person among them, because all those who owned lands or houses sold them, brought the proceeds of the things that were sold, and laid them at the _____ _____. This was then _____ for each person's basic needs." (Acts 4:33-35)

The testimony of the resurrection of Jesus Christ given by a believer in full faith and assurance is powerful in its effect. They were being unified in the faith and of one accord. The result? There was no competition among the saints and each saw the other as an equal. What great grace indeed! That is nothing more than a move of the Spirit to break all dividing walls and cause impressed hearts to beat in time with one another!

🙢"Many _____ and _____ were being done among the people through the hands of the _____. By common

Charisma

consent they would all _____ in Solomon's Colonnade." (Acts 5:12)

This is in line with the above verse (Acts 2:42-43). The people agreed to fellowship and be in line with the apostles' teaching and signs and wonders were being manifest.

❧"But Peter and the *Apostles* replied, "We must *obey* God *rather* than men. The God of our fathers raised up Jesus, whom you had murdered by hanging Him on a tree. God exalted this man to His right hand as ruler and Savior, to grant repentance to Israel, and forgiveness of sins. We are witnesses of these things, and so is the Holy Spirit whom God has given to those who obey Him." (Acts 5:29-32)

Do you see this as an either or? Obey God or obey man ~ most times these things are in conflict. Have you experience this in your own life?

_____

The apostles were so convinced of the ministry the Lord had given them that even in the face of adversity they would not back down. They had already resolved to face their opposition and remain steadfast. Have you already resolved that when you are faced with opposition from man that you will obey God? If given the option to take the 'easy way out' and stop teaching the gospel message will you persist in it anyway knowing you serve the God of eternity? Decide in advance before you are put to the test.

❧"They had them stand before the _____ , who _____ and _____ their hands on them." (Acts 6:6)

This is the first mention of the apostles laying hands on people to pray. Jesus did this and therefore the apostles would no doubt follow suit. When these seven men were chosen for duty it did not happen casually but they were instructed to appear before the apostles in order for them to lay hands on them and pray. No matter what the duty is for which you have been called to minister to God's people you are richly qualified! Those He has called He has also equipped! We are not impoverished and the blessing we receive when those above us pray and lay hands on us is a blessing to be received by all.

❧"On that day a _____ _____ broke out against the church in Jerusalem, and all _____ the _____ were scattered throughout the land of Judea and Samaria." (Acts 81b)

Charisma

One thing truer than gold; God's purposes *will be* fulfilled in this earth. No contriving of man and no power of hell will *ever* stop the purposes of God. Not ever. Persecution broke out indeed and those that were to scatter, scattered. Those that were to say, stayed. God has been and still remains on His throne...at all times.

ε "The _____ Barnabas and Paul _____ their robes when they heard this and rushed into the crowd, _____: "Men! Why are you

doing these things? We are _____ also, with the same _____ as you, and we are _____ good news to you, that you should _____ from these worthless things to the _____ God, who made the heaven, the earth, the sea, and everything in them." (Acts 14:14-15)

Paul and Barnabas *love* Jesus and gave their lives to honor Him and bring Him glory. When Paul observed a man in Lystra who was unable to walk since birth demonstrate faith for healing, he spoke as the Spirit directed him and told the lame man to stand to his feet. The crowd observed the man as he jumped up and walked around and they proceeded to declare Paul and Barnabas must be gods. Paul and Barnabas would not have anyone rob God of His glory and were so distraught at the idea that they mourned by tearing their robes. Someone operating in the Spiritual gift of apostle will be certain to direct all glory to the living God that made the heavens and the earth.

ε "But after Paul and Barnabas had engaged them in _____ argument and debate, the _____ arranged for Paul and Barnabas and some others of them to go up to the _____ and elders in _____ concerning this _____." (Acts 15:2) "When they arrived at Jerusalem, they were _____ by the church, the _____, and the elders, and they reported all that God had done with them." (Acts 15:4) "Then the _____ and the elders assembled to consider this matter." (Acts 15:6)

The controversy was whether Gentile Christians must be circumcised and keep the law of Moses. Because an agreement could not be reached, Paul and Barnabas went to the elders in Jerusalem in order to convince the apostles there.

So why was there a controversy? There were two divisions of teaching. Apostles that taught the Jews or the circumcised and the apostles that taught the Gentiles or the uncircumcised. The apostolic council assembled to accommodate these differences while respecting the authority of the Mosaic law. What was the result?

Charisma

🕮 "As they traveled through the towns, they _____ the decisions reached by the _____ and elders at Jerusalem for them to observe. So the churches were _____ in the faith and _____ in number _____." (Acts 16:4-5)

Oh the power of being of one accord with believers! The apostles and elders reached a decision and that decision would be carried out in the Christian church. The churches were strengthened because they were all of one accord and believers were added! We fulfill the purposes of God when we have unity in the faith. If you operate in the Spiritual gift of apostle you will teach the foundational truth of the Gospel of Christ in such a way that the is unity in **truth**! This unity builds faith and confidence and stirs the hearts of non-believers.

🕮 "For I think God has displayed us, the _____, in last place, like men condemned to die: We have become a _____ to the world and to angels and to men." (1 Corinthians 4:9)

The Corinthians would understand this passage because they were familiar with the arena in which victims were used for the sport of entertainment. Paul also knew all trials were subject to God's ultimate control for His own sovereign purposes and used this sort of allusion several times. (1 Corinthians 9:26, 1 Timothy 6:12, 2 Timothy 4:7) In this imagery, the apostles (like the criminals brought in the arena for the last show of the day with no means of escape) were made a spectacle to the jeering crowd as they struggled in their trials against evil. (Hebrews 12:1, 10:33, Romans 8:36)

In the arena of Roman games, men were forced to cut one another to pieces and even the victor did not escape alive. It reminds me of the manner in which we can cut one another to pieces with our words for the soul purpose of being superior. No one who enters this arena comes out intact. (Galatians 5:15) Do we realize how many eyes are upon us when we enter the arena with prideful words? Do we think about how it effects our testimony? May God have mercy on us.

🕮 "Am I not _free_? Am I not an _Apostle_? Have I not seen Jesus our Lord? Are you not my work in the Lord? If I am not an _Apostle_ to others, at least I am to you, for you are the seal of my apostleship in the Lord." (1 Corinthians 9:1-2)

Those strong in faith are ready to deny their rights (freedoms in Christ) for the good of others. Paul is indicating that he has done this in service of those he aids as an apostle. Do we appreciate the service of others on our behalf or are we quick to judge their motives? If you operate in the Spiritual gift of apostle this will also be a consideration in your own life. Please read further (verses 3-23) for additional supplementation.

What stands out to you in the reading?______________________________

____

❧"And God has placed these in the __________...Are all __________? Are all prophets? Are all teachers? Do all do miracles?" (1 Corinthians 28a,29)

Our sovereign God is brilliant and uses wisdom when placing ministry gifts in the church (the congregation). Not all believers need to operate in every gift in the assembly but when we come together in one accord we minister to one another using the gifts He has entrusted to us.

❧"As for Titus, he is my partner and coworker ___serving___ you; as for our ___brothers___, they are the ___messengers___ of the churches, the glory of Christ. Therefore, show them ___proof___ before the churches of your ___love___ and of our boasting about you." (2 Corinthians 8:23-24)

Paul is exhorting the brethren to love the apostles (messengers) because of the work they do to serve the believers and Christ. The brothers were sent by the church to bring honor to Christ in their service. Do you know someone in ministry that because of their work all you could do was give audacious praise to God? (Galatians 1:24)

In this verse Paul has identified some as apostles of the churches (2 Corinthians 8:23) as opposed to apostles of Christ which seems to indicate there are different kinds of apostles. (Jude 1:17 as an example)

❧"But I will continue to do what I am doing, in order to deny the ✻opportunity of those who want an opportunity to be regarded just as our equals in what they boast about. For such people are __________ __________, deceitful workers, ___________ themselves as apostles of Christ. And no wonder! For _____________ disguises himself as an angel of ___________. So it is ______ great thing if his _____________ also ____________ themselves as servants of ______________. Their destiny will be according to their works." (2 Corinthians 11:12-15)

An apostle of Christ will speak from the brilliantly perfect foundation that Christ already laid down ~ nothing to add and nothing to take away! His work is flawlessly complete and there is no other perfection available on this planet that can be added.

Satan disguises himself as an angel of light. Therefore, there are false apostles that will disguise themselves as apostles of Christ. Satan's servant will disguise themselves as righteous and will lay down Satan's foundation which is cloaked as truth only in hopes of deceiving the elect.

God calls and sends apostles as He sees fit. Any type of teaching that suggest we need to restore order to bring about the Messiah's return to earth is false teaching; it does not line up with the Word. There is no amount of order we can restore that will usher in the return of Christ. When the Father tells Him to return He will return because it is completely in His hands.

&"The signs of an _____ were performed with great endurance among you — not only signs but also _____ and _____." (2 Corinthians 12:12)

&"Paul, an _____ — not from men or by man, but by Jesus Christ and God the Father who raised Him from the dead." (Galatians 1:1, see also 1 Corinthians 1:1, Ephesians 1:1, Colossians 1:1, 1 Timothy 1:1, 2:7, 2 Timothy 1:1, and Titus 1:1)

Paul is an exemplary example of what a person operating in the Spiritual gift of apostle would look like. Read his books for further insight if you possess this gift.

&"So then you are no longer foreigners and strangers, but fellow citizens with the saints, and members of God's household, built on the _____ of the _____ and prophets, with Christ Jesus Himself as the _____. The whole building, being put together by Him, grows into a _____ sanctuary in the Lord. _____ also are being built together for God's _____ in the Spirit." (Ephesians 2:19-22)

The gospel message is the foundational work that is spread by apostles with nothing added and nothing deleted. The divine purpose of the apostle is to go out and equip Christ's church with right doctrine. This right doctrine the gospel message of Jesus Christ. "For no one can lay any other foundation than what has been laid down. That foundation is Jesus Christ." (1 Corinthians 3:11)

Charisma

🕮 "This was not made known to people in other generations as it is now revealed to His holy _____ and prophets by the Spirit: The Gentiles are co-heirs, members of the same body, and partners of the promise in Christ Jesus through the gospel." (Ephesians 3:5-6)

The apostles assignment is the equip the church with right doctrine.

🕮 "And He personally gave some to be _____, some prophets, some evangelists, some pastors and teachers, for the training of the saints in the work of _____, to build up the body of Christ, until we all reach _____ in the _____ and in the knowledge of God's Son, _____ into a mature man with a stature measured by Christ's fullness. Then we will no longer be little children, _____ by the waves and blown around by every _____ of teaching, by _____ cunning with cleverness in the techniques of deceit." (Ephesians 4:11-14)

As you have probably noticed, this verse is repeated multiple times throughout this study. The reason is because it is extremely profitable to understand why God gave people with these gifts to the church. ==Someone operating in the Spiritual gift of apostle will have has their goal: 1) training of the saints in the work of ministry, 2) building up the body of Christ until we all reach unity in the faith and knowledge of Jesus, and 3) mature growth which is measured by Christ's fullness.== Thank you Lord.

🕮 "But I considered it necessary to send you _____ — my brother, coworker, and fellow soldier, as well as your _____ and minister to my need." (Philippians 2:25)

Here is another example of someone serving as an apostle. The word messenger here is the Greek word translated elsewhere as apostle.

🕮 "Although we could have been a _____ as Christ's _____, instead we were _____ among you, as a nursing mother _____ her own children." (1 Thessalonians 2:7)

People are drawn and receive much easier the gospel message when communicated with gentleness, compassion, and love. These seeds we plant may not take root immediately but will be remembered and revisited fondly by those who have an ear to hear. It is our duty and privilege to do nothing less. What an honor to live by such a great and holy calling!

As apostles of Christ, Paul thought they were appropriate to make requests from those they served but chose instead not to be a burden to them. Believers, let's think deeply about how we allocate our resources. How do you value those that lead you in the truth?

🕯"Therefore, holy brothers and _____ in a heavenly _____, consider Jesus, the _____ and high priest of our confession; He was _____ to the One who appointed Him, just as Moses was in all God's household. For Jesus is considered worthy of more glory than Moses, just as the builder has more honor than the house." (Hebrews 3:1-3)

If you have accepted Christ Jesus, you belong to His household of faith and are companions with other 'pillars' in the faith that have gone before you ~ you have a heavenly calling! Jesus was the first apostle and remained faithful to the One who appointed Him. If you operate in the Spiritual gift of apostle look to Jesus as your ultimate teacher and leader and remain faithful! In all our trials, in all our unanswered questions, in all our desperate darkest hours, faith *must* remain. Faith...must...remain because you have a extraordinarily responsible mission.

The following verses relate to scoffers in the last days:

🕯"I want to _____ a genuine _____ with a reminder, so that you can _____ the _____ previously spoken by the holy prophets and the _____ of our Lord and Savior given through your _____." (2 Peter 3:1b-2)

The Word of God is powerful. It is has the mind blowing power to miraculously transform us to resemble Christ. (1 Corinthians 2:16) Christians cleansed minds are to be repeatedly stirred up so that they are effective and energetic in the work of sanctification.

In the last days we expect to see false teachers and apostles as well as scoffers. What will they scoff? They will ridicule the salvation offered through Jesus Christ, minimize sin, and belittle our faith. Strengthen us Lord.

🕯"But you, dear friends, _____ what was predicted by the _____ of our Lord Jesus Christ; they told you, In the end time there _____ be _____ walking according to their own ungodly _____. These people _____ divisions and are unbelievers, not having the Spirit." (Jude 1:17-19)

The specific form of mockery is not stated but could also include Jesus' delay in His second coming or His not returning at all. Have you experienced a scoffer? Please share:

_____

Charisma

ᛞ"I know your works, your labor, and your endurance, and that you cannot tolerate evil. You have _____ those who call themselves _____ and are not, and you have found them to be _____." (Revelation 2:2)

You are Divinely Inspired and Victoriously Anointed. Through prayer and the Word you are continually being sanctified and equipped with the mind of Christ. We must have discernment to test those who call themselves apostles. This in no way means we are justified to have a critical spirit! We must know the Word in order to determine if what is being taught lines up with the Word. If it does not, it is to be dismissed. Check out what Jesus says in Acts (below) for additional insight.

"Be on guard for yourselves and for all the flock that the Holy Spirit has appointed you to as overseers, to shepherd the church of God, which He purchased with His own blood. I know that after my departure savage wolves will come in among you, not sparing the flock. And men will rise up from your own number with deviant doctrines to lure the disciples into following them. Therefore be on the alert, remembering that night and day for three years I did not stop warning each one of you with tears." (Acts 20:28-31)

ᛞ"Rejoice over her, heaven, and you saints, _____, and prophets, because God has executed your judgment on her!" (Revelation 18:20)

Who will rejoice? Heaven, the saints, the apostles, and the prophets ~ all those that belong to the Lord! The fall of Babylon was orchestrated by an act of God's sovereign justice. The destruction of nations should serve as a warning to us not take on their acts of unholiness. God will avenge His people by executing judgment on the unrighteous because of their treatment of His saints who desire only to promote the cause of Christ.

Prayer

By Your power and strength I will never desire to know Your miracles more than I desire to know the Miracle worker. I am able to bring truth to Your people in such a way that equips and edifies them for victorious ministry work by the assistance of Your Spirit alone! I desire to be Your gentle and compassionate messenger, speaking the foundational gospel message that has been declared on the pages of Scripture. Your word says we should strive to have unity in truth with the Spirit. There is power in being of one accord with believers! Increase my faith and enable this to occur within my church. Fill me to overflowing with Your Spirit as my desire is to stir the hearts of non-believers and lead them to You. In Jesus name amen.

Prophets, God's Reformers

The aim of a prophetic ministry is to turn believer's hearts toward matters that concern God's heart. The prophet will seek to bring about reformation in the believer. The Spiritual gift of prophet is best defined as one who speaks for another. This is a person who delivers messages God has shared with him for the building up of His church. A prophet is a minister who can teach with an anointing and has been in ministry for some years. The Messiah personally gave prophets to His church so that the saints could develop and form habits in the work of ministry and to build up the body of Christ for acts of service. This is to be continued until we all reach unity in the faith and unity in the knowledge of God's Son. The aim is to grow into mature people with our never ending growth to be measured by Christ's fullness. (Ephesians 4:11-13)

Zechariah was a prophet and he spoke a prophecy over his son John saying, "And child, you will be called a prophet of the Most High, for you will go before the Lord to prepare His ways, to give His people knowledge of salvation through the forgiveness of their sins." (Luke 1:76-77)

John the Baptist was a prophet and he gave the Lord's people knowledge of salvation through the forgiveness of their sins. Teaching people in this way does not make one a prophet but this is foundational teaching for a prophet.

Prophet Examples

God sent **prophets** to help His people (Luke 7:16, 16:29, 16:31, 24:25, John 8:52, Acts 11:27, 13:15, 13:40, 26:22, Hebrews 1:1, Revelation 10:7) and **prophets** remained in the church after Jesus' death (Acts 13:1, 15:32, 21:10). The Lord spoke to people through **prophets** (Matthew 1:22, 2:17, 2:23, 4:14, 12:17, 13:35, 21:4, 26:56, 27:9, Luke 18:31, Acts 3:18) and His words were fulfilled. Unfortunately, people do not always accept **prophets** (Acts 7:52, 13:27, Romans 11:3). Jesus was a **prophet** (Matthew 13:57, 16:14,

21:11, 21:46 Mark 6:4, 8:28, Luke 4:24, 7:39, 13:33, 24:19, John 4:19, 6:14, 7:52, 9:17) and He came to fulfill the law and the **prophets** (Matthew 5:17). The **prophets** of old longed to see and hear the works of Jesus (Matthew 13:17, Luke 10:24). John the Baptist was a **prophet** (Matthew 11:9, 14:5, 21:26, Mark 6:15, 11:32, Luke 1:76, 20:6, John 1:23) David was a **prophet** (Acts 2:30) and Anna was a **prophet** as well (Luke 2:36-38). In meetings, only 2 or 3 **prophets** should speak and the rest should evaluate spiritually what is being said (1 Corinthians 14:29). **Prophets** can not find honor in their household or hometown (Matthew 13:57, Mark 6:4, Luke 4:24, John 4:44). Thanks be to God that He will avenge the blood of His **prophets** (Revelation 16:6, 18:20, 18:24)!

Besides Jesus, John the Baptist is an example of a New Testament prophet whose prophetic ministry was driven by the desire for people to radically transition from their old ways towards the marvelous things of God. Prophets are sent by God to revive the hearts of His people and to align them with His truth.

Listen to John's love for Messiah as he speaks, "He who has the bride is the _____. But the groom's _____, who stands by and listens for him, rejoices _____ at the groom's _____. So this _____ of mine is _____." (John 3:29)

The groom is the Messiah and the bride is the church. John saw his role as one preparing the heart of the bride to receive their groom. As John hears the voice of the groom approaching, the fulfillment of his much awaited expectation draws near to him and his joy is made complete!

If someone is operating in the Spiritual gift of prophet, their goal is to train the body of Christ for a work in ministry by edifying them in truth. This must continue until the church is unified in faith and filled in knowledge of God's son. You could say this is the job description of the prophet. The message of God given by the prophet even though it is given to many, will be received as a personal and sobering directive. A prophet will be found teaching words of warning as well as the value of repentance in the life of a believer. God's prophet will know through God's love poured out in him that they must commit to walking a narrower path than others. They therefore will be brokenhearted when they become aware of personal mistakes. A person operating in the Spiritual gift of prophet is different than someone operating in the gift of prophecy. Just because someone gives a prophecy does not make them a prophet.

Charisma

A prophet typically works within a local congregation. Whereas an apostle usually has a broader ministry as demonstrated by its Greek word apostolos meaning, 'one sent on a mission'. (biblehub.com)

Paul stated in 1 Corinthians 14:37, "If anyone thinks he is a _prophet_ or _spiritually gifted_, he should recognize that what I write to you is the Lord's command."

The apostle is not speaking to the pride and arrogance of false prophets in determining whether what he speaks is truly right. When we receive Jesus as Savior we also receive His Spirit. Some people are content to stop there and they remain babes in Christ. (Hebrews 5:13) Paul is saying it is harder for the inexperienced (or babe) to evaluate if what he is saying is from the Lord if that person has not been trained; therefore not having the skill needed to evaluate. Someone spiritual is not inexperienced but has knowledge of spiritual things. They are able to recognize their endowment of Spiritual gifts and is not indifferent to them. Therefore, if someone is a prophet or if someone is spiritual let them evaluate and recognize that the things written come from the Lord.

"Two or three _prophets_ should speak, and the others should evaluate. But if something has been revealed to another person sitting there, the first _prophet_ should be _quiet_. For you can all prophesy one by one, so that everyone may learn and everyone may be encouraged. And the prophets' spirits are under the _control_ of the prophets, since God is not a God of _disorder_ but of peace." (1 Corinthians 14:29-33)

I can not type this loud enough...God is not One of disorder! We MUST be able to discern what is from God and what is counterfeit. The Spirit does not manifest Himself and cause disorder, confusion, or humiliation. It will not happen. If there appears to be a spiritual manifestation and disorder, confusion, or humiliation occurs this is your warning flag. There is no need to be alarmed or frightened. We should not be amazed when a wicked spirit manifest. Don't we know they exist? With God comes honor and peace ~ not an odd freak show.

If God brings a message for a prophet to speak (even more than one) it is to bring repentance and edification. The spiritual person should evaluate and make certain it lines up with the Word.

Jeremiah was an Old Testament prophet and his divine appointment was "to _uproot_ and tear down, to _destroy_ and demolish, to _build_ and plant." (Jeremiah 1:10)

For some nations Jeremiah was to uproot, tear down (tear in pieces), destroy, and overthrow and for others he was to build up and plant. As prophet he was called to warn not only the Jewish people but all that had an ear to hear! Prophets who have messages to deliver from God must be strong and courageous in the Lord; to fear Him more than fear the wrath of man. ==Pray for prophets. They will be more aligned with God than with ANY man and thus subject to loneliness and condemnation (from man).==

God speaks to His prophets. ❧"Listen to what I say: If there is a _prophet_ among you from the Lord, I make Myself _known_ to him in a _vision_; I speak with him in a _dream_." (Number 12:6)

We are accustomed to seeing the world through fleshly eyes and human experiences. If you are a prophet of God, His ways will be represented to your mind. (Genesis 15:1, 28:12, 46:2, Daniel 8:18, 10:8) God's presentation of His ways can be received either through a vision when you are awake or a dream during your sleep.

Can you imagine having God's ways represented to your mind? What a blessing. The way you are accustomed to seeing things through your human experience is suddenly overtaken by the power of God and you see or hear is His aim. ==The intent is not that we marvel that God invaded the prophets mind and soul but that He intends for His people to *receive* instruction and to *act* on it.==

In the last days Joel 2:28 tells us, ❧"After this I will _pour_ _out_ My Spirit on all humanity; then your sons and your daughters will prophesy, your old men will have _dreams_, and your young men will see _visions_."

We should expect to hear from God's prophets!

Characteristics of Prophets

✳ Have an ear adapted to the voice of God ✳
✳ Motivated for God's presence more than approval of man ✳
✳ Deliver words of encouragement ✳
✳ Motivates others towards repentance ✳
✳ Equips the church with right doctrine ✳
✳ Intercessor ✳
✳ Edification through love ✳
Teachable

People have been accused of killing the prophets because their flesh does not care to hear and agree with what the Spirit says.

🕮 "Woe to you, scribes and _Pharisees_, hypocrites! You build the tombs of the prophets and decorate the monuments of the righteous, and you say, If we had lived in the days of our fathers, we wouldn't have taken part with them in shedding the _prophets_' blood. You, therefore, testify against yourselves that you are sons of those who murdered the prophets. Fill up, then, the measure of your fathers' sins! Snakes! Brood of vipers! How can you escape being condemned to hell?, This is why I am sending you _prophets_, sages, and scribes. Some of them you will kill and crucify, and some of them you will flog in your synagogues and hound from town to town." (Matthew 23:29-34)

Even though Jesus was speaking specifically to people in His time that does not mean we are immune from behaving the same way in this generation. Let's not be hypocrites. If God sends us a prophet, let's already decide to listen and not condemn because our flesh does not care to hear or agree. God forbid. (This does not mean we do not discern who is a prophet and who is not.)

🕮 "Jerusalem, Jerusalem! She who kills the _prophets_ and stones those who are _sent_ to her. How often I wanted to gather your children together, as a hen gathers her chicks under her wings, yet you were not willing! (Matthew 23:37, Luke 13:34)

🕮 "Woe to you! You build monuments to the _prophets_, and your fathers killed them. Therefore, you are witnesses that you approve, the deeds of your fathers, for they killed them, and you build their monuments. (Luke 11:47-48 similar to Matthew 23)

The word monuments signifies a tomb or grave.

Prophets have told us:

🕮 "However, the Most High does not dwell in sanctuaries made with hands, as the _prophet_ says: Heaven is My throne, and earth My footstool. What sort of house will you build for Me? says the Lord, or what is My resting place? Did not My hand make all these things?" (Acts 7:48-50)

🕮 "Now all this took place to fulfill what was spoken by the Lord _through_ _the_ _prophet_: See, the virgin will become pregnant and give birth to a son, and they will name Him Immanuel, which is translated "God is with us." (Matthew 1:22-23)

☙"He stayed there until Herod's death, so that what was spoken by the Lord __through__ __the__ __prophet__ might be fulfilled: Out of Egypt I called My Son." (Matthew 2:15)

☙"Therefore, whatever you want others to do for you, do also the same for them — this is the Law and the __prophets__." (Matthew 7:12)

☙"When evening came, they brought to Him many who were demon-possessed. He drove out the spirits with a word and healed all who were sick, so that what was spoken __through__ __the__ __prophet__ Isaiah might be fulfilled: He Himself took our weaknesses and carried our diseases." (Matthew 8:16-17)

☙"So when you see the abomination that causes desolation, spoken of by the __prophet__ Daniel, standing in the holy place" (let the reader understand), "then those in Judea must flee to the mountains!" (Matthew 24:15 To read more of this warning read through verse 28.)

☙"Then what was spoken through the __prophet__ Jeremiah was fulfilled: They took the 30 pieces of silver, the price of Him whose price was set by the Israelites, and they gave them for the potter's field, as the Lord directed me." (Matthew 27:9-10)

☙"Concerning this salvation, the __prophets__ who __spoke__ about the grace that would come to you searched and carefully investigated. They inquired into what time or what circumstances the Spirit of Christ within them was indicating when He testified in advance to the messianic sufferings, and the glories that would follow." (1 Peter 1:10-11)

Note: This is only a sampling of things Scripture reveals regarding what prophets have told us. Anything Jesus said would fit under this category. The verses included here are because they are introduced with something like "spoken by the prophet" or the 'prophet said". This is by no means exhaustive.

False Prophets:

When there are true prophets of God than we can expect false prophets of Satan because he tries to mimic what God does in order to serve his own unholy ends. False prophets cleverly make you question the authority of Scripture as well as arrogantly dispute the inerrancy of the Word. Salvation is not taught to be a gift given through Christ alone but achieved through works. Another sort of false teaching deals with joining a particular group, religious or not, in order to receive salvation. This also is an erroneous doctrine.

• "If a __prophet__ or someone who has __dreams__ arises among you and proclaims a sign or wonder to you, and that sign or wonder he has promised you comes about, __and__ he says, 'Let us follow other gods,' which you have not known, 'and let us worship them,' do not __listen__ to that prophet's words or to that dreamer. For the Lord your God is __testing__ __you__ to know whether you __love__ the Lord your God with all your heart and all your soul. You must __follow__ the Lord your God and fear _____. You must __obey__ His commands and _____ to His voice; you must worship Him and __hold__ __fast__ to Him." (Deuteronomy 13:1-4)

• "As for the __prophet__ who prophesies peace — only when the word of the prophet comes __true__ will the prophet be recognized as one the Lord has __truly__ sent." (Jeremiah 28:9)

• "Your __prophets__ saw visions for you that were __false__ and __worthless__; they did not reveal your __sin__ and so __captured__ your fortunes. They saw oracles for you that were __false__ and __misleading__." (Lamentations 2:14)

These false prophets did not uncover the people's iniquity but instead said many extremely foolish things. They paint false pictures of denial and fill people with false hope. No one can be saved from exile when their sin is not pointed out.

• "__Beware__ of __false__ prophets who come to you in sheep's clothing but inwardly are ravaging wolves. You'll recognize them by their fruit. Are grapes gathered from thorn bushes or figs from thistles? In the same way, every good tree produces good fruit, but a bad tree produces bad fruit. A good tree can't produce bad fruit; neither can a bad tree produce good fruit." (Matthew 7:15-18)

• "False messiahs and false __prophets__ will __appear__ and perform great __signs__ and __miracles__ to lead astray, if possible, __even__ the elect. Take note: I have told you __ahead of time__." (Matthew 24:24-25)

Charisma

☙"Woe to you when __all__ people speak well of you, for this is the way their ancestors used to treat the __false__ prophets." (Luke 6:26)

==When someone is speaking God's word, it will not appeal to everyone. People seem to be much more willing to give praise to the one that builds up their hearts as opposed to confronting their sin nature.==

☙"When they had gone through the whole island as far as Paphos, they came across a sorcerer, a Jewish false __prophet__ named Bar-Jesus. He was with the proconsul, Sergius Paulus, an intelligent man. This man summoned Barnabas and Saul and desired to hear God's message. But Elymas the sorcerer (this is the meaning of his name) opposed them and tried to turn the proconsul away from the faith. Then Saul — also called Paul — __filled__ with the Holy Spirit, stared straight at the sorcerer and said, "You son of the Devil, full of all deceit and all fraud, enemy of all righteousness! Won't you ever stop perverting the straight paths of the Lord? Now, look! The Lord's hand is against you. You are going to be blind, and will not see the sun for a time. Suddenly a mist and darkness fell on him, and he went around seeking someone to lead him by the hand." (Acts 13:6-11)

☙"Then I saw three unclean spirits like frogs coming from the dragon's mouth, from the beast's mouth, and from the mouth of the __false__ __prophet__. For they are spirits of __demons__ performing signs, who __go out__ to the kings of the __whole__ world to __gather__ them for the battle of the great day of God, the Almighty." (Revelation 16:13-14)

☙"But the beast was taken prisoner, and along with him the false __prophet__, who had performed the signs in his presence. He deceived those who accepted the mark of the beast and those who worshiped his image with these signs. Both of them were thrown alive into the lake of fire that burns with sulfur." (Revelation 19:20)

☙"The Devil who deceived them was thrown into the lake of fire and sulfur where the beast and the false __prophet__ are, and they will be tormented day and night forever and ever." (Revelation 20:10)

Prayer

Assist me Lord to be profoundly effective in turning believer's hearts toward things that concern you and to things you love. Empower me to speak in ways that bring reformation to every person that has an ear to hear. Strengthen me to deliver Your powerful message with an anointing that sets fire to the hearts of Your believers so they are prompted to minister to You in ways You desire. I long for Your presence more than I pine for the approval of man. Equip me with a passion to communicate Your message which in turn sparks people to radically transition from their old ways toward Your marvelously distinctive ways. I ask to revive hearts and align them with the truth of the Message by the magnificent unsurprising power of Jesus Christ of Nazareth. Amen.

The Evangelist ~ Bringing People to Christ

"Everything is from God, who reconciled us to Himself through Christ and gave us the ministry of reconciliation: That is, in Christ, God was reconciling the world to Himself, not counting their trespasses against them, and He has committed the message of reconciliation to us. Therefore, we are ambassadors for Christ, certain that God is appealing through us. We plead on Christ's behalf, "Be reconciled to God." (2 Corinthians 5:18-20)

As Christians, Christ's ministry of reconciliation has been committed to us! Whether or not you operate in the Spiritual gift of an evangelist, we are *all* given the ministry of reconciliation to share with a lost world. This truth we share is the compelling message of good news and how hearing the gospel has the power to change people!

Another example of this is found in Matthew 28:18-20. "Then Jesus came near and said to them, "All authority has been given to Me in heaven and on earth. Go, therefore, and make disciples of all nations, baptizing them in the name of the Father and of the Son and of the Holy Spirit, teaching them to observe everything I have commanded you. And remember, I am with you always, to the end of the age." So all Christians are equipped to evangelize and this is done by the many varied ways we serve as a witness for the cause of Christ.

As with any Spiritual gift, some are given an extra ability through faith to be profoundly effective in bringing people to Christ. Evangelism is the obvious first step before any work of teaching or other type of discipleship can begin.

Someone operating in the Spiritual gift of evangelism (euaggelistēs) will go beyond just sharing faith stories as a method of evangelizing but will preach the gospel with a zeal, with an ability to tailor their message to specific individuals, and will have the willingness to arrange their schedules in order to make themselves available to have an opportunity to bring someone to Christ. The Spiritual gift to evangelize will come with an additional portion of faith, influence, and skill in the ability to know what, when, and how to say just the right thing that will awaken someone to their need of Christ. Some might say this is one of the easiest gifts to spot because the gifted person is very focused on the urgency for others to be saved. There are many solid evangelist you can read about to study their individual successful styles. A great one to start with is Billy Graham.

Please open your Bible and prayerfully consider these verses as you complete the following blanks:

"The next day we left and came to Caesarea, where we entered the house of _____ the _____, who was one of the Seven, and stayed with him." (Act 21:8)

Philip is a New Testament example of an evangelist. Please read Acts 8:26-40.

Who spoke to Philip and also told him to join the chariot?
_____

What 2 questions did the eunuch ask Philip?
_____
_____

What can you say in summary about Philip from this passage? How did he use his gift of evangelism?
_____

Peter is also an example of a New Testament evangelist. Please read Acts 2:14-42.

How would you describe the way Peter evangelized the crowd?
_____

What techniques did he use?
_____

What was the end result in both of these examples?
_____

In the example of Philip and Peter they both needed to be well familiar with the Gospel message. If you operate in the Spiritual gift of evangelism you too will be very comfortable reciting and conversing about the life of Jesus, His ministry, crucification, and rising from the dead. As you think through these topics you will become aware of how you can communicate about Jesus and speak of His saving grace to many different types of people and in their specific walk of life in order to make it profoundly impactful to them.

❧"And He personally gave some to be apostles, some prophets, some ________________, some pastors and teachers, for the training of the saints in the work of ministry, to build up the body of Christ, until we all reach unity in the faith and in the knowledge of God's Son, growing into a mature man with a stature measured by Christ's fullness. Then we will no longer be little children, tossed by the waves and blown around by every wind of teaching, by human cunning with cleverness in the techniques of deceit." Ephesians 4:11-14

I absolutely love how informative these verses are. Here we have instruction regarding the purpose of apostles, prophets, evangelist, pastors, and teachers. We are to train the saints in the work of ministry and build up the body of Christ UNTIL we ALL reach unity in the faith and in the knowledge of God's Son. We are to be mature and the plumb line is Jesus Christ. We are also to have faith, to stand strong, and to not be deceived. Amen!

❧"But as for you, be serious about everything, endure hardship, do the work of an ________________, fulfill your ministry." 2 Timothy 4:5

If you operate in the Spiritual gift of evangelism be serious, endure hardship, stand firm, and don't give up. Fulfill your ministry. This is a message really for all! Is your gifting important enough to you that one of the things you do when you wake up is to plan how you will fulfill your ministry for the day? That really is not an unachievable goal. Live intentionally and you will fulfill your ministry the Lord has laid before you precious feet.

Characteristics:

❊ Have a burden for the lost ❊

❊ Speaks the plan of salvation with clarity, conviction ❊

❊ Creatively speaks the salvation message ❊

✻ Adept at modifying their message based on the audience ✻
✻ Builds relationships with unbelievers ✻
✻ Can witness to strangers ✻
✻ Can overlook fear of rejection ✻
✻ Speak of faith to people everywhere they go ✻

What to watch out for:

✻ Frustration when others don't seem to witness to strangers like you do
✻ Just because a 'televangelist' makes a mockery of Christian faith or Spiritual gifts this should not hinder your gifting and impact
✻ Thinking you are doing 'the most important work' with evangelism ~ it is only a temptation of pride
✻ Critiquing others work
✻ Be part of a ministry group ~ don't think you should go it alone.
✻ Make every effort to be spiritually mature ~ as you plant seeds in non-believers they are also watching you as they learn.
✻ Being around nonbelievers means you could be influenced by behavior you are trying to avoid. Therefore, maintain self control and your personal relationship with Jesus.
✻ As a Christ follower, *you* be the influencer.

Prayer

Thank you Lord for the amazing impact evangelist have had on individuals lives. We need them in our communities. Empower me to be bold and fearless in the face of opposition. Provide opportunities for me and equip me with knowledge and discernment to know just what to say to an unbeliever that will direct them to You for salvation. I welcome those you have given the Spiritual gift of evangelism to and I will do my part to evangelize those I am honored to come into contact with. I desire to maintain my spiritual disciplines so that I can be a faithful witness to you at all times. All glory and honor is yours. Empower me by the faithful name of Jesus. Amen.

The Shepherding Role of Pastor

The Greek word poimēn is translated in many versions of the Bible as 'pastor' and has the meaning of shepherding. The shepherding ministry should always make its goal leading people to Jesus as the chief Shepherd (1 Peter 5:4) or the head of the church. God personally gave pastors (used as a *noun* and defined as shepherds, Eph. 4:11) to train the saints in the work of ministry and to build up the body of Christ for unity in the faith and in the knowledge of Jesus. (Ephesians 4:12-13) Shepherding is also used as a *verb* in 1 Peter 5:2 to describe how shepherding should be done. Within the definition of the word shepherd (poimainō) we find an explanation of what shepherding as a verb looks like (Strongs biblehub.com). The shepherd 'guards and guides' God's flock. In John 21:18 Jesus even tells Peter that His sheep need to be fed. (John 21:17) The Spiritual gift of pastor is also associated with the gift of teaching.

Many in the church may find themselves taking part in the shepherding ministry. This includes the pastor, elders, small group leaders, teachers, and so forth. The purpose of the shepherding ministry in all of these roles is to guide Jesus' sheep in becoming more like Him.

Peter calls Jesus the chief Shepherd (1 Peter 5:4) and Paul calls him the great Shepherd (Hebrews 13:20). Jesus even informs us He is a good shepherd (John 10:11). Jesus was willing to sacrifice himself in order for his sheep to thrive, being built up by his loving care. Someone operating in the Spiritual gift of the shepherding ministry (pastor) will following the example of the chief Shepherd.

If shepherding entails guarding, guiding, and feeding God's sheep what would some solid examples of this marvelous gift look like?

How about guiding the sheep regarding what is needed in the world such as discernment?

"And I pray this: that your love will keep on growing in knowledge and every kind of discernment, so that you can approve the things that are superior and can be pure and blameless in the day of Christ." (Philippians 1:9-10)

"Dear friends, do not believe every spirit, but test the spirits to determine if they are from God, because many false prophets have gone out into the world. This is how you know the Spirit of God: Every spirit who confesses that Jesus Christ has come in the flesh is from God. But every spirit who does not confess Jesus is not from God. This is the spirit of the antichrist; you have heard that he is coming, and he is already in the world now." (1 John 4:1-3)

How about guiding the sheep regarding how to be equipped for spiritual warfare and the hazards of Satan?

"Finally, be strengthened by the Lord and by His vast strength. Put on the full armor of God so that you can stand against the tactics of the Devil. For our battle is not against flesh and blood, but against the rulers, against the authorities, against the world powers of this darkness, against the spiritual forces of evil in the heavens. This is why you must take up the full armor of God, so that you may be able to resist in the evil day, and having prepared everything, to take your stand. Stand, therefore, with truth like a belt around your waist, righteousness like armor on your chest, and your feet sandaled with readiness for the gospel of peace. In every situation take the shield of faith, and with it you will be able to extinguish all the flaming arrows of the evil one. Take the helmet of salvation, and the sword of the Spirit, which is God's word. Pray at all times in the Spirit with every prayer and request, and stay alert in this with all perseverance and intercession for all the saints." (Ephesians 6:10-18)

How about the necessary nourishment that is critical for a victorious life?

"But He answered, "It is written: Man must not live on bread alone but on every word that comes from the mouth of God." (Matthew 4:4)

"Let the message about the Messiah dwell richly among you, teaching and admonishing one another in all wisdom, and singing psalms, hymns, and spiritual songs, with gratitude in your hearts to God. And whatever you do, in word or in deed, do everything in the name of the Lord Jesus, giving thanks to God the Father through Him." (Colossians 3:16-17)

Let's take a look at 1 Peter 5:1-4 and break down the instructions Paul gave the elders (name of an appointed office of those who were chosen to feed and oversee the flock of Christ) in regards to shepherding God's sheep. Paul exhorted these elders to:

(1) Shepherd God's flock that was entrusted to them
(2) Watch over it willingly, not grudgingly
(3) Not shepherd for what you get out of it but because you are eager to serve God.
(4) Not exercise control over those entrusted to you, but be an example to the flock. When the chief Shepherd appears, you will receive the unfading crown of glory. (A person in this position is responsible to the chief Shepherd)

The Psalm below illustrates what a well guided, well guarded, and well fed flock looks like. Beloved, this flock is led by the Good Shepherd but let's follow this positively divine example and move out in the agape love that flows freely from Him so that we can operate full-throttle in the shepherding ministry He has purposed.

The Good Shepherd
Psalm 23

The Lord is my shepherd;
there is nothing I lack.
He lets me lie down in green pastures;
He leads me beside quiet waters.
He renews my life;
He leads me along the right paths
for His name's sake.
Even when I go through the darkest valley,
I fear no danger,
for You are with me;
Your rod and Your staff — they comfort me.
You prepare a table before me
in the presence of my enemies;
You anoint my head with oil;
my cup overflows.
Only goodness and faithful love will pursue me
all the days of my life,
and I will dwell in the house of the Lord
as long as I live.

Jesus "protects His flock like a shepherd; He gathers the lambs in His arms and carries them in the folds of His garment. He gently leads those that are nursing." (Isaiah 40:11)

🕮"When He saw the crowds, He felt _____ for them, because they were weary and worn out, like _____ without a _____. Then He said to His disciples, "The harvest is abundant, but the workers are few. Therefore, pray to the Lord of the harvest to send out workers into His harvest." (Matthew 9:36-38)

Do you know Jesus' love for you? I pray you do. Jesus Himself saw the crowds; the crowds He continuously ministered to, and He felt compassion for them. It does not state that He felt wearied or annoyed when He saw them. He felt compassion. That is our Jesus. That is who our heat beats for. He sees us when we are weary and worn out. He desires to shepherd us and lead us into His peace and comfort. Are there any fitting words that express a heart that is thankful for this? I cannot find them but I know when we are in that place He does not need our words but sees the adoration our heart has towards Him. If you are operating in the Spiritual gift of pastor or shepherd this is how you will look upon the sheep that have been entrusted to your care.

This verse implies we will not be weary and worn out if we listen to our shepherd who is operating full-throttle in their Spiritual gifting because they will keep us away from folly that causes us to be weary and worn out (if we listen and stay close). I think it is interesting to expand on the word 'weary' and see the word 'harassed'; to expand on the word 'worn out' and see the word 'thrown aside in haste'. Do you know that your enemy will harass you whenever he gets the chance and then throw you aside without any care where you end up when your use to him is drained? Stick close to the Shepherd because He treats you with compassion. Thank you Lord.

The Lord intends for us to have a shepherd.

A shepherd that will go out and come back in before us. (Numbers 27:17)

The Lord spoke out against shepherds that did not feed and tend His flock. His complaint was that they did not strengthen the weak, heal the sick, bandage the injured, search, seek, and bring back the strays and lost. Instead the shepherds ruled over them with violence and cruelty. Because the sheep were scattered due to the lack of good shepherds they became prey. (Ezekiel 34)

Again, the Lord spoke about what happens when the sheep have no shepherd. "For the idols speak falsehood, and the diviners see illusions; they relate empty dreams and offer empty comfort. Therefore the people wander like sheep; they suffer affliction because there is no shepherd." (Zechariah 10:2)

🙢"All the nations, will be gathered before Him, and He will _____ them one from another, just as a shepherd separates the sheep from the goats. He will put the _____ on His _____ and the goats on the _____. Then the King will say to those on His _____, "Come, you who are blessed by My Father, inherit the kingdom prepared for you from the foundation of the world." (Matthew 25:32-34)

It is the Shepherd's job to determine the sheep from the goats. Even though the sheep and goats may mingle during the day and separate at night. The sheep are usually referred to as the righteous and the goats referred to as the wicked. The Shepherd will soon make distinctions between those that are His and those that are not. There are even distinctions that will be made within the Church.

🙢"Then Jesus said to them, "Tonight all of you will run away because of Me, for it is written: I will strike the _____, and the sheep of the flock will be scattered. But after I have been _____, I will go ahead of you to Galilee." (Matthew 26:31-32 Also found in Mark 14:27)

When your shepherd is struck down at the hand of the enemy do you scatter because of fear and doubt or do you remain together knowing you will be stronger together than you will be individually? When Jesus was brought to death on the cross God brought the disciples together again so that when Jesus returned He found them all together in the same place. We should not be surprised if the enemy is after our shepherd. He knows that sheep are prone to scatter if there is no shepherd. Pray for shepherds! They need wisdom, endurance, peace, discernment, knowledge....

Jesus told his disciples that after His resurrection he would "go ahead" of them to Galilee. It reminds me of Moses asking the LORD to appoint a shepherd "who will go out before them" (Numbers 27:17) to guide them and the LORD appointed the One that would do just that.

🙢"So as He stepped ashore, He saw a _____ _____ and had compassion on them, because they were like sheep without a shepherd. Then He began to teach them many things." (Mark 6:34)

With a melted heart I read again that Jesus has compassion when He saw the crowd. I tell you fellow believer, I need that compassion how about you? The crowd was behaving like sheep without a shepherd. Since we are told Jesus began teaching them many things I have to wonder if what He saw was a crowd of harassed looking people that had no one to build them up in truth and they felt downcast and full of despair. Can you imagine how their sorrow turned to joy as Jesus began teaching them just the thing they need to hear to reverse their state of mind? Praise God!

🙵"In the same region, _____ were staying out in the fields and _____ _____ at night over their flock." (Luke 2:8)

Shepherds are self-sacrificing, remaining in the fields tending their flocks through the night watches. Shepherds pray for the flock they have been entrusted with - regardless of the hour.

🙵"When the angels had left them and returned to heaven, the _____ said to one another, "Let's go _____ to Bethlehem and _____ what has happened, which the _____ has made known to us." (Luke 2:15)

These shepherds were waiting for the coming Messiah. They gave the example that one should at once seek to find Him.

🙵"After seeing them, they reported the message they were told about this child, and all who heard it were amazed at what the _____ said to them. But Mary was treasuring up all these things in her heart and meditating on them. The _____ returned, _____ _____ _____ God for all they had seen and heard, just as they had been told." (Luke 2:18-20)

The shepherds heard from the Lord and went at once to see for themselves. When they witnessed this amazing truth they praised and gave glory to God! Shepherds go before us and return to the sheep giving examples of how to give praise and glory to God.

🙵"The one who enters by the _____ is the _____ of the _____. The doorkeeper opens it for him, and the sheep hear his voice. He _____ his own sheep by name and leads them out. When he has brought all his own outside, he goes ahead of them. The sheep follow him because they recognize his voice. They will never follow a stranger; instead they will run away from him, because they don't recognize the voice of strangers." (John 10:2-5)

The only door we enter through is Jesus. He is the door and there is no other. Jesus is the ultimate Shepherd. This verse tells us He calls his sheep by name and leads them. Do you recognize the voice of the Shepherd? Do you know His Word well enough that when you hear another Word you know it is strange and run away? This is accomplished by loving the Shepherd and having relationship with Him and knowing the Word so that you can discern truth from an imposter.

🙢"I am the good _____. The good shepherd lays down his life for the sheep. The hired man, since he is not the shepherd and doesn't own the sheep, leaves them and runs away when he sees a wolf coming. The wolf then snatches and scatters them. This happens because he is a hired man and doesn't care about the sheep. I am the good shepherd. I _____ My own sheep, and they know Me, as the Father knows Me, and I know the Father. I lay down My life for the _____. But I have other sheep that are not of this fold; I must bring them also, and they will listen to My voice. Then there will be one flock, one shepherd." (John 10:11-16)

A personal relationship is built between the shepherd and the sheep and they both know the sound of each other's voice. The shepherd not only cares for the sheep in the fold but also looks for His sheep that are currently not in the fold as well as ones that have wandered away.

🙢"Now may the God of peace, who brought up from the dead our Lord Jesus — the great _____ of the sheep — with the blood of the everlasting covenant, _____ you with all that is _____ to do His _____, working in us what is pleasing in His sight, through Jesus Christ. Glory belongs to Him forever and ever. Amen." (Hebrews 13:20-21)

Searching for peace in the midst of discord and chaos? Follow the shepherd and the blood of the everlasting covenant will equip you with the good you need to do His will. God's purposes for you are high and we should reach for nothing less than that. We don't settle for haphazardly trying to reach His goal for us we aspire for nothing short of His will in our life. This is accomplished by the power of the Cross, Resurrection, and Ascension. Let's exchange our failures for His victories and have it forever settled in our minds that the Shepherd through His everlasting covenant has the power to cleanse us from sin and make us holy even bringing us into eternity. THIS is our unshaken and unmovable confidence.

ᴥ"For you were like _____ going astray, but you have now returned to the _____ and Guardian of your souls." (1 Peter 2:25)

We can't help but think of Isaiah 53:6 here. If we are like sheep going astray is it because we are wandering away with our heads down, completely focused inwardly on our own misery? We therefore are unaware of the predators who are anxiously waiting to attack those who happen to be alone and wandering. The Shepherd is not the one we want to wander away from. He is the one we want to run to when all seems impossibly lost. The flesh would suggest that such sin must only be dealt with in solitude but that is exactly where the enemy attacks. Stay with your Shepherd, He will guard your soul when you need it most and set your feet right back down on His solid foundation.

If you operate in the Spiritual gift of shepherding, be on guard for yourselves and for all the flock that the Holy Spirit has appointed you to as an overseers. Shepherd the church of God with the boldness He has equipped you with because He has purchased His church with His own blood. (Acts 20:28)

Prayer

Thank you Lord for our pastors and teachers! I do not want to know where I would be without them. Assist me in training Your saints for ministry work as well as edifying them in love so that we will all be strongly unified in faith and insightful in the knowledge of You. Guide me as I continually look to you for wisdom in how to guard and guide your flock in a way that honors You. You have entrusted me with your flock and I intend to be yielded to Your Spirit continually in order to serve in a way that honors You and brings You glory. I look to you to fill me continually with compassion for Your people. Show me ways I can tend to your flock and support them in prayer. I want to follow the example You gave as you were the most perfect Shepherd. I ask and receive in the powerful name of Jesus. Amen.

Jesus, The Ultimate Teacher

Matt 7:21-23

<u>**N**ot everyone operates in the Spiritual gift of teaching (didaskalos) but we are all equipped to effectively communicate the gospel to each person in our sphere of influence. Think of a teacher as someone who instructs.</u>

<u>Someone operating in the Spiritual gift of teaching should not instruct outside the revelation and enabling of the Spirit.</u> God is Spirit and we can not expect to teach others about Him if we do it without the Spirit's influence. It is completely nonsensical. The Spirit of God is who teaches us about God. The natural man can not understand the things of God without the Spirit. The Word is spiritually discerned and therefore we need the Spirit to first understand the Word and then to be able to teach the Word. "For I passed on to you as most important what I also received." (1 Corinthians 15:3a) And, "But the Counselor, the Holy Spirit — the Father will send Him in My name — will teach you all things and remind you of everything I have told you." (John 14:26) Paul taught the Corinthians what he himself received from the Lord. Anyone desiring to instruct will wisely seek the Lord for understanding and enlightenment on a topic before they assume to teach someone else. This person will know that the Spirit ministers to them in truth and that they have received truth to impart to someone else with an ear to hear.

"I came to you in weakness, in fear, and in much trembling. My speech and my proclamation were not with persuasive words of wisdom but with a powerful demonstration by the Spirit, so that your faith might not be based on men's wisdom but on God's power." (1 Corinthians 2:3-5) The problem with being transformed merely by the intellect of man is that as soon as another person comes along with a more compelling intellect you will leave your current position and switch to the more interesting "flavor of the month". However, if your faith is established because of a powerful demonstration of the Spirit how can mere man with a different presentation ever steal you away? Once you have been taught by a compelling move of the Spirit nothing else will do.

What is the purpose of teaching or being taught anyway? So that we gain a never ending amount of intellectual scriptural knowledge? Hardly. Although scriptural knowledge is immensely useful, it is not the end game. Spiritual growth and development is what we strive for as teachers and as students. An intellectual pursuit without spiritual growth to me is nothing more than training for a position as a Pharisee. What feeds our hungry spiritual need and thus promotes healthy growth is the Word of God taught through an anointed teacher.

So what about preaching verses teaching? A simplified way of thinking about it is preaching is proclaiming the Gospel (usually to the unconverted) and teaching then follows up the preaching. A teacher typically stays with a group and teaches the wise.

I love the example of teaching given in Nehemiah 8:1-8. "All the people gathered together at the square in front of the Water Gate. They asked Ezra the scribe to bring the book of the law of Moses that the Lord had given Israel. On the first day of the seventh month, Ezra the priest brought the law before the assembly of men, women, and all who could listen with understanding. While he was facing the square in front of the Water Gate, he read out of it from daybreak until noon before the men, the women, and those who could understand. All the people listened attentively to the book of the law. Ezra the scribe stood on a high wooden platform made for this purpose. Mattithiah, Shema, Anaiah, Uriah, Hilkiah, and Maaseiah stood beside him on his right; to his left were Pedaiah, Mishael, Malchijah, Hashum, Hash-baddanah, Zechariah, and Meshullam. Ezra opened the book in full view of all the people, since he was elevated above everyone. As he opened it, all the people stood up. Ezra praised the Lord, the great God, and with their hands uplifted all the people said, " Amen, Amen!" Then they bowed down and worshiped the Lord with their faces to the ground. Jeshua, Bani, Sherebiah, Jamin, Akkub, Shabbethai, Hodiah, Maaseiah, Kelita, Azariah, Jozabad, Hanan, and Pelaiah, who were Levites,, explained the law to the people as they stood in their places. They read out of the book of the law of God, translating and giving the meaning so that the people could understand what was read."

What stands out to you from this passage? Please indicate below by including points from the position of teacher and student.

1. Students listened and bowed down
2. _____
3. _____
4. _____
5. _____

Charisma

6. _____

The teachers read God's word to all the people who could listen with understanding and they listened attentively to what was being said. The words had such an impact on them they said Amen and worshiped God by bowing their faces to the ground! This is an expository style of teaching. If you are familiar with debating, an expository speech is one of the 'platform' style of speeches in which you inform or 'expose' a given topic to your audience using a variety of teaching techniques depending on your audience.

Please open your Bible and prayerfully consider these verses as you complete the blanks:

"Then all your children will be _taught_ by the Lord, their prosperity will be _great_, and you will be established on a foundation of _righteousness_. You will be far from _tyranny_, you will certainly not be _afraid_; you will be far from terror, it will certainly not come near you. If anyone attacks you, it is not from Me; whoever attacks you will _surrender_ before you." (Isaiah 54:13-15)

Now this is the result of victorious teaching! Every day we should *give our hearts and minds and tune or ears to the Lord in order to be taught by Him.* It will be well worth our time. Victorious Christian living is purposeful Christian living.

If you operate in the Spiritual gift of teaching your ministry should reflect the way the Lord designed it and not what is acceptable in our generation. He personally gave teachers with the job of: 1) training the saints in the work of ministry and 2) building up the body of Christ. Teachers are to continue in this until we all reach unity in the faith and in the knowledge of God's Son. We are to mature in Christ always using Him as the plumb line. (A plumb line in Scripture represents what God uses as precepts to restore His people.) When this Spiritually influenced type of teaching occurs we will no longer be like little children, tossed by the waves and blown around by every wind of teaching that is based on human cleverness; rooted in deceit. (Ephesians 4:11-15)

As a teacher, the Gospel you proclaim should be equipping God's holy people for service. As a listener it is *our* responsibility to hear **and respond, which results in our further sanctification.** Are you sitting under a teaching that motivates you to repent, to serve, to deny the demands of self, and to crucify the flesh? This is the empowering truth of the Gospel that should be taught with tenacity. As this truth is taught we should always remember to do so in love. (Ephesians 4:15)

❧ "A _teacher_ approached Him and said, _Teacher_, I will _follow_ You wherever You go!" (Matthew 8:19)

Jesus' teaching brought not only regular folk but Pharisees (ex: Nicodemus) and here the example is a scribe. Scribes often came to tempt Jesus and so it seems the scribe might have been more interested in the prestige and status of Jesus' ministry and what it might ultimately bring for himself. Was this why the scribe offered his service to Jesus after he had witnessed His miracles? Did Jesus see his true motivation which caused him to answer in verse 20 that He had no place to even lay his head indicating there was no glamor to be found in His ministry? Only Jesus knows. What we do know is that we do not follow a ministry or get involved in teaching for the glamour we can obtain for ourselves. It is all about serving the Lord which extends as an outpouring of our heart.

❧ "When the _Pharisees_ saw this, they asked His disciples, "Why does your _teacher_ eat with tax collectors and sinners?" (Matthew 9:11)

The Pharisees probably witnessed the healing of the paralytic but they most likely would not have gone into the tax collector's house and dine with them. Were they standing outside making comments clearly expressing their disapproval of Jesus' choice of dinner companions? Someone operating in the Spiritual gift of teaching will teach to the wise and to any who desire such wisdom, regardless of their current season in life. Thank you Jesus and thank you teachers willing to offer ministry to those that are lost as it most likely comes at a cost.

❧ "Then some of the _Pharisees_ and _teachers_ said to Him, Teacher, we want to see a _miracle_ from You." (Matthew 12:38)

Some students will ask the teacher for proof that such a teaching is true. As instructors, we direct them to the proof already offered in the Scriptures. Just as Jesus did to those scribes and Pharisees asking for a sign. Jesus response was that there would not be any other sign except the sign of the prophet Jonah. Is the proof already revealed in Scripture enough for you? And teacher, do you know enough about the Scriptures in order to point to ample examples for your hungry student?

❧ "When they came to Capernaum, those who collected the double-drachma tax approached Peter and said, Doesn't your _____ _____ the double-drachma tax? Yes, he said. When he went into

Charisma

the house, _____ spoke to him first, What do you _____, Simon? Who do _____ kings _____ tariffs or taxes from? From their _____ or from _____? From strangers, he said. Then the sons are _____, Jesus told him. But, so we won't _____ them, go to the sea, cast in a fishhook, and take the first fish that you catch. When you open its mouth you'll find a coin. Take it and give it to them for _____ _____ _____. (Matthew 17:24-27)

When Peter was asked if his Teacher paid the tax it brought a question to his heart. Jesus sensed this and taught him Kingdom truth *in love*. For the tax payment Jesus could just as easily have given Peter the coin required but used the opportunity to also teach him a lesson regarding the importance of doing work with his own hands by 'fishing' for the coin. We operate with the skill and gifting we have and He provides the outcomes. Jesus' teaching is always multi-dimensional. I absolutely love this characteristic of Jesus.

☙"Just then someone came up and asked Him, *Teacher* what *good thing* must I *do* to have eternal life? Why do you ask Me about what is good? He said to him. There is *only* One who is good." (Matthew 19:16-17a also similar to Mark 10:17, Luke 18:18)

Is there any good we can do to have eternal life? No good whatsoever. It is an undeserved gift of grace. There is no act we can do to ever make ourselves 'good' or to 'earn' a place in the Kingdom. God is good. Because of His goodness we receive the gift of eternal life. This is a fundamental educating element of the Gospel of Christ for anyone operating in the Spiritual gift of teaching.

☙"They sent their disciples to Him, with the Herodians. *Teacher*, they said, we know that You are truthful and teach _____ the *way* of God. You defer to no one, for You don't show _____. Tell us, therefore, what You think. Is it lawful to pay taxes to Caesar or not? But _____ their _____, Jesus said, Why are you *trying to trap* Me, _____?" (Matthew 22:16-18)

The Pharisees were busy trying to trap Jesus in His words. The Pharisees did not receive grace and therefore did not operate in grace ~ then or now. You may know a Pharisee. Love a Pharisee but don't be a Pharisee. There is no perfect teacher other than Jesus so we can all expect to make errors. If someone is teaching, offer your hand of grace to them just as you expect grace extended to you when operating in your Spiritual gifting. Let's not waste time arguing with a Pharisee and let's not waste time acting like one.

teaching and edification go together

🕮 "They do everything to be observed by others: They enlarge their phylacteries, and lengthen their tassels. They love the place of honor at banquets, the front seats in the synagogues, greetings in the marketplaces, and to be called 'Rabbi' by people. But as for you, do not be called 'Rabbi,' because you have __one__ Teacher, and you are __all__ brothers." (Matthew 23:5-8)

The key phrase here is: 'to be observed by others'. Pride has a tendency of offering to puff us up when other people take notice of us. Phylacteries are the boxes that hold scripture (scrolls containing parts of Exodus and Deuteronomy) which was secured to the arm and the forehead. Can you imagine, the more scripture you know the more you put into your 'box'. The bigger the box the more you know ~ dangerous ground for sure. Teachers, it is not that we know more but what are we doing with what we *do* know? Are we ourselves being transformed as well as those we teach? Unless Scripture is making a transforming impact on our heart, memorizing and acquiring more knowledge is no more useful than a trinket that collects dust on the shelf.

What about titles? There is nothing wrong with the title of teacher as long as it does not breed superiority. If we are operating primarily out of love than the title is meaningless. The goal is serving in ministry with whatever gifting we have been entrusted with. Help us Lord to settle the pride issue and heed the warning signs when it dares creep in.

🕮 "A fierce windstorm arose, and the waves were breaking over the boat, so that the boat was already being swamped. But He was in the stern, sleeping on the cushion. So they woke Him up and said to Him, __teacher__! Don't You __care__ that we're going to die? He got up, __rebuked__ the wind, and said to the sea, Silence! Be still! The wind ceased, and there was a __great__ calm. Then He said to them, Why are you __fearful__? Do you __still__ have no faith? And they were __terrified__ and asked one another, Who then is this? Even the wind and the sea obey Him!" (Mark 4:37-41)

As I read these verses my eyes swell with tears. The Spirit reveals the truth of Scripture to us in a way that always reveals and points to Jesus. Do you see a personal application in your own life? A fierce trial from seemingly out of nowhere comes your way. The testing is so difficult it seems to overtake you. You know Jesus is there with you but why does He seem to be doing nothing? You cry out to Him, Jesus! I know you see my struggles, so why does it seem you don't care? When the time is right, the Prince Warrior rises and you are delivered from the trial! However, there is a loss. You do not rise with Him and share in the glorious victory. You instead are asked, "Why did you fear? Do you STILL have no faith?" There is no condemnation in Christ Jesus only opportunity. A question asked from what you consider to be your Rock, is only to provoke a desire for change.

Now...please receive this. They were TERRIFIED when they witnessed the One with all authority rebuke the wind and sea. The description of what the disciples faced during their thoughts of death never described terror. Their terror came when they witnessed the *power* of the Son of God.

Here is a question for your heart. Do you fear a trial that may even threaten life as you know it *more* than you reverently fear the Son of God? I find it fascinating that during these times they called Him Teacher. Did they learn the powerful lesson from the Teacher? I bet so. What about you? Let's have a heart pliable enough to allow the Teacher to instruct us gently through the pages of His Word as opposed to having us walk it out on the scorching pavement of life because we are resistant to Him. Amen. Either way, if we learn we win.

"He also told them a parable: Can the blind guide the blind? Won't they both fall into a pit? A disciple is not above his __teacher__, but everyone who is __fully trained__ will be __like__ his teacher." (Luke 6:39-40 similar to Matthew 10:24 and John 13:16, 15:20)

This verse is a warning to be on guard for accepting wrong teaching. If this happens, both the teacher and the follower turn out hopelessly lost. The students of these false teachers surely will not turn out to be wiser than the instructor. We must be aware of whose teaching we follow because we do not want to be in the category of the 'blind leading the blind' or we will be worse off than we started.

As students, we must discern if the one teaching us is Spirit led and decide for ourselves if we should follow their teaching. Also a teacher must, to the best of their ability, ensure that *they* are being led by the Spirit. Mentors *in the Word* are extremely helpful in this regard. We should at all times be aware of the tremendous influence we have regarding the people entrusted to us. It is a huge responsibility not to be taken lightly.

Jesus protected His followers from false teachers such as the scribes and pharisees. Paul also warned people to be on guard regarding the gospel men preach. The warnings are there for a reason. Let's have our hearts wide open but also our eyes. Discern by what spirit men are teaching the gospel before we follow their teaching. This does not mean we should have a critical spirit and claim no one is right until we deem it so. This is an equally dangerous place to be. If we are reading, studying our Bibles, and praying for discernment this will be an excellent resource and light for our path. See 2 Corinthians below.

🙠"For such people are __false__ apostles, __deceitful__ workers, _____ themselves as apostles of Christ. And no wonder! For __Satan__ disguises himself as an angel of light. So it is _____ thing if his servants _____ disguise themselves as servants of _____. Their destiny will be according to their works." (2 Corinthians 11:13-15)

This verse regarding false apostles is the only place in Scripture where this wording is found. A similar theme is found in Revelation 2:2. What we need is discernment or we will not be able to distinguish between the true and the false. Satan attempts to copy activities of God as well as his servants. We are told in Scripture to test the spirits to discern if it is from God. Students, we have the Spirit of the Living God residing in us (if you have accepted Christ as Savior) and therefore are able to do things in the Spirit. Period. Teaching about discernment is a MUST in this age as we should anticipate Satan's schemes to increase as Jesus' 2nd coming approaches. As someone operating in the Spiritual gift of teaching we should not only know what the Scriptures say but teach others so that they are aware that there is a counterfeit in the world and his aim is to deceive. We are the victors and God does not intent for His children to be deceived. It is time to rise up and stand firm and to teach others to do the same.

🙠"When the __Pharisee__ who had invited Him saw this, he said to himself, This man, if He were a __prophet__, would know who and what kind of woman this is who is touching Him — she's a sinner! Jesus replied to him, Simon, I have something to say to you. __Teacher__, he said, say it." (Luke 7:39-40)

Jesus knew what Simon was thinking and He used it as a teaching moment. When you hear a comment directed either at yourself or someone else, consider it a teaching door of opportunity. If operating in the Spiritual gift of teaching you should not be afraid of teaching truth because of what someone else might think or say. The opportunity for teaching will come at times we will least expect and we should always be prepared for giving instruction in love. At times you will meet with someone that is deceived and you must lead them into the truth in love. Do not be afraid of their rejection or harsh words - it needs to be said under the gentle leading of the Spirit.

🙠"Again the next day, John was standing with two of his disciples. When he saw Jesus passing by, he said, Look! The __Lamb__ of God! The two disciples heard him say this and followed Jesus. When

Jesus turned and _____ them _____ Him, He asked them, "What are you looking for?" They said to Him, _Rabbi'_ (which means "Teacher"), where are You staying?" (John 1:35-38)

John the Baptist was a teacher and had disciples. John, being led by the Spirit of God did all his teaching with the goal of pointing people towards Jesus. When John exclaimed that he saw Jesus, the Lamb of God, his disciples left him to follow Jesus. If at any time you are so vital to someone else that they continually need you to see Jesus, it is time for you to decrease so that He can increase. (John 3:30)

☙"You call Me _Teacher_ and _Lord_. This is well said, for I am. So if I, your Lord and _Teacher_, have washed your feet, you also _____ _should_ wash one another's feet. For I have _set_ you an _example_ that you also should do just as I have done for you." (John 13:13-15)

Oh indeed He is Teacher and Lord! Come into our hearts and be our Teacher, Lord! As Teacher and Lord he served those he taught. He has given the example so let's go forth and not only teach but serve, in the name, power, and love of Jesus.

☙"You then, who _____ another, don't you _____ yourself? You who preach, You must not steal — do you steal? You who say, You must not commit adultery — do you commit adultery? You who detest idols, do you rob their temples? You who boast in the law, do you _____ God by breaking the law? For, as it is written: The _____ of God is _____ among the Gentiles because of you." (Romans 2:21-24)

It is essential that what we teach others is also the same instruction we give ourselves to live by. It is important that the non-Christian world does not have the impression that Christians are hypocrites - teaching one thing and living differently.

☙"For the time will come when they will _____ _____ sound doctrine, but according to their _____ _____, will multiply _____ for themselves because they have an itch to hear something _____." (2 Timothy 4:3)

The Greek lexicon for 'sound teaching' is 'healthy teaching'. (biblehub.com) Have you ever been the person or been around a person who is unable to tolerate healthy habits? Their body is not trained for it, does not see the benefit or the point. The same is true for the mind, heart, and soul to receive healthy teaching. If we are trained for it nothing else will do. If we have an unhealthy mind, heart, and soul then healthy teaching does not go down well.

🕭"Although by this time you ought to be _____, you need someone to _____ you the _____ principles of God's revelation _____. You need milk, not solid food." (Hebrews 5:12)

If you have the Spiritual gift of teaching but you are not operating in that gift as you should it is time to repent and begin again. Is there something in your character that is causing you not to put the time and effort it requires to understand the deep things God? Let it not be so teachers.

🕭"Not _____ should become _____, my brothers, knowing that we will receive a _____ judgment, for we all _____ in many ways. If anyone does not stumble in what he says, he is a mature man who is also able to _____ his whole body." (James 3:1-3)

The Spiritual gift of teaching requires communicating. Whether verbally or in the written form, it requires much communication. With communicating there are many opportunities to stumble over what we say. If you teach a false gospel you are in a class by yourself as far as judgment. If you misspeak because of a lack of understanding, correct it and move forward. Being frozen because of any kind of fear is a work the enemy. If you have been given the gift of teaching then teach with the level of faith and revelation you have been given. If you make an error, repent if need be and make the required correction. But far be it that you do not operate in your gifting because you are a grip of fear by the varied 'what ifs'.

🕭"There was a man from the _____ named Nicodemus, a ruler of the Jews. This man came to Him at night and said, _____, we know that You have come from God as a _____, for no one could perform these _____ You do unless God were _____ him." (John 3:1-3) "How can these things be? asked Nicodemus. Are you a _____ of Israel and don't _____ these things?" Jesus replied." (John 3:9-10)

Thank you Jesus for anointed teachers you have sent to instruct us in ways you desire. We are blessed! If you operate in the Spiritual gift of teaching let's ask the Spirit for guidance when we need it and not put ourselves in the position of Jesus ever having to ask us, "You are a teacher and do not know these things?" Teaching requires reading, studying, research, and other types of preparation. Let's not slack teachers. Do you really want to?

Teaching Examples

Paul was a herald, an apostle, and a **teacher** (1 Timothy 2:7, 2 Timothy 1:11). Prophets and **teachers** are found in the local church (Acts 13:1). As **teacher**, Jesus was frequently asked how to reconcile the law of Moses with His New Covenant teaching (Matthew 19:16, 22:24 22:36,

Mark 10:17, 10:20, 12:14, 12:19, Luke 18:18, 20:28). People asked Jesus, the **teacher** for His healing (Mark 9:17, Luke 9:38). Skeptics tried to trap the **Teacher** (Mark 12:14, Luke 20:21, John 8:4) so we should not be dismayed when the same happens to us. Jesus, as **teacher** can look past the surface question to see the depth of the conflict from which the question has arisen (Luke 10:25). Some will be offended when the **teaching** of truth opposes their way of thinking (Luke 11:45). Jesus **taught** lessons about the Passover (Matthew 26:18, Mark 14:14, Luke 22:11). Jesus could **teach** in a way that would silence His opposition (Luke 20:39). Jesus' true followers allowed Him to be their **teacher** and educate their souls in order to meet their deepest needs (Mark 5:35, Luke 8:49, John 11:28, 20:16). Jesus astonished the crowds with His **teaching** (Matthew 22:24, Mark 12:19, Luke 20:28). When necessary, Jesus had to **teach** by correcting in order to adjust people's erroneous thinking (Mark 9:38, 10:35, Luke 12:13, 19:39). As **teacher**, Jesus prophesied (Mark 13:1) and **taught** about the signs of the end of the age (Luke 21:7).

Prayer

Thank you Father for giving us teachers that are willing to devote themselves to learning and researching in order to bring truth to us in a way in which we can understand. If you have given me the Spiritual gift of teaching, equip me with the fortitude and stamina needed to teach Your people in a way that brings unity in the faith and glory to You. Provide for me companions in the faith that serve either as mentors or co-laborers to help guide my steps and provide support. I resolve to hold back nothing I have that would be beneficial in teaching others your ways. You are the perfect teaching example, help me to follow You exclusively. In Jesus name I pray and receive. Amen.

A Helper with Good Counsel

"A wise man will listen and increase his learning, and a discerning man will obtain guidance." (Proverbs 1:5) Anyone who attempts to accomplish God's will might find themselves standing on a wobbly point balancing between having much to gain and much to lose. If we are wise, we will have helpers surrounding us who are operating full-throttle in their Spiritual gift of helping. The word guidance in Proverbs 1:5 and 11:14 (see below) are similar to the Greek word translated 'helping' in 1 Corinthians 12:28.

"Without guidance, people fall, but with many counselors there is deliverance." (Proverbs 11:14) It is interesting to note that the word 'people' here is figuratively seen as 'flock'. (http://qbible.com/hebrew-old-testament) Someone operating in this gift help the Lord's flock. Helpers can provide the guidance we need in our ministry work. If you have been in ministry work long you know this to be true. One person going it alone will not do much but with a person operating in the Spiritual gift of helping our efforts are multiplied for His glory!

God supplies people within His group of believers with varying gifts to support the body of Christ. Antilēpsis is the Greek word identified as 'helps' in 1 Corinthians 12:28 and is similar in meaning to the word 'serving' in Romans 12:7. Someone operating in the Spiritual gift of helps supports the day-to-day functions of a ministry in often unnoticed ways by assisting in carrying the burdens of others. It is a delightful behind the scenes type of ministry.

The helping gift is primarily about assisting a person compared to the gift of service which is generally oriented around tasks. Joshua had the gift of helps and he ministered to Moses. Joshua was there to help Moses. As seen in Exodus 17:10, "Joshua did as Moses had told him." Joshua was so faithful in his helping ministry that when Moses died, God chose Joshua to take over leadership of His flock.

❧"In every way I've shown you that by _____ like this, it is necessary to _____ the _____ and to keep in mind the words of the Lord Jesus, for He said, 'It is more blessed to _____ than to _____.'" (Acts 20:35)

Charisma 263

Helper probably also has gift of mercy

The word 'help' in the above Scripture is a different Greek word but nonetheless identifies for us that we should help the weak and we will be blessed by giving of ourselves. The weak can be considered anyone sick or without strength as well as anyone needy or poor.

As Christ followers we all are to work hard and help the weak. Let's remember that the one operating in the Spiritual gift of helping will do these things above and beyond what someone would do that does not operate in this gift. You are equipped by the Spirit to help in ways in which other people are not inspired.

What about, "It is more blessed to give than to receive"? We begin with the foundational truth that all things we do are done through God's agape love. This kind of love is characterized as sacrificial love. We are blessed when we give of ourselves and it brings pure joy to others when we bless them with our help. Giving is the product of God's agape love in us poured out to others. If this love is not the source of our giving then the question is, does the two-way blessing occur? Does the giving then become nothing more than habit?

"But I considered it necessary to send you Epaphroditus — my brother, coworker, and fellow soldier, as well as your messenger and minister to my need." (Philippians 2:25) "Therefore, welcome him in the Lord with all joy and hold men like him in honor, because he came close to death for the work of Christ, risking his life to make up what was lacking in your ministry to me." (Philippians 2:29-30)

Epaphroditus operated in the Spiritual gift of helps and was found faithful in that role to such an extent that Paul desired for him to be honored.

Epaphroditus assisted Paul because the ones in Philippi were prevented (due to illness?) from doing so. He was so spiritually motivated to assist even when it became more difficult than it first appeared. He was motivated by the Spirit for the works sake to continue helping others in their need that he became seriously ill. It is not clear if he was sick from over-exertion, from caring for infectious people, or from the burdens of his journey. Paul wanted the service of such men as Epaphroditus to be honored because Epaphroditus work for the cause of Christ was esteemed more than the outcry of his flesh.

Do we labor full-throttle for the cause of Christ to such an extent that we see it to completion even if it means we might suffer loss? I pray Lord that we are not so weak in spirit that as soon as the work gets hard we draw back in order to nurture our flesh. We seek balance Lord and above all we seek to have a heart that will put your work above pacifying the demands of the flesh. The cause of Christ is the banner under which we boldly offer our help.

If God gives a gift He has a definite purpose in mind for it and He intends we also view it as valuable. Some might be tempted to think it is not as 'flashy' as another gift. However, in order for ministry to reach and serve as many people as possible, the Spiritual gift of helps is a necessity. As Christians operating within the body of Christ we should all be willing to help each others. Someone operating in the Spiritual gift of helping would offer more than the occasional helping hand. This gifting would empower a person to look for ways they could serve by helping and be quick to offer their assistance.

We are to **help** our brothers and sisters through the Spirit of Jesus Christ who enables us (Philippians 1:19) so that they lack nothing (Titus 3:13) and their burdens are lightened (1 Timothy 5:16). The Spiritual gift of helping directs us to **help** those who work hard (Philippians 4:3, Romans 16:2) and to **help** those who are weak (1 Thessalonians 4:14, Acts 20:35). When this **help** is received, ministry is able to thrive (2 Corinthians 1:16).

Characteristics of Helpers:

✸ Drawn to those overburdened or overwhelmed ✸
✸ Regularly offers their assistance to others ✸
✸ Follows the lead of others ✸
✸ Volunteers in response to a need ✸
✸ Enjoys working with people ✸

Prayer

Thank you Lord for providing people to come alongside others as ministry supports for Your people. It is through the Spirit of Christ that enables us to help our brothers and sisters so that their burdens are lightened. I am grateful that through this gift of helping the hard working brethren can be assisted as well as those who are weak. Lord I know that help is always needed in order for a ministry to thrive! If I operate in this Spiritual gift open doors that allow me to fulfill my role in ministry the way you have envisioned for me. I know that through my help I am helping You reach those you desire to reach. I am willing Lord, therefore, grant me opportunities to offer my help. My desire is to advance the cause of Christ and to bring you glory. Amen.

The Leadership of Administration

The Greek word kybernēsis is translated as administration or managing and is usually associated with leadership. When looking at Scripture where this word is found it is associated with such things as steering or piloting ships. Just like someone steering a ship, a person operating in this Spiritual gift will keep a church or ministry group progressing toward its intended destination. This person is gifted at navigating during 'storms' as well as keeping in mind the currents, under tows, rocks, and other dangers that threaten to get the 'ship' off course.

Someone in charge of 'steering a ship' controls the direction the ship is headed which includes all the people 'on board'. Because of this, "God's administrator must be blameless, not arrogant, not hot-tempered, not addicted to wine, not a bully, not greedy for money, but hospitable, loving what is good, sensible, righteous, holy, self-controlled, holding to the faithful message as taught, so that he will be able both to encourage with sound teaching and to refute those who contradict it." (Titus 1:7-9) Thank you Lord for those you have equipped to operate in this Spiritual gift.

Here are two verses that use a form of the word kybernēsis in association with guiding ships:

⋆"But the centurion paid _____ to the _____ and the owner of the ship _____ _____ to what Paul said." (Acts 27:11 You will be blessed by reading the entirety of Acts 27:9-44 to see the full example.)

The Centurion believed the advice of the master of the ship over the wisdom of God spoken through the mouth of His servant Paul. When we seek advice in the troubled areas of our lives do we look to someone merely because they have experienced the same sort of trial or do we seek the wisdom of someone with an experienced walk with the Lord? Which one would you think would offer the sagest guidance 'guiding your ship'? If you operate in the Spiritual gift of administration expect to give advice based the guidance of the Spirit and not strictly based on experiences in the flesh.

❧"...for in a single hour such fabulous wealth was destroyed! And every _____, seafarer, the sailors, and all who do business by sea, stood far off as they watched the smoke from her burning and kept crying out: Who is like the great city?" (Revelation 18:17-18 You will be blessed by reading the entirety of Revelation 27:9-20)

Let's pay attention and not 'guide our ships' into the waters of fleshly endeavors in anticipation of finding our hopes met there. If we are motivated to guide ourselves by the worldly economy and bypass God's economy we will steer ourselves to sorrow and lament for things we should have never raised up to a place reserved exclusively for God. Make certain our advice in all things point toward God and His plan for us which is outlined in the pages of the Bible and not on the storefronts of this have-it-now mentality.

Characteristics:

✻ Take charge ✻
✻ Can manage/lead projects and/or people ✻
✻ Can accept goals set by others ✻
✻ Organized ✻
✻ Attention to detail ✻
✻ Delegates to right people at right time ✻

Weaknesses to guard against:

✻ Gods church, Gods plan, not ours ✻
✻ Pray before projects so you don't drift in the wrong direction ✻
✻ Putting projects before people ✻

Anyone operating in this gift will be wise to ensure they do not venture beyond the authority given them or *expect* the pastor or any other person in a leadership position to come after them in authority.

Ezekiel 27:8 describes the people's pilot or shipmaster as wise men. The wisdom of someone operating in this gift of administration will be able to assemble, inspire, and oversee others toward an intended aim with wisdom at the helm.

🞜Please read Exodus 18:13-27 which outlines Jethro's advice to Moses on how to operate in the administration or managing gifting. Prayerfully consider this as you strive for God's best in the ministry group He places you.

🞜What was Jethro concerned about in verse 18?

_____

🞜What was Jethro's advice to Moses in verse 21-22?

_____

_____

🞜What was the result in verse 26?

_____

🞜How can you see this applying to someone operating in the Spiritual gift of Administration?

_____

Prayer

Thank you Jesus for your managing leaders. Help me keep projects on course as You lead and direct me. Strengthen me so I become blameless by maintaining Spiritual morals. By a work of my will I choose not to be arrogant, hot-tempered, addicted to wine, a bully, or greedy for money. Instead, I desire to be hospitable, loving what is good, sensible, righteous, holy, self-controlled, and able to hold on to the faithful message I was taught. In this way, I will be able to encourage with sound teaching and will be able to refute those who contradict your message. If you have allowed me to operate in the Spiritual gift of administration assist me to do it well as I yield to your most Holy Spirit. In Jesus name I ask and believe. Amen.

Spiritual Gifts Profile Tool

There is no reference in Scripture regarding the requirement to complete a Spiritual gifts questionnaire in order to identify your Spiritual gifts. This is only a tool to help you determine where you might begin using identified gifts in ministry to God. The following questions were taken from Scriptures that discuss the gifts as well as from definitions of the words. The Spirit of God determines which gift each person should possess. If you study the gifts, complete the profile, pray, and work in ministry, it should be enough to guide you toward an accurate identification of your Spiritual gift. The observations of others as they observe your work in ministry is also beneficial in determining your Spiritual gift. Three gifts are not included in this profile. Prophet is not included because prophecy is more common and very similar. Teacher is not included because 'teaching' is similar and the Spiritual gift of 'teacher' is commonly associated with 'pastor'. Speaking in different languages is not included but interpretation of languages is included.

Directions

By working on your own and at your own pace, select the best response to all of the following statements. There is no need to spend too much time on any one item and there are no right or wrong answers.

Please write the best number in the blank

- 0 - Not At All
- 1 - Very Little
- 2 - Somewhat
- 3 - Periodically
- 4 - To a Great Extent

_____ 1. I am able to apply biblical principles to difficult circumstances.

_____ 2. I often see great faith and boldness demonstrated in others when I operate in my Spiritual gifting.

_____ 3. I feel compassion towards the sick and pray for them frequently.

_____ 4. I am motivated to preach the gospel with a zeal.

_____ 5. I feel led to train the saints in the work of ministry, to build up the body of Christ in faith and in knowledge of Jesus, and to care for their well-being.

_____ 6. I am drawn to someone who seems overburdened.

_____ 7. I strongly believe edification of the body is done when all understand the message. I have been used to interpret in the past.

_____ 8. I am able to test the message and conduct of others for the protection and strength of the group.

_____ 9. I have no reason for fear or agitation because I trust God fully in all situations.

_____ 10. I often feel the urging to speak words that edify, encourage, and bring comfort to the body of Christ.

_____ 11. I would gladly offer my own personal belongings to someone in need.

_____ 12. I pray for the sick often because it is one way I express Spiritual love.

_____ 13. I often have a surge of faith and see it demonstrated in others as well before I operate in this gift.

_____ 14. I can accept goals set by others.

_____ 15. I prefer to guide people instead of managing tasks.

_____ 16. I can guide others to continue striving towards operating in their God-given potential.

_____ 17. I often see and meet practical needs and like to do it quickly.

_____ 18. I see glory given to God with a sense of awe, wonder, and fear.

_____ 19. I often sense God is working to edify the church and bring glory to Himself through an interpretation of another language someone spoke.

_____ 20. I can encourage others to grow in the grace and knowledge of the Lord.

_____ 21. I am generally able to interpret circumstances accurately.

_____ 22. I know God gives a sudden surge to me and a word will come confidently to believe without a doubt that as I act or speak in the name of Jesus it shall come to pass.

_____ 23. I can perceive when something is not quite right about a person when I interact with them.

_____ 24. I am not quick to speak an interpretation given by God because I understand only 2 or 3 are to speak in a meeting. God desires order not disorder.

_____ 25. Signs and wonders often accompany my teaching.

_____ 26. I do not fear that as I give to others that I might suffer lack.

_____ 27. I trust that God will work spiritual health through physical healing.

_____ 28. I have a strong desire to demonstrate compassion for someone when they are facing difficult trials or are suffering.

_____ 29. I feel moved by the Spirit to speak the words God gives me.

_____ 30. If given the choice I would rather meet physical needs rather than spiritual needs.

_____ 31. I view trials as opportunities for spiritual growth.

_____ 32. I have an ability to adjust my message based on the hearer while maintaining the truth of the Gospel.

_____ 33. I greatly enjoy seeing people learn and apply Scripture to their lives in victorious ways.

_____ 34. I am adept at keeping a group progressing toward its intended destination.

_____ 35. I receive a surge of faith and divine word in order to substantiate the abundance of the Spirit.

_____ 36. I regularly desire to offer my assistance to others.

_____ 37. I often pray with bold faith regarding the healing of others.

_____ 38. I can sense when a person is acting in agreement with God's will as well as when the enemy is influencing a person or situation.

_____ 39. I receive impartations from the Spirit regarding truths I would not otherwise have known.

_____ 40. I am in prayer regarding where God would desire a group or ministry to go and I provide guidance to reach that goal.

_____ 41. I am willing to set aside money for opportunities to help meet someone's need.

_____ 42. I have a tenacious desire to plant a church or be a missionary.

_____ 43. After studying Scripture I often receive spiritual insight which urges me to speak out.

_____ 44. I can speak the Word of God and I know that it strengthens me.

_____ 45. I am quick to volunteer in response to a need.

_____ 46. I often pray for my understanding to be illuminated and I receive understanding to know what to do.

_____ 47. I am willing to arrange my schedule in order to have an opportunity to bring someone to Christ.

_____ 48. I can sense when others need assistance and I am open to opportunities to provide my aid.

_____ 49. I am willing to stick-it-out with someone and see them through their trial and suffering.

_____ 50. I personally witness the power of God demonstrated in what seems to be impossible situations.

_____ 51. I am able to delegate to the right people at the right time to ensure goals are met.

_____ 52. I memorize and meditate on Scripture so that I can speak truth to someone in need and I look for opportunities to do so.

_____ 53. I can test the intentions of someone within or outside the group.

_____ 54. I often receive and declare the revelation of God's word.

_____ 55. I recognize that God owns all things and I have a strong desire to be a responsible custodian.

_____ 56. I try to be in God's will continually and be available for His use.

_____ 57. I have delivered messages to other people that have come from the Lord.

_____ 58. I am able to develop steps needed to effectively reach the ministry's goal.

_____ 59. I enjoy meeting the immediate needs of others.

_____ 60. I don't mind following the lead of someone else.

_____ 61. I often demonstrate God's love by revealing the truths of Scripture to people.

_____ 62. I am resourceful and desire nothing in return when I give to support a ministry.

_____ 63. I can easily empathize with others. I see myself as the instrument through which God brings comfort to those in need.

_____ 64. I have an ability to uncover unknown circumstances and truths.

_____ 65. I know I have been successful when I see others growing in their spiritual journey with the Lord.

_____ 66. I lean more towards offering someone Spiritual help as opposed to physical assistance.

_____ 67. I frequently turn to the Scriptures to seek solutions to challenges and help others see spiritual solutions to their difficulties.

_____ 68. I can speak of my faith to people everywhere I go.

_____ 69. A priority in my life is laying the foundation of Christ as laid out in the Bible, even if it is accompanied with worldly loss.

_____ 70. I often determine my moral decisions from the starting place of a reverential fear of the Lord.

_____ 71. I am able to share a message from God that brings a person closer to Him and towards His intended purpose for them.

_____ 72. I see God's wonders occur as confirmation of His supreme authority during my ministry work.

_____ 73. I feel compelled to investigate Biblical definitions of words for the richer meaning and then share them with others.

_____ 74. I can often sense if someone is operating under the inspiration of the Spirit or merely expressing their own thoughts and feelings.

_____ 75. I enjoy and have the ability to witness to strangers.

_____ 76. I have a wide range of study resources and know how to research important topics.

_____ 77. I prefer to encourage someone by urging them toward Christlike choices as opposed to just empathizing with them.

_____ 78. I enjoy working with people.

_____ 79. I have a desire to teach Scripture to God's flock; desiring none of them to wander away.

_____ 80. I feel assured to fully trust God even when those around me do not feel the same.

_____ 81. I have a skill in managing projects and people in order to achieve positive results.

_____ 82. I trust that God can and will heal people in His sovereignty.

_____ 83. I can inspire others to assist in making the ministry vision a reality.

_____ 84. I have received spiritual knowledge about a situation which has caused people's faith to increase because of it.

_____ 85. I am quick to forgive and slow to judge.

_____ 86. I often receive divine revelation concerning what is spoken in another language.

_____ 87. I am willing to take the initiative to guard, guide, and nourish God's flock.

_____ 88. I study the Scriptures to determine how God might feel on a matter.

_____ 89. I am willing to make personal sacrifices if need be in order for God's people to thrive.

_____ 90. When I extend forgiveness to someone I always do it cheerfully.

_____ 91. I feel I can effectively communicate to others what the Bible says, what it means, and how to apply it.

_____ 92. I can research information and present it in a way others can relate to.

_____ 93. I am driven to do my part to equip the church with right doctrine.

_____ 94. I am willing to not only verbally give spiritual direction but also lead others by going ahead as a guide.

_____ 95. I enjoy knowing I can lighten the load of others to help fulfill the vision set forth by the leadership within the ministry I serve.

Directions

After you have completed the profile please complete the table below. Each gift has five questions each. In the boxes below, write the score you indicated for each of the statements and total the amounts across each row so that you will have a grand total for each gift. The numbers in the boxes below correspond with a number in the Profile Tool.

						Total
Prophecy	10	29	43	57	71	
Service	17	30	48	59	95	
Teaching/ Teacher	33	61	73	91	92	
Exhortation	20	31	52	66	77	
Giving	11	26	41	55	62	
Leadership	15	16	40	65	83	
Mercy	28	49	63	85	90	
Wisdom	1	21	46	67	70	
Knowledge	39	64	76	84	88	
Faith	9	22	44	56	80	
Healing	12	27	37	81	82	
Miracles	2	13	18	50	72	
Discernment	8	23	38	53	74	
Interp. of Tongues	7	19	24	35	86	
Apostle	25	42	54	69	93	
Evangelist	4	32	47	68	75	
Pastor	5	79	87	89	94	
Helper	6	36	45	60	78	
Administration	3	14	34	51	58	

Charisma

Directions

Look over the grand totals for each of the above gifts. Begin with the highest number and work to the lowest number. Write the name of the gift with the highest grand total on the first line on the left below. Each gift should be written on a line below starting with the highest grand total and ending with the lowest grand total. If a gift has the same grand total as another just continue writing the gifts down with those gifts coming one after the other. Next, shade in the box below to correspond with that gifts grand total number. The first box goes from 0-5, then 6-10, then 11-15, then 16-20. You will have a pictorial representation leading from left to right indicating which gifts you appear stronger in.

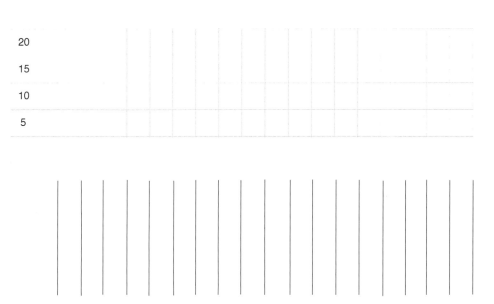

"He has given us the privilege, since we have been rescued from our enemies' clutches, to serve Him without fear in holiness and righteousness in His presence all our days." (Luke 1:73-75) You are divinely inspired and victoriously anointed, go serve and minister to your King. You are well equipped!

Made in the USA
Lexington, KY
31 January 2017